100 Reviews

Backwards

London

Matthew Arnatt, David Batchelor, Kate Bush,
Alex Coles, Tommaso Corvi-Mora, Sacha Craddock,
Alexia Defert, Emma Dexter, Dustin Ericksen,
James Faure Walker, Dan Fox, Mark Gisbourne,
Penny Govett, Mark Harris, Charles Harrison,
Matthew Higgs, Susan Hiller, Peter Lewis,
David Mollin, Niru Ratnam, Andrew Renton,
John Roberts, John Russell, Julian Stallabrass,
Gilda Williams, Andrew Wilson

Alberta Press

In this book Matthew Collings, Cornelia Grassi and I chose the writers. We also chose (on the basis of their supplied lists) what shows the writers wrote about, from the period 1987–2002.

The bare minimum was done to the writing in terms of editing – some rationalisation of name/date styles etc. and some cuts from the longest texts. I'm grateful to all the writers for their time and concentration.

I supplied two reviews when one of the proposed writers became ill.

Matthew Arnatt 2002

1 **Abracadabra** (Tate Gallery, 1999). 'Abracadabra' remains a playroom in the memory. Maurizio Cattelan's dead horse 'Twentieth Century' (1997) has been definitively flogged and removed to the knacker's yard. His *Subuteo* table 'Stadium No. 1' (1991) placed in the centre of the space (eleven a side), seemed somehow saddened by Italy's performance in the last World Cup. The mixture of magic and fairy tale is no longer with us in the same way. The innocence of Keith Edmier's lily pads 'Victoria Regia (First and Second Night Bloom)', dissipated. Maybe we don't believe in fairies and lily pads any more. What remains is an accusatory child and the social remit of imaginings. This side of the millennium the magic tricks have returned as the 'illusions' they always were – then again it always was a bit like Tommy Cooper… an amusing magic that didn't quite work. The comedic suicidal violence in Cattelan's squirrel 'Bidibidobidiboo' (1996) has come back to haunt us in the wake of recent events, a singularly innocent event in a world that has continued its mass murder into a new century. We always thought that twenty-one was the number of a coming of age, but it hardly seems so now.

Does an interest in banality and the commonplace still have its virtue? Just, but it clings on through a tenacious habit (amongst others the French artist Elina Brotherus sustains it), and I am glad to say Pierrick Sorin's video pranks still continue to amuse. This exhibition had a decidedly French feel and sought to generate an interest in a new generation of French language artists (it was a Pompidou-Tate exhibition by Catherine Grenier and Catherine Kinley). Xavier Veilhan was shown recently at The Curve, Barbican and continues to do much the same thing i.e. the theatricality of his works 'The Weightlifters' and 'The Astronomers' (both 1997) has hardly been updated. Patrick Corillon's 'The Ticket

Gates' (1993) and Oskar Serti's 'House' (1997) reveal that issues of threshold and narrative are relevant, something shared by Paul Noble in his ongoing saga of Nobson Newtown (I have yet to get around to playing the game 'doley'. In the light of contemporary employment reality, as with so many English satirical postures, it appears little more than a form of nostalgia). Vik Muniz's cibachromes of his chocolate-surface paintings (derived from news photographs) have been turned into the perfect market commodity art. On another front Emma Kay may be running out of things to remember, like myself in this instance; she will have to move towards remembering what she remembered remembering. (Not withstanding her work still has the ability to generate some intellectual interest, and that's to say, as we move into a century of rhetoric busy making a high-art out of misremembering: that's where her energies should be further concentrated – intentional misremembering.)

The overwhelming 'Eurocentricity' of 'Abracadabra' has only dawned on me recently, evident certainly in 'The Flowers (Les Fleurs)' (1988) the nonsense botany of Patrick Corillon derivative or at least comparable in form to that of Edward Lear. To what extent they were intentionally Carroll-like given the then Tate Gallery's propensities, is hard to establish. In fact the role of storytelling has magnified itself in this second reading of the show. The same Euro-Hegelian pose is true of philosopher-artist-social theorist Eric Duyckaerts' 'The Loop' (1996) which sets up endless chains of objects by analogy arranged in a loop configuring the sign of infinity. Brigitte Zieger's games and investigations of imaginary spaces remain prescient, as do Marie-Ange Guilleminot's emotional dresses. The interdisciplinary jamboree, the elision of forms and categories, are now to be found in almost every art journal. When is a building a dress, a dress a painting, a sculpture a building? And so on.

Momoyo Torimitsu's suited and robotic Japanese businessman dragging himself across the floor remains a constant – not much has changed economically. The eccentric Patrick van Caeckenbergh has continued to be just that (i.e. eccentric), his inventories of the fantastic and real grow ever larger, and one imagines him becoming a hybrid entity between a magician, the alchemist Paracelsus, and the polymath Giordano Bruno. Caeckenbergh's world is somewhat exceptional for it is seemingly a-temporal, a strange world of extremes that extends from sellotape to the wunderkabinet, a baroque mind that will never be fully structured by the world. The title of the show is almost certainly derived from Caeckenbergh's 'ABRACADABRA' (1984–1990) (a search for the ideal magic charm, the work itself with passing time, become less magical). Katy Schimert has sunk without trace and one senses may have been included due to the visual similarity of some of her work with that of Jean-Michel Othoniel (too abject and a Frenchman too many?). She added themes of narrative, metaphor and analogy, and the archetype. Fernando Sánchez Castillo's works, derived and applied from Derrida's concept of the destabilising power of play, were something that I missed first time around and which brings us back to where we began, namely the playroom. In this respect my response is not fundamentally different in terms of the frame placed around the exhibition. Though many of the arguments have been replaced or reinterpreted, a singular quality remains true of the show's installation, and may be related to Nietzsche's famous observation on artists "He has halted at games that pertained to childhood." It is through this child-like aspect, the Froebeling tendencies of artists like Tom Friedman, that the frangible sticking plaster world of the child is still with us. And, if the exhibition did not originate the idea, it was clearly present in 'Abracadabra'. Or, as Tommy Cooper's famous magic showed, it's done "Not like that … like that!" Mark Gisbourne

2 **Acting Out** (Royal College of Art, 1994). I'm no critic, I believe in it but can't be bothered. Writing about video and film is especially hard because I like it too much. Why analyse it? It's self-defeating – and I like all of it, all the shit and the good stuff. Discriminating between good and bad means accepting the insolubility of criticism, at least on the level of personal choice. That's neither an informed decision nor necessarily a passion. I like talking about the difference.

This show has both. Residing between film and video, its tension is off-set by architectural comforts like – soft cushions and sofas, privacy and space. Artists Steve McQueen, Roman Signer, Vito Acconci, Cheryl Donegan, John Lindell, Shona Illingworth and others, make work about difference. The curators added content at the level of the gendered body and its coded appearance in video, hard to theorise about.

Since Roland Barthes made film a luxurious complex of terms and inexpressable pleasures video has collapsed everything. Video is the best way for common culture to describe and stretch or contain the limits of the body as an infinite series of impulses, and work of the 60s and 70s is interesting for still claiming the homeostasis of sexual difference. Between Acconci, Signer and Donegan, rebel-transgressors are funny guys – and gals, but funny how? Roman Signer is funny because he pushes his body to the limit, an aesthetic take on slapstick, he risks death defying dangerous explosives and gets away with it. A 19th Century schoolboy prankster. Vito Acconci is an American male feeding off his own admissions of psychic dishonesty; very Yankee Doodle. Cheryl Donegan enjoys simulating oral sex with a milk bottle, not as metaphoric consumption but as an infantile pleasure, in real time, every durational drop, and we love its trashy garage soundtrack. Pierrick Sorin masturbates in black stockings, arse to the camera, miming to his own voice singing a nursery rhyme recorded as a child. Very strange and French, mixing eroticism with memory (very Alain Robbe-Grillet) and getting off. Maybe not so strange. It's what I do everyday. Not very British, the French.

What was curatorially really shocking was the combined Donegan/McQueen race/gender/porn *glissement*. Video was significant for its DIY simplicity of means and distribution – cheap and peppy, repeatable and easily forgotten. RCA relaunched the vessel 'curating' as a contemporary aesthetic moving from autonomy into image technology and design. Video's nostalgic years, the scratched, half sensed, flickering image of the body and the portrait, offered a last glance, bathed in a grey arc-lamp light, of somatic allure; in primitive film's lost aura, history's face itself. The transgressive cinema from the 60s restaged by curating as an imperative of video/film content (the 'body') ostensibly destroys artists' intentions in the slide from an audience's supposed naivety to sophistication straight back into – naivety via curatorial oversight.

Who advises these students and where do they come from with this kind of historical styling? Video once placed an accent on the authentic mode of address by its soulless present tense and uncomfortable focus upon the body's liminality. It abolished the space-time of criticism with its speed of transmission. Video theory is curiously defunct because there is no real analogous standpoint. If now taking the standpoint of the subaltern, of the minority works, misses the mark, it's because it's too late for form/content documentary dichotomies – however good a few pragmatist autuers. There is no transgressive sublime now because of the absolute essentiality of the electronic flow. Film looks better digital, and TV is all mixed up film/video/digital. The show didn't QUITE get up to date – to look at for instance – the body the way a *McFlurry* would look at us. Peter Lewis

3 **Philip Akkerman** (Andrew Mummery Gallery, 1998). I had known of Philip Akkerman's work since the mid 80s after I had been living in Brussels and was making regular trips to Holland. Although instantly repelled by the paintings' brutal appearance I could not help being attracted by their obsessive mania. The idea of somebody just painting self-portraits seemed to me to be a pretty fruitless exercise, and yet, I couldn't shake the idea of the paintings from my head. It was to be about 12 years before I was to see Akkerman's work again, after Andrew Mummery mounted his first London solo exhibition (I saw the exhibition a few days after it ended, the paintings no longer being hung, but leaning against the walls). This show was a survey of work from the earliest paintings in 1981 to a group of five or six paintings from 1998, and quite clearly showed that the meaning of the paintings did not just reside in what they looked like. (Is art ever about what it looks like?) The paintings are more often than not just of his head and shoulders with the head turned so you get a three-quarters face. The early portraits were painted in muted colours (grey being the predominant colour) and appeared crudely painted in an approximation of social realism, yet the more recent paintings had a much more highly-keyed palette and a madder and more symbolist/expressionist way of rendering the head. These paintings also looked back to a Northern quasi-miniaturism of the 16th and 17th Centuries, a sense which is emphasised by the fact that Akkerman paints on board (a few years ago his work was successfully sprinkled around the rooms of the Maurits-huis Gallery in the Hague). However, it isn't the self-portrait, or even the changing way in which the paintings are made that is important, so much as the single-minded strategy of doing what he does. The fact that Stanley Brouwn was his tutor at art college maybe gives one indication of what I mean. Akkerman's self-portraits are as much the fulfilment of a conceptual activity as are the comparative measurements thrown up by Brouwn's practice. Closer to home, Akkerman's self-portraits have a similar force to Alan Charlton's completely different grey paintings. In 1975 Charlton had used a quotation of Giacometti as an epigraph for his own work – "the adventure, the great adventure, is to see something unknown appear each day, in the same face. That is greater than any journey around the world". In one sense this also applies to Akkerman, although not in the way that Charlton is using it to underline the way that each grey painting is different from each other grey painting. Akkerman's work is not about this quality of difference, and is best understood as a body of work where the measurement

being used in the paintings is not bound up with sight so much as with a representation of time. Taken together, as in this exhibition, time unfolded before us
between the stark objectivity of the early paintings and the more dandyish role-
playing of recent years. Andrew Wilson

4 **American Abstraction** (Tate Liverpool, 2000). From the White House the
myriad hues of the colour-field painters converge prismatically.

Maybe it is Washington and not New York or Los Angeles that is the centre of
North American cultural production in the early 60s after all. The list of the cultural
militia filing through the newly vamped State Rooms of the White House would
certainly suggest so. Any single party could include Gore Vidal, Mark Rothko
and Mary McCarthy, all lapping up the warm succulent tones dripping from Stan
Getz's tenor saxophone. And that's not even to mention Jackie and Jack.

True, the Kennedy's weren't into the latest paintings being whipped-up across
town. More them was the iconic 'Mona Lisa', brought to Washington by the French
Minister of Culture, Andre Malraux. No matter though: it is through the attitudes
of the period that correspondences can be drawn today. And while the contem-
poraneous work of the Pop artists is more in keeping with the notion of 'the new
frontier' – its embrace of new mediums and manipulation of iconography and so
forth – the colour-field painters maintain the aesthetics of the double standard so
key to the Kennedy era. They also share an insistence on both upholding and re-
fining the traditions of their respective mediums with an openness and clarity of
means that is truly illusory. Key amongst those artists is Kenneth Noland. Together
with Morris Louis and other 60s alumni, he plays a key role in this exhibition – a
slightly belated nod to the mid-90s international re-ascendance of colour-field.

Noland's concentric circle series produced some of the most stimulating
paintings of the late 50s and early 60s. 'Drought' (1962) is exemplary, and easily
matches one of Jackie's *Cassini* evening gowns for eloquent configuration.
'Drought's' inner circle of deep red appears the most opaque; its outer circle the
most transparent. Noland here plays the palpable off the ethereal not through
counterpoint but by balletic sequencing. The minute variances in handling everywhere felt in the painting bespeak a sensibility that is highly attuned to the medium.
With its loose brushwork, the outside rim of the outer circle appears to hover,
while the tighter inner circles – beginning with the red and proceeding through
black, yellow and cobalt – spin away from the viewer. Earlier paintings from the

series rendered this outer circle so loosely that it too appeared to spin with the rest of the motif, seemingly throwing off excess paint. Besides their emphasis on touch – which differentiates Noland's paintings from much geometric abstraction, both then and now – it is the confinement of the circles within a square format that animates them. So, too, does the fact that the canvas between the outer circle and the enclosing shape of the frame is often left bare.

Colour-field caused a great critical fracas. For Leo Steinberg it was Detroit not Washington that was the correct city in which to conceptually situate the work – more precisely, the Ford automobile plant there; apparently, their streamlined decor and economy of means rendered the paintings analogous to the factory production line. These very same qualities meant that for Harold Rosenberg Noland's paintings were better suited to the furniture department in Saks Fifth Avenue rather than Andre Emmerich's. The affirmative prose of Clement Greenberg and Michael Fried didn't help the situation either. Perhaps if they hadn't nailed (in both senses of the word) the work down so well its fate would have been quite different, the comments of other contemporary critics more favourable, the judgements by historians today more gracious. As it stands, it is too often assumed that Max Kozloff had the last say on these paintings in his rap on the cold war penned during the paranoiac atmosphere of the Nixon administration. Since then few have been able to consider the painters outside of the remit imposed by Kozloff's writings; either that or the paintings have been subsumed under the rubric of eye candy. Exceptions have come with the writings of Lane Relyea and Barry Schwabsky, both of whom tend to approach the paintings with an openness once characteristic of Lawrence Alloway's writing. But despite the individuality of their respective takes on colour-field, whatever their generation, these critics share a disinterest in how it is partly the political undertones bubbling away beneath each painting's surface that make them so interesting, their aesthetics of the double standard so appealing. As one surface gives way to another only to contradict it later, so the spotlight of the critic is constantly refracted. These gems sparkle. Alex Coles

5 **Rasheed Araeen To Whom It May Concern** (Serpentine Gallery Lawn, 1996). It was a couple of months or so since I had been let down by Orozco. Now finally, one of the artists central to my doctoral research was having a show, and not only that, at one of London's major institutions. Or almost – Rasheed

Araeen was showing on the garden outside the Serpentine whilst the gallery was closed for refurbishment. I got out of the tube at South Kensington, and walked up towards the park. The area reeks of empire – the Albert Hall, Imperial College, the statue of Albert which at the time was under scaffolding. So it was kind of an appropriate place for Araeen's work. His work in the 80s had mostly been paintings and installations, but 'To Whom It May Concern' harked back to the stuff he did in the 60s and 70s which I think is great but is mostly ignored. It was a big lump of scaffolding – a huge cube of uprights and verticals criss-crossed all over by supporting bits. It was aggressive, messy and big. Standing on the outside you could peer into the inside and it looked like a dysfunctional jungle of steel. I liked the impenetrability of it – so much so that when I found there was an opening and a corridor leading into it, I felt a bit ambivalent about its worth. There were some people wandering inside it – and a few more outside, prodding bits of the scaffolding, which pleased me. As I walked around it I can remember thinking about a quote from Gerard Manley Hopkins – something like "My life has been nothing but scaffolding". I can't remember it exactly now. I think I was also thinking about a quote from Wittgenstein, that may or may not have had anything else to do with scaffolding. But even more, I was thinking about the insistent outsideness of the lump of scaffolding, and the way Araeen believed he and other artists from Africa, the Caribbean and Asia of his generation had never been accepted by the art world. And here he was finally, at the Serpentine. Or at least, here he was lodged in Serpentine's garden, stuck outside of its walls. Typical, I guess. Part of me wished that the scaffolding loomed over the Serpentine a bit more, but part of me liked the way it seemed kind of resigned to its fate. Albert, of course, would re-emerge from his scaffolding, all shiny and new, but Araeen's scaffolding would simply disappear, leaving nothing for me, aside from the memory of cool, burning anger and the undeveloped film that I carried around in my camera for months, before I misplaced it. Niru Ratnam

6 **Aristocracy** (Gallery Westland Place, 2001). Was it really that weird? If I'd written on it at the time I might have flattened it out into something intelligible but at this point it's only the eccentricity that has settled into memory. If I hadn't known anyone I might have slipped out at the start, but Dirty Snow were playing later and Martin Tomlinson was behind the event. They'd been in a music video I'd been working on so there was no way I could leave.

can be viewed safely as historical artefacts. Perhaps there is pleasure in mourning an old, lost generation, and with it the great emotions and grand ideals of past times, knowing that an insurmountable barrier protects the modern mourner, as the industry around World War 1 literature seems to attest. Yet the pleasure in seeing these pictures may be more subterranean than that, if the identification flits between victim and perpetrator: who cannot ask themselves what they might be capable of in the circumstances portrayed?

Rut Blees Luxemburg's photographs of London at night – council estates and multi-storey car parks – are shot on large cameras at long exposures, and are lit by streetlights. They are often of neglected or down-at-heel places, and the results are a mix of warmth (partly lent by the jaundiced tones of the sodium lamps) and distance, longing and a vicious pleasure in the details of decay, as she engaged, as many German photographers do, in a simultaneous combat with and mourning for modernism, and perhaps for analogue photography.

'Liebeslied', a show at Laurent Delaye Gallery and a book (so my memory of the former has no doubt been altered by looking at the latter) moved on from the ruins of modernist architecture to dwell upon smaller scale and more intimate aspects of the nocturnal urban landscape. It is a slow examination in which light is burned slowly onto film over seconds and minutes. The city at night is surveyed slowly as though it were the landscape of a lover's body, with the Thames lapping against some steps, puddles in a muddy backstreet, undergrowth casting areas into deep blackness, the combination of blurry and sharp shadows of branches falling over a wall. The city at night, then, as seen by someone in love wandering alone, metaphors proliferating. As in many photographs, perception is bent by desire, as light is bent by water, unreliable colour becomes its agent, and a specific vision is formed – here pictures as memory capsules containing a melancholic, nostalgic and romantic dose.

The work engaged me because of its proximity to my own interests, forcing a recognition in me, and at the same time naturally a distance and an evolving critique. It also stays in the head because it was a show seen with friends, at a time when there was a group of people, including Rut, who I'd see at shows regularly for drinking, laughing, discussing, joshing. Laurent Delaye is a small gallery and would attract a particular crowd: to walk in at a private view and find those people was to be wrapped in warm belonging and congeniality, and those feelings strongly affect the way I viewed the works. That is a good part of the reason for private views, of course: inviting a specific group of people, warming them with alcohol and each others' company is an effective way to propagate the work. It isn't that such crowds are not critical – they can be highly so – but that they are a consensus-forming machine. I've often got a lot from attending closely to what the machine says; yet there also seem to be times when it is necessary to not engage with it, especially when you need to think about the basis of all such cultural and social exclusivity, those left outside.

I saw the last show in the company of my little daughter, who was then eighteen months old. I don't get to see so many exhibitions these days because of her, and I don't mind much. She sleeps for a while after lunch, though, and when I feel energetic enough to negotiate London transport with toddler and pushchair, I can see a show in that time. This is what I tried to do with William Eggleston at the Hayward, but she wouldn't sleep. So I saw part of the show with a rocking motion as I moved the push-chair back and forth, and sung to her through some of it, at the same time gazing at Eggleston's recent pretty, gentle pictures of Kyoto, not dwelling on them much but trying to gut them for their point in the shortest amount of time. And part of it pursuing my little girl round the gallery, her squawking loudly with delight at being able to explore a new space and see new people, or with her in my arms looking at pictures. You look at pictures differently, naturally enough, like this: you find yourself saying things like, "there's a flower" a lot. It's as if (in Bourdieu's schema) your social capital had suddenly been drained away, and you are reduced to looking at art only to identify its subject matter. I think she liked the colours, though, as did I.

Wandering with a camera is something I no longer do much either, which bothers me a bit more than not seeing shows. Seeing Eggleston's pictures brought back a taste of that activity, of the strange mode of attending to the world that is required by the lens, of photographers' tricks to bring diverse objects, shadows and reflections into an arrangement that speaks of an occult coherence. Looking at the earlier pictures that made Eggleston famous, of uncanny fragments of domestic interiors, parking lots, diners and other flotsam of Southern Americana, even with the pictures of people (particularly of a couple of decorative girls who seem to sink under the weight of their own existence or the heat), the strong smell of loneliness arises. Photographers of this kind, those who continually put one foot before the other without knowing where they are going, who seek without quite knowing what they are looking for, haunt places and spy on objects, people and animals. The coherence they lend the world in their pictures speaks of emptiness, alienation, of the unbridgable distance between people, of the odd personality of objects photographed and their own apparent isolation and disconnection. In an old book, Raymond Williams argued that modernism favoured the voice of the exile, of those sundered from any form of community and solidarity. This still seems the typical mode of art-making and discourse, to the extent that entire ranges of human emotion and experience are exiled to expression in kitsch. With a force so cogent and complete, one must ask what function it serves, that the marks of distinction are so bleak. Is it purely the structural matter that since mass culture is so saturated with sentiment, that the only mark of distinction is disillusion, or does the cultural elite derive some positive benefit from its exercise? My daughter, running around, shrieking, lapping up the attention of strangers, her whole being attuned to wide-eyed exploration and sociability, is a living refutation of the pictures. Julian Stallabrass

11 **Atelier van Lieshout** (Camden Arts Centre, 2002). Atelier van Lieshout are a friendly bunch: if the Rotterdam based collective of designers seems preoccupied with the possible dialogue between collaborative contemporary art practices and eco design, what their work truly aims at is making us reflect on our real vital needs as opposed to the credit-card infested lifestyle we seem to pursue. Within the last two decades of artistic practice, Atelier van Lieshout's collaborative work comes to confirm a radical shift of paradigm born out of post-conceptual practices: no longer does contemporary art production seem to apologise for its ever-growing celebration of design-based materiality, but art's very relation to the once-upon-a-time repressed influences of decor and design has become an effective way to articulate a critical engagement with the pitfalls of material culture itself.

In this contemporary climate, art objects are increasingly meeting the path of industrially designed objects, a move in which art's relationship with commerce ceases to be systematically one of critique. Amid this rather celebratory mood, one which acknowledges the legacy of conceptual practices from the 60s and 70s, a polymorphous art object has managed to establish a dialogue with the broader socio-economical context (tackling issues as varied as ecology and global consumerism, as specific as the impact of scientific research and technology on the search for new forms of sustainable habitats), while nourishing its relationship with the white cube.

Thus, it would seem, the re-materialisation of the work of art does not necessarily impede its critical function. One could even observe that it is through renewed forms of materiality that art's role within social economy is best challenged, and that art's current shameless bonding with commerce can also constitute an effective way to overcome the somewhat stifling legacy of institutional critique. Enter 'Relational Aesthetics' a mode of artistic intervention where conviviality and interaction become part and parcel of the work, not in the form of carefully controlled sociological experimentations, but more with the immediacy of ad hoc social frameworks, facilitated by the exhibition space for the length of the shows. Artists whose practice could be said to be relational expose the viewer (or cultural consumer) to an experiential situation in which existing social structures of production are reflected, including those through which art itself (and the artist) are produced.

For the AVL collective, life is a complex and integrated version of work hard/ play hard, in which, so it seems – within a series of autonomous but connectable units – every aspect of post-modern existence has been eco-rationalised into multi-various usage (waste-recycling, compost-making toilet units, multi-media entertainment cells, fitness centres, etc). If private property and the right to privacy are central to your life, then AVL is not for you: at most, seeing the show may trigger reflection on those essentials in life upon which you couldn't possibly compromise (also an effect of visiting old hippy friends). But does one get into AVL as an idea (for art) or must one become a service-user in order to experience it as art?

Transforming the context of one's own life, learning to inhabit the world differently without necessarily wanting to change the world, such are components of AVL's philosophy. If modular living is about achieving some form of social transparency (these people don't share everything because they have to, remember, but because they don't mind), what appears to be a move away from the neurosis of bourgeois private interior, marks no less the manifestation of another ideology: forget the old concept of a private living sphere as an expression of one's own subjectivity, "Go Cubic!". As the global wave of domestic standardisation takes over one can doubt whether new zones of social communication or interaction are effectively being activated. Instead, such standardisation of time and space transplants the pressures of institutional (reading the commune as a form of institution too) productivity one step further into the private sphere of home: "office/living/bedroom". Conversely, such blurring of distinctions only seems to encourage the appropriation and utilisation of public space for private use (forget porosity, think other people's mobile phones).

Throughout the three galleries at the Camden Arts Centre, temporary architectural structures welcomed a blend of both bemused and radically blasé visitors, inviting friendly interaction with the various living units, providing one was prepared to remove one's shoes "before entering the capsules". Those just back from Kassel did not bother but instead seemed to enjoy looking at kids and minders climbing up and down sets of teletubby like pods, settling into various levels of light-tog duvet covered cells 'Mini Capsule Side Entrance (6 units)' (2002) or the more specific crimson-red upholstered version of what looked rather like some mobile polygamous boudoir 'Maxi Capsule Luxus' (2002). Indeed visitors did hang around each structure for more than the average few seconds of art-viewing, not unlike prospective bed buyers in *John Lewis* who dwell rather self-consciously on plastic covered mattresses trying to get a sense of what it would be like to take this one home. And it is precisely through consumerist tactics that, ironically, AVL almost succeeded in convincing us of its relevance to contemporary art.

By offering the viewer an imaginary slice of mobile and portable lifestyle, by drawing extensively on the way the mass entertainment industry has carved itself an audience for 'survival' type programmes (in which each participant invariably comes to confirm that the other is still Hell), AVL taps into a very lucrative market indeed, one that disguises contemporary art (and sometimes design) within some altruistic venture: art from the AVL people to those residing outside the free-state of AVL-Ville; for people who possibly care, albeit in some distant manner, about global displacement. In AVL-Ville, relational aesthetics meet post 80s cultural appetite for things nomadic. In theory it all sounds very good, everyone enjoying a bit of de-territorialisation as long as the happy-go-lucky nomads of AVL-Ville are only paying us a visit.

But like much of the art concerned with challenging received architectural and economic structures through the language of critical design, AVL fails to offer alternative templates of relational interaction, their operative zone remaining constricted to their Rotterdam compound. Their alternative effectively benefits no real community and one is left to wonder just what socio-economical scope cara-vans, mobile homes and other critical vehicles actually contribute, particularly when reintroduced in the white cube. Camden's curatorial decision to host AVL remained very much in step with its bold and ongoing dedication to mastermind projects which expand the genre of artistic intervention into the local community. But too many political questions pertaining to the reality factor outside the white cube were left unanswered by AVL: beside producing ethically designed proto-types, what kind of private venture exactly keeps the guys from AVL with a roof over their heads and (self-grown) food on their plate? It's unclear just how AVL's notional critique of state-centralised power-structures actually tackles the very physical materialisation of the 'displaced multitude' (migrant workers, asylum seekers and political refugees). In the end, the move towards mobile structures as a way of countering the implicit violence of state-ideology seems to turn rather rapidly into a binary and literal response. AVL's investigation into temporary struc-tures and self-sustaining living systems is perhaps no more than the friendly face of the somewhat more sinister dimension of their project: a community armed to the teeth with self manufactured weapons, reading up on survival techniques in the age of conspiracy theory, awaiting some Armageddon moment to really kick into action. Alexia Defert

12 **Beck's Futures & New Contemporaries** (various venues UK). The British art system seems fond of career staging posts, of giving artists a pat on the back for making the grade. 'Beck's Futures' and the much older 'New Contemporaries' exhibitions are graduation rituals perceived as tickets to a higher level, talent shows from which artists hope they will be plucked for glittering stardom, rubber-stamped by critical acclaim. To a certain extent, this is true. 'New Contemporaries' gives welcome exposure to those fresh out of art school – some artists soon be-come familiar as they start to crop up in other group shows, though the work may change considerably – whilst others disappear just as quickly. 'Beck's Futures', a showcase for more familiar names, comes a little later, a couple of years into the post-art school career: It's almost impossible to remember the differences between these shows from year to year, as they tend to coagulate into one big group show. 'New Contemporaries' seems to be remembered in retrospect – the sense of recognition when coming across an artist's work for the second or third time ("oh, weren't they in 'New Contemporaries' a few years

ago..."). 'Beck's Futures' is notable for its absences. Both shows are always patchy – that's the nature of them – and so to talk about them in terms of their curatorial successes and failures would perhaps be a silly exercise making for arduous reading.

At one time, the 53 year old 'New Contemporaries' was known as 'Young Contemporaries'. Over the last few years, the word 'New', (and on a subtler level the word 'Futures') has begun to stick in the throat. 'Young' may be ageist, but it at least allows for the idea that work takes time to develop, that it's at a nascent stage, perhaps a little shaky on its feet but smart enough to look after itself and head off in an interesting direction. 'New' on the other hand, implies a break, or a rupture with the past. It suggests the unfamiliar, the novel, that which has not existed before. Though 'New Contemporaries' remains essentially a survey show (whilst 'Beck's Futures' becomes a kind of Turner Prize for kids), both shows have increasingly come to appear symptomatic of an obsessive, frenzied almost, need to discover the next Big Thing. 'Beck's Futures' gathers nominations from art professionals but ostensibly leaves the final selection judgements in the hands of art stars and celebrities (in 2001 that well-known cultural pundit Marianne Faithful was one of the judges). These shows run the danger of breeding careerism (a disease rife in art schools) at the expense of nurturing ideas. Entry to the pantheon of contemporaries or beer sponsored futurists becomes more of an end in itself than the production of intelligent art. Institutions begin to play the top ten 'who's hot' game of style magazines, and patience and subtlety are run ragged by the acceleration of cultural production. Dan Fox

13 **Between Cinema and a Hard Place** (Tate Modern, 2000). In Melies' famous 1902 film 'A Trip to the Moon' the early exploits of film technology re-create for us the magical departure of six scientists for the moon. While Melies depicts at eighteen images a second the frantic activity preceding the men's departure, once landed on the moon, such activity mysteriously stops: the men lie down and within a yawn, fall asleep. Traditionally with Melies the camera stops the moment the actors cease to move, suggesting that only physical action is worthy of the moving image. Yet here, Melies' usually very precise filmic grammar appears to hesitate, inadvertently letting through – with the sleeping sequence, a few seconds of innanimate narrative. In Tacita Dean's 16 mm film 'Banewl' (1999) the spectator sits through over an hour of what Melies would

have probably deemed unworthy of filming, namely a solar eclipse lasting in all 63 minutes.

By filming the eclipse in real time, Tacita Dean created a situation in which the viewer's endurance of inaction was really put to the test: during her solo show at Tate Britain in 2001, a restless and agitated audience kept turning around, insistingly looking for a projection room as if to intimate that, since the moving image had stopped delivering action over inaction, something must have gone wrong. 100 years separate Dean's 'Banewl' from Melies' 'Trip to the Moon', and it seems in that time the viewer's acceptance of filming conventions, predicated on the cinematic recreation of 'real' time, has come full circle. What was not worthy of representation for Melies in 1902 (the sleeping scientists) is still not worthy for a contemporary audience, particularly when the only action has to do with a bunch of Cornish cows going to sleep in the middle of a summer's day. The narrative conventions of 'Banewl' appeared so far removed from her audience's expectations that most spectators had already left well before the end of the film. It seems her experimental approach to filmic narrative convention had separated the medium from its original purpose, story-telling.

Within the last few decades, the tools by which artists can conjure up a sense of the world's surrounding materiality have radically transformed. Through image-based simulation technologies artists can now generate very sophisticated and real looking information and exploit that information to recreate highly conceptualised forms of art. To carry on assuming the superiority of the three dimensional world over any other form of representation is to overlook the degree to which simulation can be disarmingly convincing in creating consensus of perceptual sensations. Is this to say the modern notion of 'objecthood' has become irremediably dislocated from the old three dimensional materiality of the world? Has video killed the world of hardware?

The early 1990s was the time when such technological mutations really began to impact, not only on the way artists make work, but also on what they make work about. If much of the art produced throughout the 80s seemed concerned with representing moments where the real and familiar ruptured, the 90s turned this concern around. Based on the title of a 1991 work by Gary Hill, the Tate Modern exhibition 'Between Cinema and a Hard Place' is one of the shows to have reflected on whether after a whole century of cinematic illusion, a shared notion of reality can still be said to inform artists and audience alike. Through a provoking juxtaposition of sculpture, installation, photography, film and video work, the exhibition presented some artistic responses to the possible shift in our perceptual range of experience. Progressively, the works on show seemed to be staging a negotiation away from the tactile three dimensional world of representation, one through which the viewer's sensory and psychological responses to the world made it possible to generate impressions of space, light, or sound. Evolving through various traditions of sculptural language with works by the likes of Christian Boltanski, Rachel Whiteread, Miroslaw Balka, Rebecca Horn, Anish Kapoor, Ilya Kabakov and Juan Munoz, the realm of the material world, one mimetically replicated by art, began to retract. Instead, recent approaches to the sculptural object (Kabakov, Munoz) guided the viewer towards hybrid forms of materiality. Matthew Barney's 'Ottoshaft' (1992), Mona Hatoum and Gary Hill's works acted like transitional objects between the hard place of the real world and a world now only partially recalled through series of fragmentary projections: Janet Cardiff's 'The Muriel Lake Incident' (1999); Julian Opie's 'You see an Office Building (2-5)' (1996); Stan Douglas' 'Win, Place and Show' (1998) or James Coleman's 'Charon' (1989), all functioned as truncated accounts of a concrete experience, yet still immensely powerful at triggering an immersive sensory environment. Just as you thought you'd seen everything about a world made up of fleeting impressions, Thomas Schütte's 'Strangers' (1992) hit you with its immobile quality. Legless and plunked into a series of chess piece looking plinths, 'Strangers' appeared as a nostalgic manifesto for the fixed object, discarded, seemingly going nowhere.

Clearly the curatorial team had heavily relied on the progress of the viewer's own body through the show to culminate in a series of highly theatrical installations – Rebecca Horn's 'Ballet of the Woodpeckers' (1986), Mona Hatoum's 'Incommunicado' (1993) and Cornelia Parker's 'Cold Dark Matter: An Exploded View' (1991). As such, 'Between Cinema and a Hard Place' became an indirect sequel to the Hayward Gallery's 1993 exhibition 'Gravity and Grace', revisiting not just the changing condition of sculpture, but also pointing to the possibility of a renegotiation of medium specificity. Alexia Defert

14 **Nayland Blake Bleep** (Milch, 1992). What is to be made out of a show named after mass-murderer Dennis Nilsen's dog Bleep? A description of the make-up of the show makes it seem horrendously over-determined: bronze

heads of Wagner mounted on poles; chocolate heads of Wagner skewered on the spikes of iron railings; hammers; a rubber body-suit tied with the same ribbon used to hang up portraits of a decapitated Punch and lap-dog; the kitchen table where the chocolate heads were prepared (one for each of the victims of Nilsen and fellow serial-killer Jeffrey Dahmer); a Herb Ritts homoerotic poster; blankets with Satan patches; and surveillance mirrors everywhere. Yet it has stayed in the mind despite its programmatic piling up of references. Not so much about mass-murder (is anything ever about what it looks like anyway?) this was based on a double foundation of diabolic scopophilia and fetish worship leaking out of the specific world of Dahmer and Nilsen but underpinning pretty much any sort of identity formation you care to mention. What is to be gained from obsessive looking and a love of (inanimate) objects? You are always going to sell yourself short – neither of the two killers could engage emotionally with anybody who was alive (apart from Bleep of course). From this angle the show mounted an assault on personal and social repression and the rather too widespread failure to invest emotion in real life and instead direct it onto inanimate fantasy (dead things and poster images), ridiculous ideals (yes, Wagner) and animals that don't answer back in any way we really understand (unless we are Dr Doolittle and who is?). This made the show one of the most unsettling two rooms to walk through in an art gallery in London in the early 90s. Looking at something and being brought up short for looking at something about looking gone wrong. Andrew Wilson

15 **Patrick Brill & Wayne Winner** (Anthony Wilkinson Fine Art, 1995). WAYNE WINNER plays the role of a psychopathic Thatcherite selfmade tyrant who laughs a lot – he spends some of his time exposing people like Florence Nightingagle as a Communist, drug-taking, Lesbian pervert. And he laughs a lot. He laughs so much you think he's going to puke. He laughed in the same way in another video where he pours chemicals and detergents down the sink and shouts "THIS ONE IS FOR YOU FLIPPER". HA HA HA HA

The only thing I remember is this video called 'The Winner' in which Wayne Winner's FLOUNCING OPEN COLLARED MAD MAN and Bob Smith's self-pitying loser play and replay the tired out and overrated dramatic/comedic configuration of the two tramps, the two comedians, the double act, the good guy/bad guy, conscious/unconscious, Bruce Nauman's domestic violence and replayed reversals, Tom and Jerry, Batman and Robin, Good boy/bad boy, on/of, on/off…

Wayne smacks Bob Smith around the face with a hairy glove. Then Wayne pisses in a cup and says to Bob "do you want a cup of lemonade?" Then Wayne asks Bob how his wife and kids are; as Bob starts to answer Wayne switches on his ghetto blaster and starts dancing. Then Wayne sells Bob a car for £3,000 – a Ford, the best car in the world but it doesn't work. Then he sells him another one.

The CRUDE CARICATURED SUB-SLAPSTICK ROADRUNNER-ESQUE TRAGEDY stutters on for fifteen minutes – a banal everyday tale of repetitious victimisation and SADO-MASOCHISTIC MALE BONDING. The film breaks down as a joke, as a theory, as a parable and technically as a video. Wayne Winner as a disjointed Nietzschean MASTER STRUTTING PEACOCK TOSSER and Bob Smith as a down-trodden weasel/victim SLAVE unable to fulfil his Hegelian destiny – stuck in a loop in a REPEAT TRAP playing out the same INFERNAL LOOP of FRIENDSHIP DOMINATION AND DESPAIR. "I'll sell you a car for three thousand pounds."
John Russell

16 **British Abstract Painting** (Flowers East, 94, 95, 96, 01). The sequence of British Abstract Art shows at Flowers East blur in my memory so I think of them now as an anthology with a confusing agenda. They were built around a core of gallery artists and their associates, one work apiece, spread across the galleries on both sides of the road, and scheduled for the slack end of summer. There was a real effort to be inclusive, and most of the expected names were there – too many perhaps. So what did they add up to? There was a touch of defensiveness, as if the message was about these artists all doing their thing – circles, heavy marks, aluminium stripes, contrived stains – regardless of fashion, regardless of the fact that 'abstraction' hadn't been a headline issue for years. Fair enough, but if these painters were to be presented as individualists, each fine-tuning a niche style, each customising rectangles, purple to grey nuances, splashes, dots, that concept was a few yards away from abstraction as a Big Idea.

Critics put down this 'kind of' painting because it was derived from formats pioneered in more idealistic, heroic, or simply optimistic epochs; it was never home-grown. They dismissed the lot as provincial, derivative and dull. These shows looked like those critics had been brought in to prove their case. Yes, there were outstanding paintings here and there, a Beattie, a Cohen, a Hoyland, an Irvin – but the overall impression was of artists fending about in a vacuum.

There wasn't much of consequence by younger artists, and nothing 'edgy': the painterly urgency looked manufactured; minimalist pictures looked foyer-friendly; a generation getting older, some better, some worse. A more cunning show – even using the same artists – would have posed questions and tested where the limits of this category lay. The implied abstract/figurative polarity is a killer – it alludes to stereotypes that should have been binned decades ago. It's nonsense to speak of painting as something heroically isolated that needs defending, that is threatened by 'media'. For one thing most of these painters were based in art schools. The strengths and weaknesses would be much clearer if they were set against, say, German and Spanish contemporaries.

There is nothing wrong with abstraction as a small idea, with a personalised flavour, perhaps decorative, idiosyncratic, academic, eccentric, comfortable, easy-listening, barmy. But I do have a problem with abstraction as a sectarian cause, abstraction as the direct line to the transcendent, the high-minded; as if this painting process is all about existential commitment, or an incantation of the spiritual world. Sometimes the obsessively worked, heavily brushed or immaculately finessed painting calls for that kind of reverential submission, and I don't want to play. Where they signal commitment, struggle, intensity, the exhalation of close-tone fusion into spiritual harmony I see repetition, mannerism, prettiness, stupidity, or just bad design. Painting is difficult, yes, but isn't it a nice trick to make it look effortless and one shot? Why this culture of heroic failure, wilful martyrdom? As someone said of Auerbach, doesn't he ever get it right the first time?

These shows did not inspire me. They prompted the thought that gallery groupings set up false hierarchies (bland paintings sell, difficult ones don't) especially when artists are working outside the limelight. From the practitioners' point of view there is a lot to be said for switching around between this and that art ideology, rather than trusting to any one approval system. In fact it is a good idea to keep out of the way of people who are certain about what they are doing. If visual imagination and ingenuity is to count for anything in painting you have to be amazingly versatile. You have to know your Rembrandt, your *PhotoShop*, your Richter. You have to know all about contrast. Re-doing Rothko isn't enough.
James Faure Walker

17 Jean-Marc Bustamante (Timothy Taylor Gallery, 2001). The gallery is sporty and consular, earthy and weirdly cosmological, with tricks-up-its-sleeves. Sort of Lacoste/ Minkowski/Blunt. It shows Enzo Cucchi, Alex Katz even (although I prefer the non raisin-eyed Brian Calvin. Less of those desperate calculating subtleties). There's a certain liberation in not agonising over some work against or in relation to some other, so I'll stop. Like the gallery in its mews is not cavalier, or libertine or privateering, but slightly *Barry Lyndon*. It's worth noting that precise Kubrick period quality.

Bustamante's photographs, C-prints from the L.P. series with the cool wall-mounted ink Plexiglas things, and a white structure. Some unrelaxed lesser artist would settle with the photographs: European lakes and palm-trees and hills, which are topographically heated, intrinsically saturated and, as pictures, hummingly uninterested in procedure. All of the Plexiglas (prints on Plexiglas) seemed alarming in the way that very good glass (and very good Plexiglas) is alarming. Pictures and things married in a totally necessary old-fashionedly relational combination, apparently. They take one off somewhere to a place where one is hot and sleepy and virtually decomposing and there is the smell of burning and a whine coming from the temple just above and to the left of the right ear. Extremely clever, all in all reminding me of Gaston Bachelard, of whom it was said: "he was so modest that probably few of his contemporaries will remember him as a young man." Matthew Arnatt

18 Care and Control (Hackney Hospital, 1995). The name of the hospital is still written on the front of the 22 bus. The hospital was a sprawling Victorian institution with walkways between blocks providing insufficient cover. In 1995 a curatorial organisation, Rear Window, set up 'Care and Control' an ambitious project aimed at being extremely respectful to the place in which it showed. A strange relationship was developed between the curator, the art therapy section, the doctors, and the remaining patients. It's hard to bring art into such a context. Hard to make it work in its own terms as well as those of the otherwise institutionalised.

A section of this enormous place had been closed down and stood still, but a large part of if it was working. Signs lead to nothing but the graffiti in the empty wards which was still very recent. The whole enormous place was caught in a state of semi-permanent transition, paralysed by the re-ordering, the re-structuring, all the re-justifying of a change of use from one thing to another, from something to nothing. Its original use as a poorhouse had got mixed with the hospital anyway, in the artists' and everyone else's, minds.

We met in the porter's lodge with its electric-fire. The processional tour was along corridors, through heavy, flapping rubber-bottomed swing-doors, past the chapel (always funny in hospital or airport) and through the day patients' territory. We avoided the real activity of the hospital except when staring down at patients in a courtyard, or hearing activity in a locked ward. We went through a hinterland of piled beds, discarded lockers and curling carpet. The old trick of staring at feet to spot the slippers was scuppered, because the artists wore the slippers and the visitors knew them anyway.

It had very much fallen to Peter Cross, the curator, to prove genuine involvement to a powerful therapy group and interested parties, and there were many. Patients in the art therapy section had been encouraged to make their own show but this must have been as difficult to place as a public Turner Prize nomination. The relation between the history of the place, its use, and the art that might 'respond', 'reflect', 'grow out of' it, just too difficult. The difficulty of it all perhaps far too pronounced. Donald Rodney, gravely ill in another hospital at the time, had a friend make his work. Jordan Baseman showed shirts spun with hair, while Derek Jarman's 'Blue' was projected in the basement. A touching equivalent to the chapel and perhaps less literal in application. Sasha Craddock

19 **Maurizio Cattelan** (Laure Genillard Gallery, 1994). For a while Maurizio Cattelan was a really good artist. For most of that time he showed in London with Laure Genillard, whose diminutive Foley Street space was the occasional home to some memorable shows. (Anyone remember Angela Bulloch and Sylvie Fleury's collaborative installation? Or Gareth Jones' curatorial debut 'Inside A Micro-cosm'?) Cattelan's second show for Genillard consisted mostly of his now (very) famous suicidal squirrel tableaux, his debut however contained what remains – to my mind at least – his best piece. In the back room, hemmed into Genillard's cramped space, was a vast canvas hopper filled to the brim with tons of rubble allegedly recovered from an Italian railway station partially destroyed in a terrorist bomb attack. Sort of a commentary on land art and, in particular, the work of Robert Smithson, Cattelan's subtle and ambiguous – at least politically – pro-vocation was far more complex and less gag fixated than his subsequent crowd pleasers. Matthew Higgs

20 **Maurizio Cattelan** (Laure Genillard Gallery, 1994). Strangely enough I didn't think much of this show when I saw it the first time; now I've come to realize that it was one of the most moving, most understated exhibitions I'd ever seen. I was disappointed that I didn't recognize that right away; maybe I missed it because I was assuming that, coming from Maurizio Cattelan, this was mostly a joke, "another fucking readymade" as he calls them, and a way out, for Cattelan, of actually having to do any work. And it is that too, but still, there was more to think about.

The show consisted primarily of a large blue cloth bag, filled with the rubble from a bombed building in Milan called the PAC. The PAC 'Contemporary Art Pavilion' was Milan's single public contemporary art space; it had always felt underused, delapidated, compromised and inadequate. It didn't really seem to have a proper curator, more a kind of governing director scouting around to fill the calendar. It had an air of desperation. I can think of no important or memorable show that's ever been there. It was an old, unobtrusive building decaying alongside a city park, and it seemed the least likely target for a terrorist bomb, which hit it a few months before Cattelan's London show at Laure Genillard. The bomb killed a man, a homeless North African immigrant whom I believe was sleeping in the nearby park. The bomb put the lumbering old PAC, already lame and defenseless, out of commission for some years. It seemed a true slaughter of innocents, a random tragedy which cost a life, and prevented Milan from making the weak claim that it, too, had a contemporary art space.

Since then the fashion houses of Prada and Krizia have opened contemporary art spaces in Milan, and these sort of take the place of a public art space. Plus, in the meantime the old PAC has re-opened, so Cattelan's show loses some of its poignancy. But the show still haunts me. The bag itself is the cheapest possible form of luggage, the kind with which an impoverished immigrant could, say, haul their life's belongings to their new country, uninvited. Usually it's full of junk, just like the rubble from the bombed PAC. It looks sort of like a body bag, and it's called 'Lullaby' – maybe to soothe the sleeping man who was killed by a stray bomb in a time of peace? The notion of lovingly picking the pieces of stone and cement off the pavement, stuffing them into the bag, ensuring it got safely to London by careful art handlers, is a beautiful ritual of mourning, I think, as calculated and pointless as the bomb itself. No I don't mind if the rubble isn't authentically from the PAC – although Cattelan promises that yes, it really is.

There weren't a lot of new generation Italian artists showing in London around 1994, and as a response to the question "what is happening in contemporary art in Italy today?" the bag of rubble stands as a forlorn reply. It is not optimistic, or showy, and installed beside Cattelan's neon sign of the crosses of calvary this, his first exhibition in London, looked surprisingly more like an empty funeral than a new beginning. I always wondered what happened to 'Lullaby' after the show. How silly to store it somewhere, so valueless and heavy and cumbersome, yet how sad to return it to Milan, where it came from. It'd be like returning heaps of charred metal to Ground Zero – the worst place for it. Did somebody buy it? Equally silly. Maybe the bag was just opened, its contents scattered in a nearby lot, like ashes on the ground. Gilda Williams

21 **Cocaine Orgasm** (Bankspace, 1995). Cocaine Orgasm was the best group show I've ever seen, honest. Or at least it was the most enjoyable art experience I've ever had – and I'm still grateful to BANK for it. If every art opening came even close to the excitement of Cocaine Orgasm, every young beautiful thing on earth would be clamouring to get into this art racket, instead of pop music or movies or fashion or whatever it is they're all clamouring to get into. It would be a different world.

The invitation to the show was rubberstamped on the cheapest Christmas card I've ever held in my hands, the kind with sandpapery glitter glued over a seasonal illustration on see-through paper, setting the enticingly tainted Xmas mood. It was December. The show was on or near Curtain Road; it was a real dump at the time, though I suspect it's been developed to unrecognizability by now.

First thing when you got there faux paparazzi sprang out at you in this richly mirrored entrance and called you by name, snapping your picture! Everybody was a star! I was enjoying myself already. Next you went up your basic East End rickety staircase, crowded with two-way traffic and heavy coats (it was really cold that night), everybody carrying a beer. As you neared the top of the stairs you noticed more and more these rolly little balls of white polystyrene (polystyrene?), littering the stairs, sticking to your shoes, like snow. Did this stuff spill from out of a crate or something? Then you got it: a-ha, the white powder connection with the show's title. You kept climbing up, to the beer table.

The main room was crammed with art: painting, sculpture, all kinds of stuff. There was a kind of machine made out of cardboard, plugged into a courgette,

I think by Bob and Roberta Smith. It was the first time I saw work by Chris Ofili. I seem to remember a Partridge Family work by Jessica Voorsanger which I really liked. Lots of good stuff. The *piece de resistance* was a giant, white, papier mache rock in the middle of the room – I innocently thought iceberg, my companions said no, cocaine crystal – bearing more (slightly lopsided) sculpture. The paintings had heaps of the little polystyrene balls piled up on the top edge of the canvas, very festive. It was great to see the artwork looking so relaxed for a change; you felt connected to the work. Do artists like that? Do they prefer sanctimony? I don't know, but it was such a break. This shockingly informal, utterly adolescent presentation made me like every single work in the show, even the ones I can't remember. I've seen work by these artists so many times since then – Bob and Roberta Smith, Voorsanger, Dave Burrows, Ofili – but it's never looked so alive, as good as it did that night.

But the best bit was this weird little side room, papier mached hideously to replicate a mysterious Arctic cave, as if carved out of the ice (great idea!), with little collages by John Stezaker, who is so good. You really got to look at the work up close, in fact you had to look at them nose-to-nose, packed as you were in a closet with the papier mache, more art-viewers, the beer bottles and the tiny balls of polystyrene. This was a truly intimate encounter with some really good work, and I loved it.

Afterwards, feeling genuinely elated, excited about art, excited about the possibilities of how it can be shown, about how much good work we'd seen, we all spilled out into the street, with everybody drinking at I think the 'Bricklayer's Arms', actually talking about art all night. Sounds awful, I know, but it wasn't. Some guy in a flashy red sports car was making his way slowly, slowly down Rivington Street, separating the crowd of impoverished, carless art lovers who were all jeering at him in a more or less good-natured way. Was this part of the show? Was everything in the world part of the show? Where did Cocaine Orgasm end? It was impossible to tell. Gilda Williams

22 **Comedie (Beckett/Karmitz)** (Anthony Reynolds Gallery, 2001). 'Comedie' at Anthony Reynolds was Beckett back at its best, made at a time when actors and film makers were convinced that 'commitment' in art meant placing one's classical training (Comedie Francaise style) at the service of experimental novelists and playwrights. Comedie (play) first performed in 1964 but jointly

filmed by Beckett and Karmitz in 1966 reads, 40 years on, like an anti-monument to the national theatre of its time. An all Durassian star cast of actors (Michael Londasle, Eleonore Hirt and Delphine Seyrig) seething in their respective clay urns, stuck in the antechamber of Hell with nothing else to do but reminisce the most unpleasant – yet pathetic – entanglements of their triangular love lives. None of the formal theatrical 'laws of unity' being observed here (time, action, place) but instead and perhaps for the first time, a systematic undoing of all structural tools. What governs the viewer's experience then is a sense that this very pre-1968 experiment was being filmed well before anyone knew what to call it, pre-empting the moment when unaccomplished and decentred forms of narrative became a flagship for deconstruction. Although the three disembodied voices appeared to circulate around the room, the pictorial quality of the film denied the viewer an all-round immersive experience of Hell. This had nothing to do with suspension of disbelief, quite the opposite. Narrative and medium appeared to be wrestling along its 18 minutes duration: a scratched soundtrack, a bile of inaudible words erupting from the protagonists (the soundtrack was carefully doctored by Beckett and Karmitz to eradicate any pause), unorthodox swaying forward of the camera, ridiculously farcical underlighting effects, and the painstaking moment of realisation that the actors are not rehearsing through the same section of a script, but endlessly reproaching one another with the same grievances. All very 'end game' we might think, but the extraordinary impact of 'Comedie' upon the contemporary viewer stemmed precisely from the realisation that what was unfolding here preceded the enthronement of Beckett as a prophet of modern absurdity. To all of us out there interested in art and who never quite got the whole Beckett Society art world thing, this was a true occasion for a redeeming second chance. Alexia Defert

23 **Melanie Counsell** (Matt's Gallery, 1989). Installation with white tiles, carpet, water, chintz, curtain and copper pipes. At one end of the otherwise empty studio (gallery is not the right word for the wonderfully raw space that Matt's formerly occupied in Martello Street off London Fields) Counsell had installed a shallow trough lined with white tiles. Within this lay a piece of sodden carpet, which was kept wet by the dripping of water from a pipe running the length of the trough, and which was wrapped with pink chintz material. The piece spoke powerfully of time passing, of decay, suburbia, of conformity gone awry, and of a

certain lack-lustre 'Britishness' coupled with despair that was appropriate to the mood of 1989. Misery, and angst were subtly hinted, yet the work remained open and ambiguous.

This was as close to a site-specific work as was possible in a gallery – Counsell had laboriously stripped the floor of its polite grey paint covering and had exposed the raw concrete beneath. This work at Matt's had a precedent created by Counsell in a deserted London mental hospital. In 2002 the vogue for site-specificity seems to have vanished – is it time for a revival? Admittedly the atmosphere of a building was sometimes used to prop up weak work, but when used effectively atmosphere can be devastating: a real example of *gesamkunstwerke* for our age. But the atmosphere of the late 1980s is hard to conjure; it was a melancholic time. We were nearing the end of the vicious Thatcher project and The Economy and house prices were starting their nose-dive. The city was still full of holes and blank spaces left by either the *Luftwaffe* or cash strapped property developers. Vast areas of London felt impoverished despite the vast amounts of money being made a few yards away. Counsell's work had something to say about this soulless world, about change and stasis, about trying to conceal rot behind flowery curtains.

The installation dated from a time when British art meant big sculpture made by men represented by the Lisson Gallery. Melanie Counsell and Bethan Huws burst upon the London scene at the same time, and quietly challenged this hegemony circa 1988/9. They made delicate and subtle installations using light, water, existing built structures, carpet. Compared to the Lisson 80s generation or the Goldsmiths generation of the 90s, their work was remarkably resistant to co-option by the market. Before London became clogged with small galleries selling work for lofts, there was this time of radical and formal experiment.
Emma Dexter

24 **John Cussans** (Cabinet Gallery, 1994).
DECKARD: Remember the bush outside your window with the spider in it.
(Rachael looks up at him)
DECKARD: Green body, orange legs... you watched her build a web all summer.
RACHAEL: Yes. (Her voice is getting very small)
DECKARD: One day there was an egg in the web.
(Rachael nods faintly)

RACHAEL: After a while, the egg hatched and hundreds of baby spiders came out and ate her. That made quite an impression on me, Mr. Deckard.

DECKARD: You still don't get it?

RACHAEL: No... I... I... don't.

DECKARD: Implants. They are not your memories...

NOT YOUR MEMORIES. MEMORY COLDSLAW. Maggot DEATH CRAZEE MUMMY OVERLOAD. PLEEEEEASE! O GOD O GOD! This show was a kind of HYSTERICAL ANTI PSYCHO-GEOGRAPHY SHOW. There was some sort of ANTI-ANTI-ANTI-ANTI-ANTI-eternal recurrence going on. Some sort of ANTI-NOSTALGIA for the future. In the catalogue John describes how if you imagine the idea of "playing tennis for fun" you set that scene in your mind by finding a lived example of a tennis court and then the rest of the narrative takes place in the geographical vicinity of this original place. He describes how this works with ANY text and he then plots out his life in relation to a series of mental scapes and zones like BLACK DEATH BUS STOP, HITLER VORTEX, DISCREET CAR PARK – memory is inscribed onto the external environment according to likeness and categorical familiarity. The environment is mnemotechnically ordered and I think he wants to smash this up – UNMAP and erase playgrounds, streets, school holidays – WHICH IS NOT THE SAME THING AS THE SARTRE-STYLE NAUSEAU AT THE COMPLICATED FUTILITY OF A TOOTHBRUSH.

He wants to kill these memories off and he asks people to stage their own deaths. He asked the gallery owner – Martin McGeown – but he refused so John Cussans got some friends to go into the gallery and pretend to shoot him. As he was looking down the barrel of the gun, Martin McGeown's last thought was "Who do I owe money to?" John Russell

25 Ian Davenport, Gary Hume, Michael Landy (Karsten Schubert Ltd, 1988). It's a question of how much you remember and how much you configure as memory. What could a review be other than a reviewing, as if you had already been here before and passed judgment?

A looking again, a looking over. Or a remembering anew. X years after the fact there's an irresponsibility that comes with forgetting, and the fictionalising of something from nothing.

These were things that I never imagined would survive as ideas, as objects, as stuff. Actually, they're probably not around any more – no-one was making them to last then. They were of a moment, for a moment. That's what makes them so important, even now. [...]

I'd never seen painting like Gary's before. I didn't understand it for a long time. There was process, there was surface – thus far it's with the textbook, but then it has a strange content – the shape of a door. The arbitrariness knocked me for six – because it wasn't about the door at all. It played at some type of simulation, but neither did it represent the door nor did it become one. The scaling was right, but it never left the wall. It never stopped being a painting. There's time in those paintings. The first ones were so grungy; all sorts of stuff was embedded in the surface. And then they got smoother. And, strangely, they still had a history.

I'd never seen painting like them, and it took me nearly a year to begin to know what they might be about. They're almost my favourite paintings ever.

Ian's I understood straight away. And it was just what the doctor ordered. A painting that played the game, but didn't succumb to any idea of expression. The paint just did what paint did. Gravity played a part, but I was beginning to see a way of painting where manual, even editorial, control was secondary to its just being there.

These, too, have a history, a layering. The surface had a tendency to crack. So if they're still around, they're probably not what they were. I don't think it matters.

Michael's clipped tarpaulins were the most aesthetic and the most wilful. Remember what we took for sculpture those days? It was all welded bricolage and art school material transformation. This was almost the least you could do with the least promising materials to hand. It was hardly sculpture.

I tried to call it all something like 'minimal diligence'. It wasn't that it looked minimalist, it was that the material – household paint, tarpaulin – had been hardly handled. I don't think I was right. Andrew Renton

26 **Willem de Kooning** (Tate Gallery, 1994). In 1994 these paintings were flying too high for the local radar. We were used to looking at paintings that took one or two problems at a time – colour, volatility, image, structure, tonality, process, surface – and whose relation to the great painting of the past was through quotation. De Kooning from the start took on the past not as history but as competition. He also evolved through a process of drastic self-criticism, so each phase is a revision, a cleaning out, a magnification, a heightening of tempo. So going into this show was quite a shock, a reminder that – for

instance – a 90 mph line can whip round a surface with the lubricated ease of a Disney virtuoso.

The show touched on a string of questions I still find hard to answer. De Kooning outlived his contemporaries, yet didn't leave any obvious trail. The cooler, minimal modes of the sixties were in reaction to his hot 'expressionism'; yet the great and gorgeous works of the seventies, and the icier works of the eighties left fellow painters bewildered. Was he just repeating himself? What on earth were these pictures about? Were they the ghosts of earlier pictures? Was he brain-dead? I heard some visitors refer to the Alzheimer years as if they went all the way back to the seventies (..."but I know he was intelligent before this because I saw a film of him talking"). In fact there was a show in Rotterdam in 1996 of the really late paintings – 1981 to 1987 – that was quite sublime, and beautiful in an unworldly way. The Tate show actually had very few pictures from the last years and ducked this issue.

I came to think of the seventies paintings as the painterly equivalent of Richard Strauss in their luxuriant orchestration, always on the edge of incoherent splendour, as if the structure was melting, slipping away, rhapsodic. I remember seeing some of these at the Serpentine show of 1978, and doing a review, and being much more perplexed. I had to do a talk at the Tate in '94 and when I checked back as to how those shows were reviewed I was struck by how dated the 'process art' of the time, e.g. Barry Le Va, looked in comparison: long hair, flares, gallery floors. De Kooning hadn't dated at all; they were still in the present tense. I think that's still the case, and there are parallels with late Picasso.

The show had omissions – 'Excavation' was one – and without the early struggling works, I missed the neurotic uncertainty and reworked surfaces that had opened my eyes in the '69 show. By the late sixties he was more or less working as a loner. For addicts there were plenty of tricks of the trade on view – blocking and pivoting the brush-stroke, curdling the oil with water, shaving the paint layers (he developed a gadget for this), accelerating the curves with kinks, the soft reds. I had known for a while that he was more a paint/brush engineer than an expressionist. A friend had stayed with him in the eighties and remarked how he worked slowly and deliberately, left to right, starting in the top left corner.
James Faure Walker

27 **democracy!** (Royal College of Art, 2000). Arriving late to the private view I had a premonition. Like Freud's own uncanny return to a street of brothels, somewhere I had tried to avoid but kept tramping back to, wished to, failed to control my desire to return to. 'democracy!' It was familiar dream work, wanting to transgress yet wanting to belong.

In my dream the first work I encounter is by Andrea Fraser. It made me nervous about institutions. The Royal College curators placed it at the front for good reason, I suspect, contrarily accommodating these practices and the conceit of the show's therapeutic postmodernisation. Everything will be alright. Everything will be real again.

Individual groups point the participant to the absorption of action within a techno-economic urban frame with a bad faith. This conditions the participants eccentricities. Annika Eriksson's real people show their polished collectables... Clegg and Guttman set up a bookshop designed for agricultural venues. No one steals the books. Is this patronising? The group names are 'branded'. Given a lead by the proto-activist 'Group Material', commercial interface is intentional and subversive. Like Plamen Dejanov and Svetlana Heger, transparency (something old-school-curating-course leaders believe in) is rejected in favour of big business allegiance. Inverting the model provided by Microsoft (who re-employ hackers), companies favour the 'perverse imp' (Zizek's term) to slide criticism into the hands of more business. These strategies are designed to raise synergy through complicity and customer care. Does it work?

Sarah Tripp's questionaire 'what do you believe?' poses questions with built-in answers: is this about the oedipal failure of the new age perverse communities? Not. Targetting a neat little niche Dave Muller caters to the LA art scene with three day events in his apartment. More a party. The rhetorical 'forum for exchange' irritates beyond belief. "Is he the fat bastard who upset my friends?" someone asks at the opening. No, Dave's the one making art right here for our own cognoscenti. OK, I guess, *but as a de Sadean?* I'm tempted to add there's no such thing as a collaboration. Only sadism as entertainment for bellowing libertines. Today's celebrations of the local could be seen as such: regressive and even fascistic, celebrating nationalism, ethnicity and not circulation – as advertised.

'Punish' is a club culture group that uses the dance floor and chill out room rather than the gallery; old news. Nils Norman offers aids to civil disobedience. Norman's fictional 'Underground Agrarians' a group of people who use the roof of a warehouse as a base for eco-political activism. Godard made a very funny (tragic) film about such a group of young Maoists in the 60s. Norman's unmoved. So am I. Rigo 00, a radical community fighter one time collaborator with Black Panther member Geronimo Ji Jaga, jailed for 26 years, for actions against democracy, sounds like the real thing at last, he may suffer from the management.

'No Problem Agency' a style agency for an imaginary artistic polit-bureau, conceived the image and signature for the enterprise's own disenchantment. Its front-page 'street' ethic is Nanterre-styled anarchy. "Zeit zum Widerstand!". Without dangerous professors and a disenchanted working class set in a marginal location (in the Paris ghetto) – we asked RCA students for less of the 99p fare. Pickled walnuts and a dry biscuit, in my day.

I'm a reluctant writer about art that makes an assumption about the political limits of the avant-garde. Peter Bürger's cool apology for the dying avant garde is itself the child of a better dada polemic, undermining the individual creation and its audience. Funny peculiar behaviour from Stephen Willats and his 'demophonic filters'... Willats' demophonic works filter behaviour. But not his own. Modernity haunts the hygenic atmosphere of the RCA. Too clean, too administered. Names, titles and organisations profilerate but it all still behaves like a business fair or the office. More management. Willats is a structuralist, Beuys a utopian, 'Superflex' a little cottage industry selling bouncy ecological balls, *Biogas* (like Tango ads), to black people, developed with the African/Tanzanian NGO – instead of giving them fuel. Does it work? Is it the new campaign in double cheese offers?. I don't trust the ethics because what is lacking is a distrust, at a primary level, by the artists' groups themselves, and there are 23 here. It's as if they believe a little too easily in what they're contributing to: an over-saturated passive mass. The catch 23 of heteroglossia is that it cannot contribute to a common civilisation in unrelated fragments; 'democracy!'catalogues that fragmented pathos. Does it work?

"There's too many!" Tubs says in *The League of Gentlemen*... and what if Stephen had turned up at the local shop? "Hello. Can I help you... at all...???" Peter Lewis

28 **Dinner** (Cubitt Gallery, 1996). Tables yawned, glasses were refilled, there was real food, a positive last supper with talk . Familiar artists provided decorative elements, videos, paintings, tablecloths and plates. The rather dank, dark

basement of the old Cubitt Gallery held the event/dinner. There was a speech, we were provided with pencils for doodling like the children who eat for free, *bambini nonpagano*, at an Italian restaurant. The exhibition, 'Dinner', which consisted of the whole situation left by the people who had come to the event/dinner, was probably badly attended.

Giorgio Sadotti knew that something like this stood a slim chance of greater success through reputation. The evening carried the quality of a disturbed patient's illustration of a snake eating its own tail. Perhaps outsiders knew they would feel sick if they came, were happy to be left out, or didn't go at all. Perhaps those who did visit the show were the sort who wanted to be there in the first place. A certain shame surrounded attending. A cloak and dagger, "I am going out and I may be gone for some time" reinforced the separation of the show itself from the not altogether unpleasant experience of making it happen. Sacha Craddock

29 **Documents Henry Bond & Liam Gillick** (Karsten Schubert Ltd, 1991).
Karsten Schubert was a blonde gallery. Though by night it was a throbbing nightspot. I'm oddly interested in how the relationship broke-up, or just stopped, and who got what, between Henry Bond and Liam Gillick: how the spoils were divided. I could probably find out. It's just interesting to know how partnerships or collaborations formally dissolve. Especially when, as with these early Bond/Gillicks, it's impossible to, really, truly, say who was the dominant partner.

These works were medium-sized black and white photographs with short texts – titles almost – locating the time and occasion of the photographs. So: '28 November 1990 London England 13.00 Michael Heseltine at American Chamber of Commerce lunch. Grosvenor House.' It wasn't a capital lunch. The photographs all pictured events: conferences, arrivals at press-conferences, seminars. I don't remember that the version of visual neutrality to do with the way the things were mounted or glazed or whatever was more Schubert than Bond/Gillick but I do remember that that version felt like a kind of experimental 'control'. One could have understood the photographs as photographs per se, or one could have paid attention to the title 'Documents'. Whatever they did they did extremely elegantly in the small yawning space between. Some people might find that a deficit, to not fully recover what they did, those photographs, in that space, even like loosing something, say – a favourite red scarf, in Town.

They had a great level of consistency, like a circle. But small variations in the degree of lack-of-animation in the subject-matter took on significance. Heseltine and partner being lively relative to: 'Men of the Year lunch (7.11.1990)', which though dark had more incident than: 'The Everest mountaineers with model of mountain before lecturing at Royal Geographical Society. Kensington Gore (8.11.1990)', which was a picture of a model of Mt. Everest, which was obviously mostly white, with black behind it.

I really loved these photographs, I thought they were heart-rendingly pretty and clever. I don't think I want to wriggle out of that. If you had held on to Victor Burgin and searched him really hard he might have had something almost as doe-eyed and engulfingly charming tucked-away-about-him from the seventies – brush the letters off it. Can't speak about Bond but I think Gillick's connection to conceptual art was to improve on it. Matthew Arnatt

30 **Itai Doron** (White Cube & The Passmore Building, 1993). My memory of this show is a little hazy, having gone to its opening after a Gilbert & George book launch. The show was in two halves: half at the new White Cube in St James's showed film stills into which had been inserted, Zelig-like, the ubiquitous face of Mr D, and the other half was in a huge warehouse building in East London. One video showed a figure (the artist) strangling himself with his tie (a sort of freaky dancing) to 'White Rabbit', in another room a Mr D/Otis Redding/ Mamma Cass nativity scene provided the focus for a number of videos from the life of Mr D – the one that sticks in the mind being Mr D dancing with a rose to the title track of 'You Only Live Twice'. The next room was dominated by a huge painting of a flying saucer with a big 'D' on it, underneath which were its landing lights and some triffid-like plant sculptures with heads of film and art stars as flower buds. And then out into the Spring sunshine. The show was particularly dreadful. Its literalism was mind numbing, its star adulation was sophomoric and the overwhelming scale and scope of the show's commercial ambition was embarrassing. Doron's Mr D fantasy remained resolutely earthbound and horrifically self-absorbed. While the found elements he used happily broke free from the Mr D construct (trying to piece together my memory of the show I remembered the soundtracks to the videos long before what actually happened in them). This was at root a desperately cruel exercise in hype, it seemed so much like an identity crisis fuelling an identity crisis. The idea that Mr Jopling was going to get Mr Saatchi to scoop up Mr D for his collection was so clearly the object

of the exercise and also, as it turned out, totally fruitless (the myth that Jopling could sell anything was here seen to be a myth). Later that night, Itai Doron couldn't get into his own party at Groucho Club which also provided the party for Gilbert & George, and even later at Gaz's Rocking Blue Jeans G&G were deep in conversation with Jay Jopling. And so the world goes on. Mr D was no living sculpture. Andrew Wilson

31 **Early One Morning** (Whitechapel Art Gallery, 2002). 'Zobop'. The title of Jim Lambie's psych-out floor seemed to provide the best description of 'Early One Morning'. 'Zobop' – synthetic, playful, poppy, absurd, almost onamatopaeic. At the time of writing, the dust has barely even formed, let alone settled, on the zappy, delinquent formalist works in the show. This kind of proximity denies 20:20 hindsight, but my initial response is to wonder whether historical precedent weighs a bit too heavily on these young guns' shoulders. The site of what could now be considered epochal shows, such as 'This is Tomorrow' and 'New British Sculpture', any Whitechapel exhibition purporting to take the pulse of tendencies within current art is in danger of crushing its subjects with the full force of professional and public expectation. Taking the title from an early Anthony Caro work and timed to coincide with 'Tra-La-La' (a mini-retrospective at the Tate of 'new generation' British sculptors such as Philip King, Caro et al), this show was perhaps hoping to position itself within the same zeitgeisty tradition.

Gary Webb's chatty fibreglass confabulations dominated the lower gallery with a fantastically lumpen presence. Absurdly pleased with themselves, these sculptures defied anyone to take umbrage at their candy-coloured excesses of formal arrangement, although Claire Barclay's spindly, hermetic hybrid looms and gibbets seemed pinned in the corner by the sheer bulky loudness of the Webb's. Shahin Afrassiabi's DIY product compositions skated happily around ever decreasing circles of sculptural potential, to the point of almost disappearing into the world. Somewhere between Eva Rothschild's wall-based works and her tentative sculptural musings there's space for the graphic immediacy of her woven images and the spooky indeterminacy of her objects to achieve a kind of happy equilibrium. But the line the wall pieces walk between visibility and invisibility suggests that wild oscillation suits the work better than calm resolution.

'Zobop' – synthetic, playful, poppy, absurd, self-referential. I'm not sure what it could mean. It's not sure what it could mean. It's far too early to tell. Dan Fox

32 **East Country Yard Show** (East Country Yard, 1990 (curated by Henry Bond and Sarah Lucas)). They don't talk about this one as much these days when they're doing the broad sweep thing. But they should.

They don't mention Gary's doors – giant, suspended, droopy versions of his paintings with the door elements (windows, fingerplates) cut out of the tarpaulin. Everything you'd been thinking about the paintings – without painting. And still curiously about it. I wish I could see them again.

I remember Sarah's installation – all corralled balls and cut out self-portraits.

My Dad still talks about Anya's ton of oranges arranged into a rectangle.

I still talk about Henry's photographs. He had gathered thousands from those one-hour photolabs – abandoned moments of intimacy and profundity. Intimate and profound only to the taker and the nearest and dearest. An anthropologist would learn much from these, I thought. The same images, the same concerns. Revisited time and again. Thousands of them. Someone who knew about such things – an art historian or some such – would confirm the composition as quite classical. Always the same composition. Thousands of golden sections cutting through same-difference sunsets. You have to walk up and down aisles of images.

None has more or less to say than another. Andrew Renton

33 **The Epic & the Everyday** (Hayward Gallery, 1994). There are two things I remember about 'The Epic & the Everyday' (bit of a naff title, come to think of it). The first was the poster, which was a kind of purplish maroon colour with Jeff Wall's magnificent 'Sudden Gust of Wind (after Hokusai)' gracing walls all over London, which made for good civic decoration. The other, more memorable, was Robert Smithson's 'Hotel Paneque', which I've wanted to see again really badly ever since. 'Hotel Paneque' was a slide show, featuring the recorded voice of Robert Smithson 'deconstructing' a wreck of an unfinished, abandoned hotel somewhere in the jungles of Mexico. 'Run down' and 'modest' barely describe the desolation of this place. The 'Hotel' was a cheap cinderblock ruin, left to the damp and the moss, a tribute to mismanaged funds, bad modern architecture and what had been a pretty bad idea in the first place: a big building in the middle of nowhere.

Did Smithson accidentally find this place on his travels to the Yukatan? However he found it, he proceeded to take a lot of slide photographs of details in the building – an electric socket on a discoloured wall, a cracked stair, a few cheap plastic chairs abandoned on what would have been the patio. But Smithson's brilliance – and sense of humour – came out in his disembodied voiceover, in which he describes each decaying detail as the product of a great architect, lovingly integrating the building into the site. Hotel Paneque, the worst heap of rubble ever conceived by human mind, becomes through Smithson's words and images one of the finest pieces of architecture of the postmodern era. Unfinished staircases become 'Piranesi-esque' features leading enticingly up to nowhere; a pool (or was it the sewage pit?) now filled with jungle turtles attests to the architect's sensitivity to the local fauna, and so forth. It was hysterical, a real dig at the pomposity of a certain strain of architecture speak, but beautiful and somehow authentic at the same time. You could almost fall for Smithson's attentive description of architectural detail, his genuine love for the place, the nagging suspicion that maybe it was all true: this really was a masterpiece, hidden in the Mexican jungle, stumbled upon by Smithson.

Smithson never lapses into a sarcastic tone, never gives in to laughter. Recorded behind his voice is the occasional unsuppressed laugh from somebody in the audience, but the comedy takes a back seat to Smithson's own extraordinary ability to see beauty where there is none. I thought of the Monuments of Passaic, with Smithson hiking over the industrial wastelands of the New Jersey shore, making it all noble. I thought of his patience and his great use of words ("one pebble moving a single foot in a million years is enough action to keep me really excited"), of 'Spiral Jetty' sinking into the Great Salt Lake, invisible and legendary. His talent wasn't just in the words and images, impressive enough, but in the radiant transformations he concocted.

I think 'The Epic & the Everyday' had a lot of other good work in it too, Patrick Faigenbaum, Andreas Gursky, but nothing was more alive than the old hotel, haunted by the ghost of Robert Smithson, resurrecting a building which had never been born. Gilda Williams

34 **Examining Pictures: Exhibiting Paintings** (Whitechapel Art Gallery, 1999 (curated by Judith Nesbitt and Francesco Bonami)). As everybody knows, group exhibitions structured around a specific technique or medium are often problematic; this show embraced diversity, doubt and failure to the extent of neutralising this risk. 'Examining Pictures' tried to describe the reasons behind

the desire to make or look at paintings. It failed (how could it succeed?), but it gave you the chance to look at some great work. Seeing 'The Studio' (1969) by Philip Guston was a real revelation. Tommaso Corvi-Mora

35 **Keith Farquhar** (Anthony Reynolds Gallery, 1998). These eight new paintings had the appearance of algebra class Modernism − wonky compasses, Venn diagrams and wipe board calculations − and were immediately refreshing. The paintings were on gloss surface or primed or unprimed linen, and used marker pen, coloured paper and paint. The images, predominantly clusters of circles, interlocking segmented circles, and overlapping halved circles, derive from the designs found on the covers of 60s and 70s *Pelican* psychology and science books − given away in Farquhar's titles such as: 'The Integrity of the Personality', 'The Phenomenology of Moral Experience', 'The Plight of the Remedial Child', or the rather more famous 'The Self and Others'. The quality of finish wasn't of the highest order, the work being marked by the casualness of the earnest schoolboy making copies of the covers of his favourite books and being unable to hide his mistakes (or rather, stop being unable to stop making mistakes). Disregarding their sources, the paintings were successful in providing an abject beginning to an idea of modernist painting: ideals might have been intact (we will make the 'New World' of 'The Self and Others') but the means were rather degraded (my marker pen is running out and, anyway, who can draw a perfect circle and colour it in with flat colour?). There were yawning gulfs between the materiality of the work, the images (copies of diagrams or models) and the titles (which both energised the work while at the same time putting the boot into po-faced process-based nostalgic Modernism). Although these paintings' sources are 30 or more years old, there didn't seem to be any whiff of nostalgia hanging in the air. For all that they appeared to be about, at root this was not Modernist painting. It is more about the poetry of making something inappropriate into a painting, in which the title is both title of the image, title of the source and title to a way of working. Sickness and healing is subject to the rational and the untenable. Andrew Wilson

36 **15/1** (Malania Basarab Gallery, 1992 (curated by Denise Hawrysio)). Denise Hawrysio ran a gallery in a top floor council flat in Vauxhall for a couple of years. 15 artists were invited to install an exhibition over two days, as is normal. What

was different on this occasion was that the artists who came after other works had been installed, were permitted, if they wished, to alter/interfere with the already placed works. Obviously everybody who took part had to sign up to the ethos of the exhibition. What resulted was that some works acquired a certain patina provided by another hand, or were moved or even obliterated. As a result 15/1 conveyed a sense of infinite possibility – there was none of the sense of closure associated with conventional exhibitions. It spawned a lot of dreaming on my part and some discussions with Denise about ways of dismantling the whole structure of an exhibition – something that happens surprisingly rarely, even within 'alternative' or 'artist-run' spaces. Which leads naturally to a question that needs asking regularly: "who is an exhibition for?" 15/1 raised the taboo subject of the implicit egotism that operates within every exhibition.

Is an exhibition there to make the artist's work look good, or is it there to stimulate and challenge an audience? Of course everyone will say both, but more often the former comes into play, and the result is that exhibition formats become dull at times when they should be at their most disarming. I wondered why no one had done this exhibition before – I believe there is an historical precedent perhaps within the Fluxus movement in New York, but this was not known to Hawrysio at the time of making the show.

One had to admire the bravery of those taking part – did some wince with pain on finding out what had been done to their work? The most memorable contributions were those of Anya Gallaccio and Denise Hawrysio herself. Anya added a filmy surface to other people's works, and Denise set about demolishing a plasterboard wall which such fury that the work has stuck in my mind for 10 years.

The other artists were: Sean Dower, Clare Tindall, Peter Lloyd Lewis, Pauline Daly, Brendan Quick, Andreas Ginkel, Amikam Toren, Graham Ramsay, Richard Makin, Adam Chodzko, Wendy Elliot, David Griffiths, Patrick McBride.
Emma Dexter

37 **15/1** (Malania Basarab Gallery, 1992 (curated by Denise Hawrysio)).
Shows in people's apartments weren't as big a phenomenon in the early 1990s as people imagine. For the most part people didn't – and probably still don't – want people traipsing through their homes. Denise Hawrysio's Elephant & Castle council flat space, along with the earliest days of the Cabinet gallery in Martin

McGeown's Brixton walk-up, were two of the more distinguished attempts to negotiate the public/private thresholds inherent to such enterprises. Hawrysio's '15/1' was probably the best exhibition ever inspired by a televison quiz show. One at a time, Denise invited 15 artists to install a work in her apartment/gallery, on the clear understanding that the artist who would install next would have full rights to completely change the installation of the works by all of the preceeding artists. Clearly artist Number 15 would have almost total power to reinstall the show to their advantage. The show seemed to be, on the one hand, about trust, mutuality and comradeship, whilst on the other it was about, deviousness, one-upmanship and in some instances plain spitefulness. (A microcosm of the art world no less.) Which of course made for a great spectacle for the viewer, akin to hearing your grandmother swear or watching nuns fight. Matthew Higgs

38 **fig-1** (Fragile House, 2000). 50 shows in 50 weeks. What a forgetable few weeks that was. Big fucking yawn. How can 50 artists appear so useless in one project? How can such apathy be induced. It crept up on me around week 17. But still those horrible minimal email invites would arrive, even when I was on holiday. And does anyone remember the web site? Yukmando. Teeny little fuck-ing boxes with teeny numbers is all I remember. I can't stand what's in my head anymore thanks to things like this. I'm going to die with things like this in my head, emerging at the last moment. Can you imagine? It's fucking tragic. No fucking God or blinding light, not even a big spider, just teeny little boxes with teeny numbers from the web site design of 50 shows in 50 weeks. It makes me neurotic. David Mollin

39 **Freeze (Part 1)** (PLA Building, 1988). Let's be honest: Freeze was a terrible exhibition. Curiously, given its subsequent and somewhat mythic status, little mention is ever made as to how staggeringly derivative, conservative and reactionary most of the work in Freeze was. With a few notable exceptions – including works by Mat Collishaw and Angela Bulloch – Freeze was little more than a tired-looking, eager-to-please student homage to the vaguely formalist, sort-of-conceptual, post-painterly abstraction and post-minimalist sculpture favored at the time by Doris and Charles Saatchi and Michael Craig-Martin (the then Goldsmiths guru). Impressive for all the wrong reasons – Clement Green-berg would have liked the show – and celebrated largely for its late 80s entre-

preneurial spirit it could be argued that Damien Hirst's curatorial debut was the worst thing that ever happened to British art. (We are certainly still suffering the backlash and consequences of its effect: the cult of the celebrity artist, the prurient tabloid-like coverage of contemporary art in the British press, Charles Saatchi's self-aggrandizing lording over British Art, the dumbing down of the Tate empire with its Conde Naste published inflight magazine, etc. ...) Matthew Higgs

40 **The Genius of Caspar David Friedrich** (Courtauld Institute, 2002). Elegant environment for a good study of his work from St. Petersburg. Particularly struck by a painting of him and his wife with their backs to me on a boat sailing towards a harbour. I felt like grabbing his wife. I lower the tone because I'm like that in the face of the sublime, or when people's backs are turned to me. I'm sure both are connected in some horrible art historical way. Nature is big and Caspar David Friedrich is partly responsible for this misapprehension, exacerbated by his deliberate rudeness. I don't know how you would paint these paintings without nature looking colossal and overwhelming. Even if you made the backs so that they covered most of the canvas it wouldn't work, because just a tiny amount of nature poking over the shoulder would still give the impression that nature was a lot bigger than man. In fact, it would make it worse. If you had them amiably posing and smiling in front that would work, perhaps. So, I draw my conclusion; nature is big when people are ignoring you. I'm just trying to think back... Snowdonia's similar. I fucking hate Snowdonia, rudeness, and the snotty sublime. David Mollin

41 **Alfred Gilbert** (Royal Academy, 1987). Just scrapes in at 1987. What a terrific show this was. Black and silver come to mind, with low lighting. Black drapes cradled baroque-roccoco-victorian silver busts and statuettes by the man who did *Eros* on Piccadilly Circus and a statue of the man who founded Barry Docks (now overseeing a waterfront development that boasts a 'Morrison's', and second only in ambition, if not funding, to Cardiff). This exhibition was, how shall I put it...Yes, an experience, and one that Norman has tried to recreate a few times since (and in the very recent past). None have hit the mark as this little black and silver beauty. A concise, tight little box all of its very own amongst some less concise, dodgy boxes that I carry around in my head thanks to the RA. David Mollin

42 **Liam Gillick Renovation Filter: Recent Past and Near Future** (Arnolfini, 2000). Depending upon the route by which you approach Gillicksville, it is either a place where the conceptual underpinnings of art practice are reconsidered in their entirety or somewhere adorned with designer objects floating on hot air. If we take the former approach – and we should (as Gillick himself advises in the last volume of this series: always give the artist the benefit of the doubt) – then we arrive at some quite stimulating results. To take the latter approach is simply unproductive. Sometimes cynicism is the correct way but most of the time it's just plain nasty.

What, then, does Gillick's practice consist of? Nothing less than a reconsideration of the legacy of conceptual art by way of a series of parallel investigations into various ideological structures, is the short answer. The accuracy with which an artist such as Lawrence Weiner makes linguistic plays over into visual puns has therefore been key to Gillick. Meanwhile, Victor Burgin's co-ordination of word and image as means to deliver a sermon on consumerism has not. Weiner has also informed Gillick's conception of site, which is not surprising given that he has a polyvalent approach to the issue rather than a laconic purchase on it. Weiner's wall texts are simultaneously generic and specific. They effect the site where they are placed, and the site effects them. Each time they are re-sited Weiner reconfigures the font, the spacing, the colour to produce a new work.

Sometimes, Gillick's installations establish an ambience that permits the beholder to surf through the gallery space, lap up the pools of light on the floor, deliberate under the platforms from which they emanate and jive with the video on display. The multifarious objects making up the installations are like theatre props abandoned on a stage and Gillick's numerous books located nearby appear to provide the script that should make sense of them all but often doesn't. Thus in the same way that his work is not site-specific, more site-sensitive, so it is not simply viewer interactive, but rather viewer reactive. The ambient situation his installations provide for the viewer is a result of the way Gillick chooses to conceive of his exhibitions neither as points of conclusion nor revelations of the diligent activity that goes into producing the work, whether process-based or purely intellectual. They are instead places where the beholder can jam in time with Gillick. Be part of his think-tank. This approach is transposed into the way his different exhibitions interrelate. Each one feeds into the next but not necessarily in a linear fashion. In the present exhibition, there is one element that was originally intended for a corporate building in Munich as a corrective gesture to an inadequately programmed sector of space. Gillick's proposal was rejected by the building's architects who choose to deal with the problem themselves. By re-mapping the element into the present exhibition, Gillick alters its implications – hence the exhibition's title, replete with its echoes of the Independent Group.

Previously, artists laboured to achieve a firm coalition between the artwork and the story or experience they wanted to trigger or communicate. Whether it was a modernist painting or a postmodern text piece didn't make any difference. Gillick's practice readjusts the binary of experience versus interpretation these two types of work depend on. Sometimes this is by setting off objects with unexpected triggers, little quirks that unsettle things he has produced that, if left on their own, may appear to align with existing codes and ideologies, which would be undesirable for Gillick. A glass of coke nestles next to one of his Plexiglas platforms; a pool of glitter twinkles on the floor; a wall text implies a narrative that seems to go nowhere. Each supplement troubles the original, resulting in a kind of altered state of meaning.

To try and arrive at the point of all this, however, is to miss the point. Sure there is some hot air in Gillicksville, but something needs to keep one afloat when traversing a show. And anyway, since when did art relinquish the right to enlist rhetoric as a conceptual devise to court the beholder? Rhetoric has simply been sublimated for too long by flat-footed pragmatism in all its disguises. Artists who call a spade a spade should use one. It's all they are fit for. Alex Coles

43 Dominique Gonzalez-Foerster (Robert Prime, 1996). This was the inaugural show of Robert Prime. The show was in three parts: two rooms – a 'photographic studio' and a 'museum gallery' – and a book, a 'guide' to Chandigarh. It belonged to the first series of works by Dominique Gonzalez-Foerster to examine exoticism, the way in which modernism has been assimilated in tropical or subtropical climates. As often with her work, it incorporated autobiographical elements without being confessional. I have always been impressed by the clarity, the emotional precision of Dominique Gonzalez-Foerster's work. I am a fan.
Tommaso Corvi-Mora

44 Douglas Gordon 24 Hour Psycho (Tramway, 1993). I remembered this long before I got there for the first time. We all thought we knew it, or at least had a take on it before we saw it. But we did not.

I can't watch the Hitchcock any more. It moves too quickly for me. But '24 Hour Psycho' takes on other inflections – something to do with when I arrived for the first time. I've seen it maybe in four or five places now, but it's still about that first time and the first scene in which you will always invest so much. A sort of transference. Despite the spacious installation, there isn't the collective resource that movies usually have to offer. There's an intimacy that stems from that singular point of arrival. No-one came in at just the same moment as myself.

So for me, it will always be about the fugitive, about Marion asleep in the desert, and the policeman's face at the window, and the drive, and the hurried(!) escape.

I've entered '24 Hour Psycho' at other moments in the narrative, but that one's the start of my Psycho, always.

Each scene can last up to an hour and so takes on an enormous burden of meaning. You see the gaze, the camera's, almost your own. But you are apart from it. Douglas doesn't seem even to be quoting from Hitchcock; it is the film itself. He doesn't even seem to be appropriating Hitchcock for himself. The film is always copyrighted Hitchcock. Douglas sees an object in it, something less transparent than a movie. He makes it material.

Something I said, but had forgotten: "The lips hardly move at all."
Andrew Renton

45 Luke Gottelier Kill The Young (One in the Other, 2001). I first met Luke Gottelier in 1998 when he was running the Germanicly *chi-chi*, 'Deutsch Britische Freundschaft' in Islington. I included him in a drawing exhibition because he made photographs that really seemed to have transported the act of drawing into some 3rd dimension. He would create a scene using studio rubbish that was just lying around: scraps of paper, blu-tac and pens etc. which he then photographed. Drawing featured heavily as subject matter in these photographs – yet in an indirect and elusive way. The viewer was allowed to peek into a private world, a place where someone played, and yet the results were satisfyingly abstract and absurd. These scenes were only related to their titles in the loosest of ways, being called things like 'View from the A361'. Then Gottelier took up painting. He felt that he had done all he wanted to do with photography, and in fact it always had been a means to an end: a way of capturing absurd situations in his studio.

At first glance the paintings had an imbecilic simplicity to them – a few lines and squiggles on an otherwise blank canvas. But there was a sense of purity about them, of going back to first principles, and also, as in all of Gottelier's work, a strong sense of play. This artist was having fun, and it was infectious. Then Gottelier's paintings became more complex and ambitious – yet still they retained a lightness of touch and joie de vivre. Gottelier moves backwards and forwards between abstraction and figuration. Importantly his work is free of the influence of photography, which is so common in today's painting. Turning his back on photography as both a source material and as a medium in its own right, Gottelier has found a liberation from the limits of description – each day he creates a new fantasy world; painting has become a kindergarten for subjectivity.

At One in the Other, Gottelier exhibited 5 square canvasses – each one an experiment in the plastic properties of paint and the dynamics of modelled form. On the floor lay a carpet of black and white photographs, (a limited edition of 1000) which could be taken away. They became soiled and destroyed as time wore on. Appropriately the visitor had to trample over the discarded ruins of the photographic, in order to view paintings of pure invention, which were blessedly free of any indexical link to the real. Oh joy! Emma Dexter

46 **Paul Graham** (Anthony Reynolds, 1994). Nine framed colour photographs of cloudy Irish skies hung in the gallery. We know they are Irish skies, not from any clue garnered from the image but from each work's title that appears on the mount of each photograph to read, for example, 'Bogside, Derry, Cease-fire April 1994'. The works continued Graham's procedure of finding images in which history and politics can be discerned in those everyday places and situations which don't readily provide such visual markers. On 31 March 1994, the IRA announced a 72 hour temporary cessation of hostilities prior to the full cease-fire scheduled for August. Graham juxtaposed a title as an element of the visual experience of looking at the work, with images that, if unreferenced, would have been generic (sky) rather than specific (the sky above a place in Ireland at a specific time in the history of that place). For Constable, the sky was the heart of a landscape painting establishing its '"key note", the standard of "Scale", and the

chief "organ of sentiment" … The sky is the "source of light" in nature – and governs everything'. Isolated, in Graham's photographs, the skies above Andersontown, Shankhill, Bogside, Craigavon, Ballymurphy and elsewhere were chosen as the only part of the landscape not touched in one way or another by the 'Troubles'. The sky became an image of an ideal Northern Ireland, while the changeable conditions he photographed reflected the unsettled and fragile nature of the cease-fire. However, more significant is the fact that the photographs existed as so much more than just metaphorical surrogates. These are documents of a particular moment in Northern Ireland – the captioning says so. The photographs indicate a state of fact that is rarely found in photography (supposedly a medium governed by fact but manipulated by artifice). They show, as did his earlier photographs of a changed Europe following the fall of the Berlin Wall, that absolutely no part of the landscape can escape the hand of history. In making photographs as mute and as seemingly about as little as they can be, Graham shows that meaning can be inscribed and found in most things chosen by the camera. History leaks everywhere and can be felt in everything. The document might appear to depict not very much, but tells us everything.
Andrew Wilson

47 Peter Halley Recent Paintings (ICA, 1989). It's funny how the black polo-necks the 80s ICA dudes are so proudly sporting disappear against Peter Halley's new paintings. Same goes for those black jeans. The only things that sing against these dark canvases are the day-glo titles that zip across the little pocket books in their hands. They look like Bibles. And the way they constantly refer to them would suggest they serve the same function. But these little books are actually collections of essays by a number of French theorists. Even *The Face* did a piece on this stuff such was its popularity back in the day.

Halley made good use of these theorists by calibrating his paintings with his writings for much of the 80s. There was a way he manhandled primary theoretical texts – warping and contorting their very lineaments in the process – which meant his were creative readings. Still, Halley's early paintings appear quite didactic now in their figure/ground opposition. The cell and conduit create a motif that goads too figurative a reading. Some of the paintings in the ICA from the late 80s expand the cell to such an extent that it obliterates much of the background and becomes almost at one with the actual canvas unit. Here the figurative element is almost obliterated and the apparent relation to the texts subsumed. Art historians didn't appreciate Halley's use of theory much. "Thinking of the use of Baudrillard by an artist like Peter Halley" Madame Krauss conjectured: "Theory thinks it gains the possibility of resistance in critical practice, but it is often recuperated and evacuated by the worst – the most trivial – artistic practice." She must find it bizarre that Halley's subsequent paintings from the late 80s mark the high point of theory in the artworld, albeit pessimistically so.

Halley's own shift away from a textual engagement with theory in the late 80s was followed by a return to the studio for a period of regeneration. At precisely the same time, theory was entombed by two disciplines: Art History and Visual Culture. Ostensibly different, both are connected by a complete inability to relate to the cutting art practices of their day. And while this is not surprising for Art History given its pledged subject, it is for Visual Culture. On the other hand, that Visual Culture is critical of both the New Art History – which was new about twenty years ago – and the *October* group is no bad thing; most certainly, its devotees are onto something when they endeavour to develop new methodological models that move in time with the artwork. So it is regrettable that as yet their efforts have yielded negligible results. Wayne Koestenbaum is perhaps an exception to the rule, flourishing under the influence of his mentor Roland Barthes.

There is however something much worse than Visual Culture's inability to use the theoretical text to write in time with the artwork, with the art historian's complete impotence when faced with contemporary practice. It's how those affiliated with it still wear black like they did when they were training to be art historians in the late 80s. And with the banal covers' the academic publishers wrap around their theory books today there is not even the day-glo flash brought by the title font of the old days for relief. Alex Coles

48 **Duane Hanson** (Royal Festival Hall, 1998). I am keen on a certain strand of American fiction that had its zenith round about the late eighties, early nineties; Richard Ford, Andre Dubas, people like that. So? Hanson had bloody realistic life-size models of American people looking depressed. Anyway, these were depressed everyday American people, wearing memorable retro American clothes. 'Depressed' in the sense that they looked it in this context. If you are put in the position of looking at people like this then they look depressed, believe you me. Catatonically depressed. I stare at depressed people making them look more

depressed the more I look. One scuttled across the ceiling while I was occupied with staring at a George C. Scott type, depressed in a Hawaiian shirt. I thought the Festival Hall was a good environment for this work.   David Mollin

49 **Georg Herold** (Paley Wright, 1991). Looking back on it, this show had the appearance of being defined by a degree of decadence and pose. Paintings of caviar (if I remember right Karsten Schubert had shown some of these separately at about this time as well); a cocaine mountain; two gimcrack vitrines, one of which was empty and the other containing multiples (the heart of the show) with images of multiples silkscreened onto the glass panes; and a sculpture made of lathes of wood with no instructions for its making into art. Reviewing the exhibition for a Belgian magazine at the time I earnestly over-egged the installation and stupidly wrote that the two vitrines (one empty, the other with objects inside and images of the objects on the glass) not only served to "extend a long-standing Modernist commentary on authenticity, absence and presence, here Herold also enacts a sort of self-ridicule through his indifference which admits a commitment to the absurd". Looking back what has kept this show in my mind is the absolute lack of the absurd, absolute lack of indifference and, strange as it may seem, absolute lack of cynicism. Herold is no Beuys and I am sure he knows it, but that is not the point. Herold's multiples, like Beuys', tapped into a prevailing social mood which, unlike Beuys, Herold satirised at the same time. Satire seems virtually a dead form in art and one wonders why. Yes, Herold mocked art and its institutions, but painting a face of Jaruzelski in caviar (or the Birmingham Six), or joining together the German and Polish flags (the Wall had only recently come down) was not just an insolent postmodern jumbling of signs – it was politically pointed as much as it was aesthetically pointed. One can witter on endlessly about multiples and authenticity and integrity and what have you (even absence and presence, if you are really desperate) – but satire? That's actually a bit tougher to take on board, because it really is an irony free zone. Andrew Wilson

50 **Patrick Heron** (Tate Gallery, 1998). Patrick Heron died within a few months of this retrospective, and it is still too soon to get a settled perspective. Since then I have not seen a single Heron painting in either of the Tates, or in any overseas collection, so does this mean he was a peripheral figure? Or that 'colourfield' painting deserves less attention than life painting? At the time of this show

there was a small show of Lucian Freud being hung next door, and I remember glimpsing them though the door, the cold muted greys, the frisson of nakedness, the picturesque poverty… and then the shock of the open sunshine of the Herons, the opulence, the stylishness.

Heron had written in the fifties of wanting to lead abstraction out of the harsh and mean-spirited abstractness of Pollock or Kandinsky into the handsome and sensuous worlds of Matisse, Bonnard and Braque, and this is what he actually did. And, yes, there was a price. At this show you had paintings of warmth and light, but there was also this aesthetic distance, a reluctance to touch anything troubling and difficult. There was no angst, and not even much revision. His painting was sublimely elegant – and often way ahead of anyone else in Britain, yet alone in the St Ives circle – elegant in the service of colour. The rhythms of his forms in his later years were identified with the Cornish landscape, but they owed much to the School of Paris, to Matisse cutouts. The scale, the breadth, the confident colour came from his original excitement with his contact with New York painting – something he found difficult to address. Yet the paintings were completely his own, written all over with his signature. Does the aestheticism matter? Taken on his own terms – where paintings just happened, without doubts or second thoughts – it doesn't. One evening at the end of the show there was a closing private view, which was extraordinarily moving, where these beautiful paintings disappeared in the fading twilight. The reds and mauves softened and lifted from the surface, an ecstatic moment.

Half of me feels these paintings, this show, was beyond criticism. It was simply one of the most beautiful things you could come across. What more could you expect? The other half has a list of questions, both about the way the show was done, and about how sooner or later we must look at Heron with the same analytical eye he himself used in his formidable early criticism.

Heron was 78 at the time, and in failing health. In the sixties and seventies there had seen a succession of Tate retrospectives of younger artists, some of the 'New Generation' school whose hard-edge and American-scented sensibility was – in part – a reaction against the more romantic and 'English' wishy-washiness of the St Ives Group. 'Bric-a-Braque' was one of their nicknames for Heron, and in the seventies Heron's apparent simplicity – cadmium reds straight from the tube – was looked at by younger painters as 'kindergarten painting'. Heron's exhibition at the Barbican in 1985 was carefully designed to be a non-retrospective. When the Tate show finally happened it was far too late. Chapters could be written on why it was that it hadn't happened at the proper time. Heron had campaigned against British capitulation to New York critical propaganda – three successive pages in *The Guardian* in 1973 – and the belligerent tone and self-justification probably hadn't won him friends at the Tate, where the disputed Morris Louis paintings held pride of place. When Heron claimed he had done his stripes first (true) and Louis might have seen slides of his work the culturati of the time smirked.

During that period Heron's paintings were gearing up with the same cranky stridency, with straight-from-the-tube colours set sharply against each other, each area disputing its boundary. These were the great 'wobbly hard-edge' paintings of the mid seventies. They were the most uncompromising and confrontational paintings Heron ever made, the most ambitious, the angriest, the least tasteful. They were first exhibited at Waddington's in 1975. The red/green jigsaw forms flipped jarringly along the meandering contours, and the flat discs and continents for the first time wove in and out and on top of each other. At the same time there was an exhibition down the road at the Rutland Gallery of paintings Heron had shown in New York in the mid sixties, much more approachable, soft edged, brushy, the colour more melodic. Though both these shows had the effect of transforming a younger generation of painters' whole outlook, the critical reaction was indifference or dismissal – no reviews were recorded in the catalogue, and I know of a review that the editor at *Studio International* didn't think worth publishing. In retrospect it seems so obvious that Heron needed edges in both art and life; that while he was digesting – despite his protests to the contrary – the hardheaded method painting of his American colleagues, he was also defining his critical terrain. The seventies paintings were punchy and real. They felt compelled into being.

If the editing of the '98 retrospective had a point to make it was that Heron's final phase of gorgeously luminous 'garden paintings' returned to the Braque-derived landscapes of his beginnings. The soft tachisme, the friendly discs nuzzling into each other of the fifties and sixties were melting back into their origins in garden fantasies. So there was a disproportionate amount of early work and of very late work. The period between 1972 and 1983 – the great years in my opinion – were represented not by one or two, but by no paintings at all. (There's a '76 painting in the catalogue but it wasn't in the exhibition.) Nor were there any gouaches. I didn't see any review that mentioned this glaring fact. It was quite an excision, but a clue as to how it came about lies in the eminent critic chosen to curate the show, regarded as having the 'best eye' in the business. David Sylvester's record as a champion of Heron's painting is curious: between 1952 and 1998 he published precisely nothing on Heron. Did Heron have anything complimentary to say about Sylvester, Bacon, or 'establishment taste' during those 46 years? Well, for his part Sylvester broke the silence in 1998; as the curator of this show he actually produced a page, or slightly less than a page of text in the catalogue, half of which is about Bacon.

The rest of the catalogue consists of reprints from earlier shows, and a rather bland and unsearching interview. Ultimately, I think it would have been more respectful to Heron's great intelligence to have challenged the image Heron wanted to control. For example, his tirades against the anecdotal, the feeble tonality and mean-ness of English painting, and American design, shouldn't be taken at face value. His idea of what was unEnglish was itself distinctly English. The model haunting Heron's whole oeuvre was really Ben Nicholson, who was also overshadowed by his adoration of Mondrian and Braque, but you can usually find a Nicholson on show in the Tate. Much as I admire Nicholson, I cannot think of any postwar painting done in Britain that matches the class of those paintings Heron squeezed out in the seventies. James Faure Walker

51 **Damien Hirst Still** (White Cube, 1995). This was in the days when White Cube operated solely out of an over-designed broom cupboard in Mayfair. I got buzzed in from the street, went up the wooden stairs and into the office on the left, which appeared to be empty, but that's because in this gallery they always hide their staff behind walls. I don't know why – it's not as if they employ ugly people. I asked to see the Hirst press files. It was only 1995 but there was an astonishing amount of stuff, several volumes of clippings, and almost all of it junk. I felt vaguely angry that there appeared to be no serious discussion of his work, any of it, anywhere. I decided to correct this. The show consisted of one work, 'Still', on one wall of the gallery. Still was a shallow, glass-fronted, polished steel cabinet, similar to the familiar earlier works but much more expensive-looking. It contained a variety of surgical instruments laid out on glass shelves. It looked clean and creepy at the same time, and immediately reminded me of a film about a psychotic gynaecologist played by Jeremy Irons. I wrote a brilliant and insightful

review that discussed Hirst's relationship with minimalism, the readymade, photography and films. I sent it to *Artforum* where some grad-school sub-editor decided to rewrite it. By the time the review was published I hardly recognised the thing. David Batchelor

52 **David Hockney Flowers, Faces and Spaces** (Annely Juda Fine Art, 1997). The exhibition title, as the exhibition itself, had a slightly pedantic tone that I really enjoyed. The still lives occupied the gallery's main floor, while the portraits were hung in a grid like formation in the space downstairs. You could tell Hockney had a great time in the studio painting these pictures, especially the still lives. Each painting showed off a new set of tricks. The catalogue included some studio shots: an unfinished painting on the easel side by side with the props used for the still life. Reality looks so drab, so banal compared to the sumptuousness and goofy elegance of the finished paintings. Tommaso Corvi-Mora

53 **Homeless Project** (Mota, 1998). This incredibly complex and tiring exhibition took place in a domestic setting. It was necessary to walk through the bedroom to see the rest of the show. Here the personal merged with the political, or public, to a point where it could have been a touch confusing, even frightening, to visit unless prepared to write about it or wash up after. The kitchen/sitting room at the back looked over a concrete patch. The front, an empty shop on the Old Kent Road, now a parking penalty advice shop, was turned into a mock office, a collection point of opinions about change, with forms asking questions like "Do you think changes will cause problems for you and if so, what might these be?" Homeless Project, initiated by David Goldenberg with the collaboration and participation of a kind of steering committee, was made possible by Frank and his girlfriend, Melissa who actually lived there and who, I think, split up very soon after. They had both come from Norwich to run a gallery and had decided to set up MOTA. Anyway, people seemed to come in there all the time; there was coffee and drink, art around the sink, and discussion about arranging more discussions. In the same way that a campaign to save a local hospital can suddenly take in the strife of Bolivian tin miners, the collaborative possibilities here were apparently endless, with no edge or boundaries and no privacy for Frank and Melissa. The art itself consisted of painting, pictures, photographs, interventions, wall and floor pieces. About 75% of those invited to exhibit were,

to which the critical dimension of performance art has all to do – perhaps more than any other art form – with its relationship to means of documentation. In the making of performance art, the issue of synchronicity between the action performed and the roll of the camera becomes key: the making of the work becomes the work as well as a synchronous documentation of the work being made. This fundamental collapse of two durations into one, (it takes as long to make the work as it takes to document it), means that performance art thwarts the traditional boundaries necessary to distinguish between the space of the artist and that of the viewer. Add to this the looping effect often dictated by the economy of gallery displays, and the temporal *mise en abime* reaches a peak. As performance art caught up with its time-based condition (too many shows in the past settled for the 'seats in front of the monitor' solution), the nature and legacy of its real object began to emerge as poised somewhere between the impossibility of its re-enactment twenty or thirty years on (though such vintage re-staging was recently attempted), and its re-evaluation as a precursory form of reality show. Against such a backdrop, the artists in this show survived the test of time extremely well: the exhibition, resorting to a series of pared down monitors economically scattered on the floor of the gallery, dramatically surfaced the tension at stake between the means of documentation necessary for the work to exist beyond its one-off execution (both through the use of the camera, the monitor and/or sound) and the actual real time physical endurance of the artists.

The works included in this show well documented the various radical attempts to jeopardise the traditional distance between the artwork and the beholder – once held the essential condition of art. Here, the great 'I am' ceased to just refer to the artist: the spectator's subjectivity too was being directly addressed and at times rather aggressively. When not directly pointed at (in Acconci's 'Centers' 1971) the beholder was thrown in and off the screen, catapulted in and out of the artist's studio space. Once the subjectivity of the audience had been so provoked, it became impossible to extricate oneself from the compulsive but partial spectacle of the artist at work. The unsettling intimacy created by the experimental use of both the camera and the monitor in relation to the artist's body never became exhausted, in such a way that watching too was endurance. In Bruce Nauman's 'Bouncing in the Corner No. 1' (1968), the camera is positioned sideways, cropping out what is there to be seen, while the sound of the performance frustratingly suggests that the viewer may be missing out. No artist explored the implication of the camera to the artist's self image as consistently as Joan Jonas. 'In Duet' (1972), Jonas re-creates, through very simple technological means, an encounter with an image of herself. Although this image is external to her, mediated by the camera onto the monitor through carefully timed choreography, she engages with it as if the materiality of the screen was irrelevant, reducing it to a mirroring device. The spectator is then made to witness a live performance of the artist with her own image, a disturbing intimacy one feels at once part of and yet excluded from. In John Baldessari's 'I am making art' (1971), the artist's deliberately exaggerated self-conscious execution of minute and self-exploratory gestures is turned on its head. The work forewarns of how an endlessly repetitive and gratuitous action could in time appear as no more than chronic bouts of narcissistic indulgence. Symptomatically, the archetypal positioning of the artist's body in front of the camera becomes part of the pathology, pre-empting to a degree a certain form of contemporary prime-time unveiling of the self and its tortured intimacy.

But there are possibly other resonances that come into play about the way the artist's body espouses the camera. The subtext of the show could indeed be read as the artist's wilfull vindication of the author function over the instrumental (secondary) role of the documentary machine. Perhaps the documentation of performance exposes two existential modes at once: the theatricality of its form closes on the transcendental affirmation of the artistic subjectivity, but not without harvesting a shadowing anxiety. (When exposed to Hans Namuth's camera, Pollock felt the need to protest that he was not a phoney.) In performing the self 'making art' for the camera, what it takes for the artist to be seen producing art uncovers not only the subject's answer to the irreducible necessity to pursue their vocation as an artist, but also inadvertently lifts the veil on just how little it takes to be 'making art'; thus displaying in full view of the camera no less than the fragile equilibrium through which the artist's subjectivity endures, the 'to be or not to be' of the whole affair: "I am the one making art, not the camera, but I am also making art for the camera." Alexia Defert

56 In & Out of Love Damien Hirst (Woodstock Street, 1991). It was quite unusual to take over a shop right in the West End near all the big, proper galleries. The shop still has an old fashioned Italian café opposite with a good ceramic tiled mural of ducks taking off and landing, half carafes of wine, spinach with eggs and bread rolls. But then, inside the shop, upstairs and downstairs, was a new work by Damien Hirst, it was so long ago that the heightened expectation was not really in fullgear (the almost Victorian gravitas of vicarious life and death stuff didn't hit quite immediately and there was no sense of extreme wealth and power. This was an installation after all, the whole place taken over for the show – not about a series of autonomous numbers). The relationship between live butterfly, dead butterfly, painted surface and cigarette remained integrated. The commodity sitting strangely well with other, more free, suggestions. In fact, the clammy, heightened hatching-heat and smelly fag ends piled up downstairs hinted at Hirst repertoire but in an unusually fallible manner. The whole process of life, death – not much truth, but a touch of reality – had live butterflies perching on the top of stretchers upstairs and butterflies trapped, caught, clogged, dead in the paint on the pictures downstairs. Hirst was still framing however, with the paintings functioning a bit in the same way as the edge of the vitrine. 'In & Out of Love' carried that insistent, comforting quality; like the *Hawaii Five O* beat in the original Motown B track of the same name. Sacha Craddock

57 **The Institute of Cultural Anxiety: Works from the Collection** (ICA, 1994). ICA competition. Conceptual liquidity. The artist is dead. Long live the artist. The Curator of Experiments has been liquidated. Marcel Broodthaers turns in his unquiet grave, an eight foot glass vitrine displayed at the Archive Museum of Eagles (white).

Jeremy Millar collects (but not really) artefacts as a sign of a modern fascination with death; seducing us by vitrine and archival list, but he's no collector, he's a curator of the sublime. We feel safer here with mediocre little things, like the locals we are, fascinated by the two bit flea-circus. Papa Lazaru's fake museum of freaky curios, we prefer our little grubby world to the leap of ambition concealed in constant anxiety. I'm not sure if this act of failure was billeted on the competition but the show had enough Angst going on behind the scene in manipulations of young artists of the not so (banal) freaky scene at that time, willing to sign their inclusion in another Nazi-massification stroke accumulation of cultural capital. To forgo discrimination in the traditional sense they are promised success within the complexity of a body called 'art' (if certainty gives way to uncertainty I too could perhaps make a success of my life and become an artist).

Mourning, Jacques Rancière eats his heart out in public and is forced to swallow intellectual pride. Theo Adorno has another fatal heart attack. Paul Virilio is discovered sniggering during communion. The sheer scale of horrid funereal conceits collected as small tokens (art objects in a museum, the uncanny ICA) a J.G. Ballard type recurrence in the atrocity cell's future-anterior, 'the eternal world of the gods', that Millar offers (as the autodidact he really is) who would never concede pity to those publics, a Curator shaking the hand of visitors to a garden of wreaths.

Mimesis is how you fake it. Design dresses up in post historical clothing. The list that Millar's institute begins to recite is replete with other names and slowly read, like the Mahler track used for *Death in Venice*, it whimpers at the end, with a puff of the mediocre.

I cheated on this one, as I searched out an archive, joining the 'Tate Research Centre'. Confusing libraries and archives I couldn't go into on a day pass. There was an archivist there who cross-referenced 'ICA', and found it missing from the ICA archive and in the wrong box file. I told her that I was writing for *100 Reviews*. We talked about collecting and of the small lost editions of less prominent shows and how much each publication would cost now. I said some unscrupulous book dealers capitalise and speculate by stocking them in their basements to accrue value. She was curious about *100 Reviews*… "What a task… 100 reviews!" I said the anxiety was not in choosing out of the thousands of shows from the last 15 years but in the necessary editing. Peter Lewis

58 **Anish Kapoor** (Hayward Gallery, 1998). This was a big show. Kapoor had taken over the whole gallery and along with an architect plotted a route that firmly guided you around a series of voids and shimmery things. Lots of critics noted the 'less is more' thing going on in the first gallery which had three voids strategically placed in the walls and floor of the vast first gallery. Very Kapoor – you look in them and go all funny. There was a big, reflecting silver apple in the second room and I think, one of his semi-circular voids sticking out of the wall. Upstairs were more voids. There was a series of concave mirrors that meant your reflection was all over the place and sometimes not there at all, but also his piece consisting of rocks saturated with blue dye. Perhaps it was there to break up the voids. And then when you were feeling voided-out there was a large rock that was polished inside so that when you looked at it it gave off a shimmery light that seemed to float by itself in front of the piece. And finally, there was an enormous red void stuck to the ceiling of the last room. Lots of people lay underneath

it trying to get down with the transcendental thing, like some scene out of *The Buddha of Suburbia*. But for me this wasn't the point at all. For me the point was that if you went to a corner of the room you could see the metallic bits of the bell structure and the illusion was destroyed entirely. I liked this greatly, even though I knew that this was not how Kapoor would have seen the piece. When I did a gallery tour of the show I made everyone stand at the edge of room and said "Look! Look! It's all an illusion". I then pattered through my theory about this and how it was all to do with a misidentification with the Lacanian other. I realised this was perhaps not what was required from these glorified walking tours when an old dear came up to me and said "You've ruined it for me now". And what's particularly strange – and I remember this clearly – is that when she said this she was beaming from ear to ear as if some veil had been lifted. But that wasn't my point at all, I thought. Niru Ratnam

59 **Alex Katz Small Paintings 1951–2002** (Timothy Taylor Gallery, 2002).
Alex Katz' 'Small Paintings' at the Timothy Taylor Gallery works a bit like a miniature identity parade of the painter's usual suspects. His favoured sitters were all there (close up portraits of Ada, Vincent et al), reappearing one after the other in familiar backdrops (beaches, fields and parks, isolated woods etc.) which, executed in such small formats (oil on board, mostly 12 x 9 in. or 16 x 12 in.) take the viewer right to the heart of the painter's social cosmology. Before you even get to engage with the rationale behind works of this scale (were they meant as works, or as studies towards some larger formats? Were these quick impressions, hastily transcribed in order to assist at a later stage the process of reminiscence for larger canvases?) the paintings trigger a perceptual operation which takes you in the opposite direction. Although Katz' small works appear to document his own part of the world very closely, the viewer soon surrenders, as the paintings call to mind his or her own databank of locations. Of course small paintings tend to do that, performing through their sheer format and in the way they beget the viewer's physical proximity, a degree of intimacy. But here such immediacy owes as much to the genial sequencing of the paintings as to the convivial informality of the exhibition. This stunning collection of Katz' small paintings had much to offer to a viewer keen to retrace some of the steps that have lead the lived world of Alex Katz to fossilize into a series of such instantly recognisable images.

As often in the paintings of Katz, the depicted subjects – young and not so young, affluent and idle, beautiful and distinguished – are busy savouring their own glamorous appearances: revelling in their narcissistic envelop, they seem happy to be contributing to the making of a good image, a series of effortlessly arrived at 'Kodak moments'. But, paradoxically, although Katz' small paintings appear to have been executed in little time, even conferring rather grotesque expressions to the sitters ('Kate' 1993, 'Black Coat' 1999), the brush marks bring them away from artifice, instead charging their vacant and leisurely expressions with disturbing life-like qualities and an overbearing presence. But even if these small formats champion, the way a story-teller might in one short paragraph, the significant detail that will epitomize the sitter's personality, there is no trace of cynicism in the painter's ability to make the subjects' respective social posturing visible. The paintings seem, on the contrary, to celebrate social and gender codes as well as emotional detachment: at times the sitters' distant expressions suggest that in certain circles social denunciation itself has become somewhat clichéd ('Maxine' 1976, 'Mrs. Kahn' 1980, 'Ace Airport', 1999). Is this precisely what Katz sees in the people he chooses to paint, an expression poised between authenticity and heightened artifice? For the subjects in Katz' paintings are not weighted down by any form of metaphysical interrogation. In many ways, their affirmative skill at just being, mirrors their status as part of a carefree American elite. So, if the source material evoked is already about glamour and visual pleasure, how can the paintings be about anything else? What the series brings to the fore is Katz' painting grammar, in turn challenging the viewer's ability to go with the brashness, the at times, disarming simplicity of the brush marks (here the earlier works, such as 'Two Boys' (1951) and 'Yellow Interior' (1953) attest to the dramatic transformation and the progressive paring down of Katz' process). To come so close to the painter's alphabet forces the viewer to reorganise his or her own understanding of how things appear through painting. The paintings become as much about the act of looking itself, as the viewer has to negotiate what will constitute a detail over the rest of the composition. It seems the details in the more monumental works assume a different function altogether.

Colour becomes a major contender with the format of the work: at times, some of the paintings appear as vibrant as backlighted boxes, with a near calligraphic inscription of objects, reminiscent almost of the accurate art of silhouetting. Elsewhere, pockets of colour carry-on erupting in unjustified violent monochromatic zones, almost indifferent to the coherence of brush marks in their vicinity ('Pale Greens' 1955, 'Study for COWS' 1984, 'Rocks and Sand' 2002). Such pockets of pure colour seem to be still forming, leaving it until later to determine what element of the composition they will be cast in: the blue of the sea, pale yellow sand or the lime green of the park. Next to the most built up and tonal brush marks a trace of pale paint surfaces, surprisingly precise in its execution, given the size. Thinned out, such tracing around the figure seems to prop it up into depiction ('Vivien-Black Stockings' 1988; 'Night Nude' 1989). On one hand, this repetitive process of thinning out the paint around the form interrupts the continuity of the figure/ground relationship and brings the cohesion of the painting to a halt. But stand back from the painting, and the very opposite takes place, this time locking the sitter into place, as if the cut out cardboard figure had found its legitimate position in the landscape through the discontinuous intensity of marks. What had initially conveyed an impression of hasty execution, the conflation of the format with the range of brushstrokes, now manages to convey a bewildering sense of the sitter's presence beyond the burden of representative accuracy. Elsewhere, touches of deep red paint flicker through a top layer of flesh coloured paint, adding to a similarly conflictual impression: a female subject who, at first glance, had appeared majestically frontal, ('Nude with Folded Arms' 1989) all sealed up in self-assurance, is now, on closer inspection, betrayed by the undercutting and vibrant glow of the red.

In many ways these paintings are about making you see the way you look at painting: on the one hand, close inspection of small works means you are given to see the handwriting that further along tries to lure you; on the other hand, the changing intensities of spaces, achieved by the variety of marks, keep on drawing you in, creating a bi-focal effect across the surface of the paint. Where Katz visits the scene of painting at night, the viewer is in for another surprisingly contrasting effect. In 'Crosslight' (1994); 'Moonlight' (1997); 'Night Ride' (1999); 'Lamplight' (2000) the encoding of total opacity is pitched right against the high intensity of a glowing white moon deceptively simplified down to white paint. In 'Rushing Brook II' (1990), the river barely glistens, the way it would appear to the lost stroller: as the materiality of water takes on the appearance of a cold slab of black marble, the painting suggests that all you could go by to find your bearings would be sound. Katz here not only translates the subtle changes operated by a new hour upon the landscape, but by showing how one corner of the world transforms, subtly refers the viewer to his larger works, bringing into visibility the way variation appears in the same. Alexia Defert

60 Alex Katz Twenty-five years of painting (Saatchi Gallery, 1998). The Alex Katz exhibition had the qualities that marked the few great shows at the gallery: a vision in organising something no other space in London could – or would – put together and a timeliness, both from a cultural and a market point of view. The paintings looked great in the spaces of the Saatchi: cool, elegant, glamorous in a subdued way. Slightly chilling but incredibly generous at the same time. Alex Katz' solipsistic endeavour has something heroic about it, to me it's as monumental as Pollock's or Barnett Newman's. My feeling is that his individualistic approach is as influential to a generation of young artists today as Jeff Koons' strategies were for the YBas. Tommaso Corvi-Mora

61 Martin Kippenberger The Beginning was a Retrospective (Karsten Schubert Ltd, 1991). Amazingly – and to London's great shame – this was Martin Kippenberger's only solo London show during his lifetime. (Equally astonishing is the fact that there has still only been one posthumous show: a sampling of his 'Hotel' drawings at the defunct 'London Projects'). We can only imagine how British art might have turned out had we had the opportunity to see a little more of Kippenberger's work first-hand in the mid-to-late 1980s. For Kartsen Schubert – at the time an occasionally great gallery showing Ed Ruscha, Christopher Wool, Victor Willing and Georg Herold amongst others – Kippenberger appeared to have made most of the show on the day of the opening. Such was Kippenberger's genius (and I think it is fair to say that he was a genius) that the resulting show was pretty much perfect. A tartan shopping trolley had been sprayed with fake snow, plastic wind-up toy soldiers crawled aimlessly across metal trays and – best of all – old shoe boxes had been gaffer-taped to Schubert's staircase making the passage upstairs perilous if not impossible. What it all meant was anyone's guess. Matthew Higgs

62 Yves Klein The Leap into the Void (Hayward Gallery, 1995).
63 Piero Manzoni (Serpentine Gallery, 1998). Piero Manzoni and Yves Klein were both young when they died but these important, well-presented and tidy solo shows respectively at the Serpentine and Hayward galleries made them

seem old. The two artists had radically embraced variety and heterogeneity of means. Both combined philosophical idealism with adroit manipulation, yearnings for transcendence with bodily abjection, and extremes of innovation with traditional ambition. In these exhibitions they were effectively reduced to manufacturers of collectables.

The artefacts resulting from their thinking and their actions were beautiful, and beautifully exhibited in both shows. Yves' sumptuous colours glowed; Piero's off-white *Achromes* modulated the white gallery walls tenderly. Performance residues or conceptual propositions were elevated to the status of relics and their incidental aesthetic appeal, instead of jolting us into questioning the traditional values of painting and sculpture as both artists intended, elicited murmurs of appreciation from connoisseurs. At the Hayward some films of Klein's events were presented to provide context, but the fascinating black and white footage of naked women with beehive hairstyles, covered in paint and overseen by a suited man, looked fairly antique and therefore irrelevant. A live performance using the painted body of a naked man under the direction of a clothed woman reversed the roles somewhat and alongside other events programmed at the Hayward during this exhibition by contemporary artists working perhaps 'in the spirit of' Klein, underlined the uneasiness of the curators in the face of problems created by an exhibition celebrating Yves Klein's work in a series of objects. Nothing so disquieting occurred at the Serpentine, where Manzoni's 'Magic Base' (a wooden pedestal with metal footplates designed to transform participants into artworks) was presented as an untouchable object to be looked at …

In these two exhibitions, Manzoni and Klein, who were audacious, critical, multifarious, energetic and articulate artists, were the victims of an art historical desire for simple closure. It was tragic. There were two huge illustrated catalogues. The work of both artists appeared to be finished, acceptable, and rather old hat.

At some point in both exhibitions it was pointed out that some young British artists were using Manzoni's and Klein's ideas forty years on, a suggestion that confirmed the extent to which those ideas, in becoming part of a commonplace art language, are beginning to seem author-less. But without an acknowledgement of the past, of the difference between then and now, nothing intelligible could be made of the objects on display apart from their sensuous and physical aspects, since their essential criticality was based on a radical departure from earlier art. The institutions' desire to assert the importance of today's remakes, while erasing temporal succession by skipping over all that's happened since the 60s, simply confirmed a lack of willingness to grasp the significance of Manzoni's and Klein's contributions to the history of ideas. It isn't very intelligent to speak glibly of the uneasy fit between the work of Klein or Manzoni and the museum as an institution, while editing the work so that it can be situated quite comfortably in a museum. If the work is reduced to a succession of attractive objects without any critical framework or intellectual content, it would be honest to admit this is a trivialization of what both artists were about.

Manzoni was 29 when he died, Klein 33, both in 1962. They might have gone on through the rest of the 60s, 70s, 80s and 90s still multifarious and audacious but not fashionable because they were no longer young, or they might have invented video or political art or some other genre. They would have learned a few things from feminism. They might have got better and better although we have absolutely no idea what that might mean, maybe simply the slower working through of ideas that came early and all at once to each of them, bursting rapidly into full flower. If they had lived longer they might have begun to seem rather beside the point (like Arman, Klein's closest friend and collaborator) or dated, or tiresome through our over-familiarity. They would both have received solo museum shows and maybe they would have refused or figured out a better way to manage them than these posthumous examples. Maybe they would have more or less given up making art, having said so much so early. Maybe their appetites for fame and recognition would have been satisfied and their researches intensified in private, like Duchamp. Maybe they would have repeated themselves even more. Maybe they would never have repeated themselves. Susan Hiller

64 **Harmony Korine The Diary of Anne Frank Part II** (Thomas Dane/ Patrick Painter, 2000). When commissioned to make work for a gallery, rather than cinematic distribution, great filmmakers like Atom Egoyan or Abbas Kiarastami have an unfortunate knack of being able to make work with all the excessive trappings of the spectacular end of 'installation art', but an almost equal degree of banality. A mastery of cinematic language or process doesn't always go hand in hand with knowing how to deal with physical space and objects within it. They have the right accessories but just don't know how to put together a decent outfit. Their recent follies for Artangel and the Venice Biennale respec-

tively, flicker like dim projector bulbs in comparison with Harmony Korine's simpler 'Diary of Anne Frank' some years ago.

The black cube presentation conditions of video art have a tendency to put me on edge as much as any tedium to be found therein. Scale and darkness often seem too sepulchral, puffing-up works into grandiose bloated parodies of themselves. In an empty Clerkenwell building on the dusty, dirty side of loft conversion, Korine's work seemed, at first glance, to follow the usual pattern, utilising a combination of structuralist multi-screen projection, layered sound and raw, gutsy hand-held camera footage denoting layered, raw, gutsy thinking. Typical of Korine's work, the subject matter was that of poverty-stricken middle-America, of small-time hopes in small towns, of those on America's fringes. Perhaps the title – 'The Diary of Anne Frank' alluded to a sense of entrapment. Perhaps it was just glib. Either way, what was striking was that Korine's Herzogian poetics made for a morally complex experience that was moving and upsetting as much because its pathos was disturbingly entertaining, as it was because of any feelings one had for the plight of those depicted. I remember the bathetic gestures of a local teen Death metal band tearing up a copy of the Bible in someone's basement seeming somehow emblematic of small town desperation. I faintly recall the rich digital blues of a figure floating in a dirty swimming pool, adjacent to Super-8 footage of an albatross in flight, with melodramatic opera resonating around the shell of the building. It still makes me sad to think of the ageing entertainer matter-of-factly stating the brutal fact that he's no longer wanted to make anyone smile or laugh. Utterly heart-wrenching and elegaic. Utterly manipulative filmmaking. I admit it – I'm a sentimental fool. I was suckered in, but at least left with my mind racing and arguing with itself. How often can you say that? Dan Fox

65 **Michael Landy Market** (Building One, 1990 (curated by Carl Freedman and Billee Sellman)). The huge industrial interior of Building One, has, in Landy's installation, been re-imagined as a vast indoor market. It is filled with structures and objects which all refer directly to the kind of basic hardware to be seen in a real street market: tiered display stands (fabricated from steel armatures and overlaid with planks and artificial grass); the same structures, pre-assembly, reduced to their component parts; stacks of *Sunblest* plastic bread crates arrayed with bewildering variety.

At first sight, it looks like a real market place, dense and chaotically grown.

Gradually though, moving through and amongst the discrete clusters of stuff, you discern a structural, sculptural logic at work. Landy has differentiated types of arrangements, and then evolved different permutations within those arrangements. Thus, the Market Stalls themselves are constructed in a variety of heights and forms, some double-tiered, some no more than rudimentary cuboids. A related sub-series 'Work' – comprised of wooden planks, steel sections and piles of neatly folded plastic grass propped and ranged along the walls – dismantles the 'Stalls' into their component parts. The 'Collect' pieces – stacks of bread crates, placed near the exits and entrances of the building – rehearse their adapted function as temporary storage systems; while the taller 'Stack' series (columns of crates towering over wheeled bases) are intrinsically moveable. Finally, the 'Appropriations' are inverted, low-level blocks, built from the same trays, and dispersed throughout the space. They refer to the most common revised function of the ubiquitous plastic crates – as display podiums filched by the high street grocer or stallholder.

In its urban aesthetic, in its seriality, and in its delineation of the part to the whole, 'Market' seems to consciously borrow the grammar of Minimalism. And yet 'Market's objects and materials remain closer to life than Minimalism's idealised geometries. Though not 'found' per se – for they are still manipulated sculpturally Landy's objects admit the existence of the real, phenomenological world, rather than retreating into the distanced, abstracted space of art. For Landy, meaning is rivetted to firm, concrete facts, to the look of the contemporary world and its material artefacts (what could be more particular to modern urban culture than the multi-adaptable plastic crate, an object so familiar that it has almost become invisible?) In choosing the most determinedly prosaic of objects, and in composing a resolutely non-hierarchical arrangement in the space – with no discernible beginning or middle, and certainly no finale – Landy forces our attentions on the minute similarities and discrepancies between like-looking things. He preserves the ordinary indifference of his objects and presents a situation which is, at the level of appearance, value-free.

The notion of value is at stake in 'Market', in another sense, in that the piece catalyses a dialectic between what is, and what isn't, art. 'Market' is composed of real, non-art objects constructed by commercial manufacturers. And yet it can only be understood as art, self-consciously created for the context of the gallery, and for consumption in the art market. It rehearses some of the distinctions between artistic activity and social activity, highlighting different categories of value (use, exchange, aesthetic) and production. Many of these ideas coalesce in the video section of the exhibition. Three video sequences, collectively titled 'Appropriation', document high-street grocers performing their daily ritual of opening up shop, as they assemble their pavement displays from plastic crates and fake grass. Landy's camera records their activity in inexorable detail. The cross-reference to the 'Appropriation' series (the crates arranged as low-level podiums) becomes obvious. As Landy 'steals' their pictures and makes them art, so the traders are caught stealing the crates. (Each bears the legend, "The sole property of Sunblest Bakeries Ltd., who will prosecute for the retention or unauthorized use of this container.")

The videos focus on the deliberateness of each vendor's routine. Landy, in his orderly filmic procedure, plagiarizes not just their objects, but their methodicalness too. He appears to assert that there is art in life: that even the most basic of activities can be seen to have a purpose and an aesthetic, and that art-making itself differs little from the kind of daily decision-making that people habitually make. And yet he knows that it does differ. He knows that the domain of art accords objects an alien value. There's a pleasing irony in the fact that *Allied Bakeries* insist any buyers of Landy's work contract not to allow the crates to revert to 'practical usage'. The owners are prepared to authorise the 'theft' only on condition that their products remain artworks not bread carriers: here use-value takes clear priority over exchange-value.

This huge Market, teeming with stalls, is conspicuously devoid of consummable goods. With its vacant surfaces, and its volatile, changeable arrangements – where many possibilities are presented but nothing appears permanent or certain – it is tempting to interpret the piece in terms of the fashionable post-modern assertion that we exist in a limitless, yet empty, market, where 'goods' are just vacuous signs, circulating continuously and completely severed from tangible need. Tempting too, to read 'Market' as a specific comment on a contemporary British art world, where the market is all, and the art itself is merely a more or less differently packaged by-product. And yet Michael Landy's Market, as you wander through its expansive space, seems to metaphorise something contrary and something more positive. It forces an awareness of your physical presence, your role, in relation to the objects. It is less a monumental totality than a mass of humanly-scaled accretions (each tower of crates, for example, no taller than our reach).

The street sounds on the videos – snatches of conversation, the hum of passing cars – subtly tune with the noises of the real street beyond the gallery. Landy's piece refers to a site of exchange which historically and to an extent, still, is premised on real human need and social relations. On the street – as opposed to the siteless market of global capitalism – real goods, of real use, change hands between real people, in a space which is endlessly, physically flexible. In its fluid materiality, 'Market' can be seen as an homage to this kind of human economy, where the products of a subject's labour are valued, and where the object has a distinct, material existence. Kate Bush

66 **John Latham** (Lisson Gallery, 1987). This was when the Lisson Gallery was a fraction of its current size, and its migration westwards along Bell Street had hardly begun. *Artscribe* was a dynamic international contemporary art magazine and frieze still meant a kind of wall decoration. This exhibition of Latham's early work – as early as the late 1950s but mostly from the 1960s, I think – simply looked wilder and fresher than almost anything else I had seen at the time. This was my first direct encounter with Latham's strange and beguiling output. All the works, and there were lots of them, contained partially burned, defaced, cut or torn hardback books that had been fixed onto canvasses with plaster, cable, string and wire. They looked energetic, improvised, and on the point of falling apart. They were pale and dirty or dark and dirty, and some had spots of primary colour sprayed onto pages of the books. By turning the pages you could change the colour of the work. They were intelligent and some were very funny. They seemed to be about information, noise and knowledge, and I thought this work belonged up there with Rauschenberg and Dieter Roth's. But I was too impressed by it to say anything in my review that was very convincing or original. I realise now that Latham must have had dozens of these works lying around for two decades or more and that for most of that time no one was very interested in them. David Batchelor

67 **Live in your head: Concept and Experiment in Britain 1965–75**
(Whitechapel Art Gallery, 2000). This show was fastened to the historical coat-tails of a much more substantial occasion, the exhibition 'When Attitudes Become Form', organised by Harald Szeemann for the Kunstalle, Berne in the spring of 1969, and shown in a different version at the ICA London that autumn. The emptily avant-garde slogan 'Live in your head' was printed on the cover of

the original Attitudes catalogue. The pseudo-address-book styling of the White-chapel publication was copied from the same source. The designer of the 1969 catalogue had a point to make. Szeemann had gone zotting back and forth across the Atlantic, collecting names and addresses and phone numbers as he traced the connections of an emergent and cosmopolitan avant-garde. 'Attitudes' was an international exhibition, offering vivid testimony to the loss of authority and loss of coherence in a modernism conceived on the lines of American paint-ing and English sculpture. But the entries in the Whitechapel's address book were restricted to British artists, with a smattering of temporary residents. Of the sixty-four individuals or collaborations listed very few (for the most part those with connections to St Martins) had made it into 'Attitudes' or into any of the other large exhibitions staged in Switzerland, Germany, Italy and the US between 1969 and 1972 – by which latter date the avant-garde moment was effectively over, its terminal celebration staged at Documenta 5.

Retrospective reconstructions are always dodgy affairs, liable to be infested by clerkish enthusiasms and compromised by the self-aggrandising activities of the disappointed. At 'Live in Your Head' some long-time art-school functionaries acquired an avant-garde history, while a lot of once casual try-ons were accorded museum potential. It might have been thought that the show would benefit from the smartening-up of disregarded fragments and the expensive enlargement of the once inconsiderable. Perhaps, as mere spectacle, it did. The exhibition was popular after all, its opening an unparalleled crush. But a high price was paid in confusion of curatorial categories. Bits of Concrete Poetry – never so much constructively 'intermedia' as pathetically neither one thing nor the other – were enlarged from their homely typewriter-and-paper prototypes into bold-looking photostats, thus confusingly aping the presentational style of transatlantic Con-ceptual Art, to which Concrete Poetry was always anathema. Several previously more-or-less unheard-of film-makers were included. Most of them seemed to be lecturers in art departments. The late and silly 'Oak Tree' by Michael Craig-Martin (who?) was accorded the status of a foundational work, alongside John Latham's more deserving 'Art and Culture'. Roelof Louw's neat pyramid of oranges reap-peared as a kind of formless heap. It was made in 1967 as a site-specific work for the now defunct Arts Lab. The idea was to provide the hippies with some vitamin C. Its reconstruction at the Whitechapel was sponsored by Sainsbury's. The oranges came big and lumpy. Those told-off to do the installation had had problems with the geometry, and had sort-of given up on it. As shown at Documenta 5, Art & Language's 'Index 01' allowed the spectator/reader to search the files of text that were indexed in the wall display. At 'Live in Your Head' the file drawers were kept locked, so that the work was reduced to an impenetrable minimalist installation. 'Index 01' now belongs to a Swiss corporation. Though it had been shown open the previous autumn in New York, it was apparently a condition of the loan to the Whitechapel that the cabinets be kept locked. Had this information been made public it might at least have saved Art & Language from the imputation that the work was designed to be inaccessible. And so on.

'Live in Your Head' was altogether a very British event, paradoxically reeking both of the art-school cubicles and common-rooms of the time and of the smartened-up academic environments in which competition for 'research' credibility is nowadays encouraged. Restricting the survey to work made in Britain no doubt allowed – or constructively obliged – the organisers to fill out the galleries with some liberal 'rediscoveries', or even 'discoveries'. But the resulting picture of a messy but *sui generis* British avant-garde served to obscure the more substantial scenario. In the mid-to-late 1960s and early 1970s modernist art and theory was both powerful and powerfully hegemonic in its American mode. It was also evidently riven with fissures and contradictions. These were conditions of the emergence of an international avant-garde tendency to which a small number of English artists made significant contributions. One factor that made those contributions distinctive, where they were, was a class hatred for the consumably artistic. It was this combination – class criticism of posh culture on the one hand, intelligent fascination with modernism in crisis on the other – that made Conceptual Art both possible and necessary. If that is not what Conceptual Art means, then all that's picked out by the term is 'anything that's not painting and sculpture but aspires to be art' – which is more or less what was collected at the Whitechapel. 'Conceptual Art' as an idle journalistic category embracing the British beneficiaries of today's curatorial fashions thus gets a spurious pedigree in the British 'experiments' of 1965–75.

At the close of 'Live in Your Head' the contributing exhibitors were sent a fat package of press cuttings – testimony to the success of the show. (The Wall Sreet Journal described the text of Craig-Martin's Oak Tree, approvingly, as 'Monty Pythonesque'. This is a fair indication of the categories under which British culture is most readily accommodated in the US.) Two points are worth bearing in mind. The first is that over the past dozen years there have been various international surveys of the art of this period, in which, out of the sixty-four artists and artistic enterprises represented at the Whitechapel, no more than five have ever been included. The second is that celebrations of artistic culture as national culture tend inexorably to misrepresent what they cannot comfortably co-opt. Charles Harrison

68 Sarah Lucas Penis Nailed to a Board (City Racing, 1992). Sarah Lucas had made wall hangings from glued together sections of the *Daily Sport* – a newspaper interested in strange, lurid sexual topics. I was shocked by her appropriation of the *Daily Sport* pictures and the choice of topics they represented: in particular a dwarf woman who describes her sexual exploits. The apparent cynicism of the whole show and the ability to make a joke of anything offended my idealistic feminist sensibilities. The game from 'Operation Spanner' worried me, while the photo montage of glistening erect penises formed into a kind of soup made me gag. Surely art was meant to be serious? In fact even bad boy Damien's subjects were existential and grand: Life, Death and God. You were left dumbly contemplating the vacuous, with no redemptive life lines in sight. Lucas had taken the material of popular media and commonplace objects and twisted them into something horrific with a few deft sleights of the appropriationist's hand.

Lucas also exhibited an upturned bicycle functioning as a plinth, ('Still Life' 1992) with a plank of wood balanced upon it, bearing little photographs of a man covering his genitals with pieces of fruit. This work flew in the face of established British sculpture of the time: it was rough and ready and lewd, conjuring numerous jokes and aphorisms involving men, women, fruit and bicycles – with ease. Lucas' provisional use of materials combined with in-your-face humour signalled a turning point for British sculpture. For an early solo show, Lucas displayed remarkable assurance: the amount of work, its placing, the variety of media; it was a little museum display in miniature. Emma Dexter

69 Christina Mackie (The Showroom, 1999). Every exhibition at the Showroom always has to negotiate the peculiarities of the space's two rooms as well as the gallery's overall wedge-like shape. Within this fractured space, 'IIP' by Christina Mackie presented another disruption. Orders of representation and recognition were thrown in disarray, creating a sense of disorientation and displacement in terms of what was being looked at in her quasi-scientific naming 'Intron Image Project'. At the heart of the show was an old scratchy drawing by Mackie of her cat, this had been converted into DNA, and the process by which this had been carried out could be mapped through various materials presented in the gallery – drawings showing how the co-ordinates of the drawing could be plotted and mapped to form the DNA's double helix structure, and a number of embroideries charting the drawing's DNA sequence. In the back space was a copse of poplar trees being cared for in hydroponic conditions. The intention was to slip the DNA material into the trees and see what might happen. On the face of it 'IIP' was absurd poetry. It was all very irrational. How can a cat drawing become DNA material? But then again, why not? On this level it was all very rational and no more scary than having a mouse with a pig's ear (i.e. very scary) – and just as creative. Over the last 50 years or so science has moved from Enlightenment rationalism towards the megalomaniacal preserve of the mad scientist out to change the world, and science companies out to rule the world (and bleed it dry). Mackie's delightfully homespun yet clinical installation negotiated this shift, yet beside the scientific scariness is the purity of the creative dream – 'what if…' to be found in equal measure in the artist's studio and the mad scientist's lair. Andrew Wilson

70 **Made New** (City Racing, 1996). Run for no particular or identifiable reason by essentially the same five people for most of its decade-long existence City Racing was – for much of that time – the best space in London. The number of great shows held at City Racing remains remarkable, especially given its perilous funding, or, more accurately, its lack of funding: shame on you London Arts Board. 'Made New' was one of the very few exhibitions at City Racing organized by an 'outsider': Andrew Wilson – bon-viveur, art historian and authority on all things avant-garde. 'Made New' was a beautifully conceived, staged, and subtle exhibition of works (by Alfred Jarry, Barry Flanagan, Gustav Metzger and Tim Mapston) that necessitated their being 'made new' on the occasion of each subsequent showing. Flanagan's 1960s pile of sand with a handful displaced from its centre; Metzger's revisting of his prophetic, ecologically minded 'cardboard' pieces of the 1950s and Mapston's astonishly ahead of their time functional/minimal sculptural 'situational' objects of the early 1970s – made for an alchemical experience in which the 'old' was magically transformed into the 'new'. Matthew Higgs

71 **Matisse Picasso** (Tate Modern, 2002). There is a somewhat judicious lyric composed by Jimmy Van Heusen and Sammy Cahn in the late 50s for a tart little duet titled 'Nothing in Common'. One of the verses goes "I love Picasso he's all style and he's all flare," to which there is the refrain, "I've seen Picasso and I think he's a square". Since this exhibition affords the rare opportunity to dish about the paintings of Henri Matisse, let's take the latter part of the couplet as being preferable.

Entering Tate Modern the heart weightens upon realising that the exhibition is replete with laclustre examples from Matisse's so-called avant-garde periods and bereft of the intimate caresses of the early Nice period. Here the curators mimic the classic modernist version of Matisse by insisting that first there came the fervour of the Fauvist period, then the magnitude of the Shchukin murals, then the chilled vapour of the Moroccan paintings, then the austere first world war period and then… nothing. Or at least not much. Not until the mid-30s when the old man returned to the ranks of the avant-garde with the Baudelaire and Joyce bookworks and the 'Barnes' mural.

What is lost in this version of Matisse's development is nothing less than some of the most sumptuous paintings made in the twentieth century. Henry McBride – critic for the New York *Sun* during the period of their production – thought so. So did Edward G Robinson – the 'little Caeser' of Matisse collectors. Maybe their tastes count, maybe they don't. One thing that is for sure though is that their tastes are in no way inferior to those of Alfred Barr, who the exhibition's curators follow. That John Golding and Elizabeth Cowling duplicate Barr's method – which, anyway, is a hangover from British aesthete Roger Fry's – means we have the first version of the 'Piano Lesson' in the present exhibition instead of the second one. The tough geometry, the pared down palette, the scratchy, anxious mark making. All of this wins over the fluid, the sensual and the fully chromatic, undeniable qualities of the second version of the 'Piano Lesson', so-titled 'The Music Lesson'.

The larger story that corresponds with this one over the respective efficacies of the different periods of Matisse's output is a distasteful one in which academics are pitted against artists and critics. For while artists have been known to bathe in the luxurious qualities of Matisse's output, academics tend to take shade in the conceptual cover provided by the paintings of the First World War period. Some shade it is too. In it they are safe from having to get to grips with a slice of Matisse's œuvre that is teeming with paintings ready to serve up their visual intelligence to the beholder on a silver platter. By extreme comparison, McBride manages to refine a way of approaching the paintings that gets something of their impact into the register of the writing. So does Clement Greenberg in his little book on him from '53. Then there are the artists – many of them. Mary Heilmann makes bubblegum out of Matisse's palette. Jessica Stockholder trashes his still life scenes and wrenches them out of the fictional recesses of the picture plane. Both Polly Apfelbaum and Beatriz Milhazes blow-up the luscious patterns that garnish his interiors into pulsating surfaces of colour. And Pae White pursues Matisse's penchant for design in hitherto unseen fashion.

To be fair to the curators, what we do get in this exhibition are some of the most delectable works from the mid-to-late-30s. In them, Matisse has shattered the intimacy of the 20s boudoirs without yet having arrived at the deserted interiors of the 40s and 50s. A work such as 'Music' is a case in point. The background of the painting is split into two: the top third consists of a palm leaf set on a black surface, the rest a cadium red laid over a lemon yellow. A sofa covered with a blanket of stinging red sits to the left, a sullen black chair to the right, and a grey green coffee table hovers in the centre foreground. Then come the two sitters. The one to the right is by far the most noticeable, partly because of her flowing pair of trousers, trimmed with yellow triangles. The red apple, the furthest forward of the objects in the painting, ties the entire room together by linking both background and overlay. Even though it is placed on top of the green coffee table, which hurtles it forward, the apple flattens the painting out by establishing a continuous plane with the blanket. The effect is so efficacious that everything in the picture dances in the same shallow space, albeit on slightly different planes.

Move in closer to 'Music' and it becomes clear how elaborate the handling of the paint actually is. At moments, it appears to complement the overall design, at others to work against it. From this distance the painting's surface breaks up in to a series of washes, scratches and scumbles. The apparently simple sense of design becomes tenser as the subtle underlayers of paint skip around the contours of the figures rather than simply being contained by them. Not to be confused with the one the Impressionists piloted, Matisse's technique allows for a bolder sense of design to come through without sacrificing the fusillade of surface effects the medium was made for.

Now move back out from the painting, until most of the room is in perspective, and consider how Music was a perfect backdrop to the scenes that unfolded before it on weekends through the 40s and 50s. In one of these scenes, McBride is perched on a couch placed just to the side of Matisse's painting, fending off the advances of a high-minded academic friend.

"Say, what's he driving at, that fellow Matisse?"

"Merciful powers have you never seen his work?"

"Sure, but the more I see of them the more my head spins... but if there is an idea in it I'd like to know what it is."

"The idea? My poor academical friend, that's what you'll never get from me.... Explanations do not explain! When a picture can be explained it's already en route for the garret." Alex Coles

72 **Matter & Fact** (The Collection Gallery, 1993). The main point of this show, its main focus, was the space itself. Katherin Hamnett's old shop had an entrance that was both long ramp and catwalk, at the end of the room was a mirrored wall which allowed you to see the whole show twice; the arriving visitors were the models, the stars. But only one artist really played with this, Hilary Lloyd's video was seen on three monitors placed on unicol stands against the end, mirrored, wall. Each monitor showed the same video but out of phase with each other. The video showed a group of people from an 80s-revival club dancing wearing their own clothes (often designed by Hamnett). The rest of the show rather blurs in the memory. There were the sort of placards taken on demonstrations leaning up against a wall (I think), the slogans were sort of politicalish and I think it was by Martin Boyce. There was something to do with football (a goal's net and posts I think) by Neil Miller (the show's curator); Brighid Lowe had painted some circles; Louise Messaoudi was performing at the opening by keeping very still, but I didn't realise it at the time; Dinos & Jake Chapman showed their autoerotic machine (brain, dildos, shampoo standing in for spunk, hammers) which was shown later in a non-operational state in a show curated by Gregor Muir in Hoxton Square (pre-Lux); also in the show was work by Neil Chapman, Patrick McBride, Stephen Murphy and Simon Starling which is too difficult to describe. Given my poor memory of the show, why has it stuck in the mind? The theatre of the space as harnessed by the show was one, small, aspect (later, it provided the space for Jade Jagger's first exhibition and then became Moegens Tholstrup's restaurant,

'Collection', beloved by It Girls). The other was that it was possibly the first time I had seen work by Hilary Lloyd in a gallery setting: seemingly frivolous, yet highly considered and framed; video as time, as document, as structure and as sculpture. Andrew Wilson

73 **Minky Manky** (South London Gallery, 1995 (curated by Carl Freedman)). This was one of the first shows I saw when I moved to London. I found it interesting that Gilbert & George were the only artists from the previous generation that could be included in an exhibition like this; not Richard Hamilton, nor David Hockney nor Stephen Willats. There was one work that I thought incredibly powerful and suggestive that really stayed in my mind: 'Where does it all end?' by Sarah Lucas. Tommaso Corvi-Mora

74 **Modern Medicine** (Building One, 1990 (curated by Carl Freedman, Damien Hirst, Billee Sellman)). When I arrived for the private view Damien was still punching plastic swing ticket tags into the pieces he was making with Angus. He walked around the space, talking about the installation, whilst continuing to make the work.

I liked that very much. Andrew Renton

75 **Bruce Nauman** (Hayward Gallery, 1998). This show made me realise how wrong I had been about Nauman. If I thought of him at all it would be his upturned face spewing water of 'Fountain' or the casts of his knees with a bit of neon. If minimalist art was about slabs of granite and curator-controlled architecture; if Robert Morris was the interesting one who made the Tate into an outward-bound gym; then Nauman was the clown with the plastic cup. The early videos where he just marches around on a line I had thought of as just boring – there were plenty of student imitators who could do boring. This time around my senses were more receptive: boots echoing on the floor, the claustrophobic corridor, the colours of the flashing neon. I came to sense all of these as having an insistent presence, like the force field of sculpture.

Upstairs was something really special, a magnificent installation with huge projected heads mouthing semi-coherent slogans about sociology and other ologies. The performer with the speaking part was bald and impassive, and the heads must have been at least eight feet high. There were similar video installations downstairs, but with narrative or political messages and they demanded a different kind of attention. I preferred the raw and semi-coherent mutterings of these monumental sculptural heads. They were synchronised to be confusing, with the voice tracks overlaid and interfering with each other. James Faure Walker

76 **Virginia Nimarkoh** (ICA, 1994 (Mis en Scène: Claude Cahun, Tacita Dean, Virginia Nimarkoh)). ICA ICA ICA ICA OK OK OK 1993 or 1994. ICA. Some time in the past. 1994, or 1995. My memory is rotted by Alzheimers but if I concentrate hard I can see some arse prints – red and framed, with an arse print/ink pad chair in front; and wallpaper decorated with murder-blood-death-splashes and maybe one of those eyes on the end of a bit of bobbly wire, or have I just seen the photograph? Or a dream? And so turning once more, I turned and stepped up further steps, past the reflective wall of vanity and self-knowing, thrice more I turned and then into the upper chambers. And there was a large scale photograph.

I can remember the photograph. A young black woman with a late sixties, medium-afro, waiting in the road, the road seemed like it was in the countryside, maybe with a coat and a bag. I think she was wearing white gloves or maybe the coat had white trimming. It stuck in my mind. I thought it might be the British countryside and I thought that a black woman in the English countryside in the 1960s would have looked UN-NATURAL. Also it reminded me of the famous Cindy Sherman 'Film Still' with her dressed up like Marilyn, with white hair and a white bag – which was like a negative of this image of a black woman, with black skin and the black bag – with some things that are black in one photo, white in the other and some things that are white black. But maybe both were wearing white coats. Cindy Sherman's photo is to do with IDENTITY and so is Virginia Nimarkoh's but it is also to do with BLACK and WHITE (which is also to do with identity but not so much when it's to do with a pair of white gloves). Where does the COMPOSITIONAL and the FORMAL end, and where does the CONTENT begin? It reminded me of a John Stezaker collage where a woman is holding a black cat but when you look closer you realise that the cat has been cut out of the photo and remains as a black silhouette. Is this something which is there or is it the excised shape of something else? John Russell

77 **Gabriel Orozco Empty Club** (St. James's Street, 1996). I started at the wrong end of St. James's Street. Before that afternoon, I had not realised that this wide, slightly stuffy and officious street was St. James's. Same as like I never realised Pall Mall was 'Pall Mall' but had always known that The Mall was 'The Mall'. Whatever, this just wasn't my part of town. Although since that time I have visited 'Che' on a few occasions, each time leaving with a sizable credit card receipt and wondering what the point of cigars is. The building that housed Orozco's installation was at the top of the street – the Royal Academy end. It was a disused gentleman's club if I remember rightly, and it was a sunny, warmish weekday afternoon when I visited. I'm convinced that I had seen Orozco's show at the ICA before 'Empty Club' and been oddly moved – especially by the photos of pairs of scooters in the corridors. But the dates don't quite seem to fit – officially they were the other way round, which is odd. Anyhow, by this stage I had been working on my PhD on postcolonial art for two years and I was just getting into the swing of things. I had also realised that the artists I was researching weren't the artists who were getting a huge amount of exhibiting opportunities. So when I saw the ICA show I felt kind of that it was my type of work, even though Orozco wasn't one of the artists I was researching. The themes chimed with all those great ideas that were banging around in my head. I think I went back home and read an article about Orozco – possibly in *frieze* – that confirmed I was right to be moved. Or perhaps I had just read the *frieze* article before 'Empty Club'. My memory's shot to pieces.

Whatever I had seen or read I do remember that when I strolled into 'Empty Club' I was filled with that excitement when you know that what you're going to see will be brilliant. There was an Artangel person at the door. I liked Artangel as well – 'House' was great, and had played a large role in articulating what I was angry about a couple of years previously when I had been angry about something or other. Orozco and Artangel – well, it had to work. The installation was spread out over a number of floors. I think you had to climb stairs to get to different floors, or perhaps there was a lift. And I think I might not have started at the bottom but the top. Each floor was given over to an English leisure pursuit such as crown green bowling or billiards. I think Orozco was trying to make something that gently satirised the arcane nature of gentle English sports, whilst additionally creating something fun that also had bits of larger ideas about identity and imperialism and so forth floating in and out. He failed. I now perceive that I did not realise this immediately. Instead my disappointment was gradual and unbelieving. I can remember pretending to like the first floor and perhaps even the second. I think it might have been by the third, as I forlornly looked at an outsized picture of the English cricketer Alex Stewart that I realised that I had been mistaken. At least, I think it was an oversized picture of Alex Stewart – instead of details I remember a slightly embarrassed deflating feeling – as if someone I had put all my hopes in of being great was just tootling away in mediocrity. The whole installation looked rushed – jokey ideas which fell apart in execution, lost in the dusty interior of the abandoned club. And nobody was here. There were no crowds milling around to see this Mexican sensation, amazed at the irony of importing the third world into the hallows of the first and laughing as notions of Englishness were trashed. Empty Club – too fucking right, I thought.

The visit was turning into a bad experience. This was the afternoon that was going to confirm to me that all that postcolonial, third-world stuff I was doing was no longer marginal, but striding across the art world as the new big burning issue that no-one could escape from. Yet, Orozco – in whom all these hopes were perhaps unfairly invested – had blown it. Gabriel! You were my chance of escaping researching and teaching increasingly embittered accounts about race and nation in a small new university in the Midlands – a big show here and postcolonial theory would have been all the rage in the art world. And more importantly it could have been my passport to that proper shiny art world. And you blew it! I might have even wondered around again but this time full of spleen, anger and invective. Back to driving up the motorway to no-hoper galleries and ill-attended conferences in Coventry and Leicester for me, I thought as I emerged full of nervous anger back onto St James. Niru Ratnam

78 **Performance (Edge)** (St John Ambulance Headquarters, 1993). The point of this moment, or extended moment, survives and becomes a bench-mark for teaching and almost everything to do with performance. How long should a performance go on for and what is the right and appropriate time to stop? The bicycles were parked outside an undiscovered patch right there in the centre of Clerkenwell. The performance was part of a whole programme. The rest eludes me. This is what remains. A woman spun around and around, and around, time lay heavy. The very presence of the tree in the centre of this cloistered courtyard provided some comfort; surely when this whirling performing dervish reaches the

tree she will stop because she has to stop sometime and there is no other indication that she might. But no, the whirling goes on. Two boys lie precariously on
a roof in the corner of the courtyard and beckon to their friends to come up.
Maybe she'll take her clothes off? They stare in disbelief. And still this goes on.
This is part of 'Edge', a festival taking place across London. Venues have been
discovered, reclaimed, turned out, churches have been emptied of pews and
folding chairs, trap-doors have been opened, and here the Ancient Order of St.
John, with its relationship to the ambulance service, carves a perfect temporary
art place in the heart of the city. Sacha Craddock

78 **Stephen Prina** (Karsten Schubert Ltd, 1989). This exhibition of ten works
from his series 'Exquisite Corpse: The Complete Paintings of Manet' formed the
first London solo exhibition of Stephen Prina. It was also one of the very few
exhibitions from that period that has been impossible for me to forget. Quite why
it made such an impact is rather difficult for me to understand as the work is so
understated and dry. Each work in the series consists of two framed elements.
The first is an offset lithograph showing the complete paintings of Manet, each
reduced to postage stamp size and each painting represented by a single block
of yellow ochre as if in silhouette (or like a blank image for a painting in a catalogue raisonné which has been destroyed, lost or whereabouts unknown). The
second, hanging to the left of the print is a sheet of paper covered in a yellow
ochre ink wash. The sheet of paper corresponds in size to the painting by Manet
that it stands in for. The ink represents nothing more or less than the painting it
stands in for, but not figuratively as it is just a wash of colour broadly applied; the
catalogue raisonné's dead hand of history, framed. This is a framing of history
that both frightens and appalls, and for an art historian pretty unnerving stuff.

   In many respects this exhibition was a provocation to the viewer. Images were
covered over, scale changed, a body of work – one birthplace of Modernism
(according to TJ Clark) – had been rendered, perhaps even neutered, by a programmatic series. But no. This isn't a rendering or a neutering, but a critical
investigation – like much of Prina's work – into the institutions of art, both as
dead body and as rebuilt system. Once art enters an institution (whether it is one
called 'history' or another called 'museum') it breeds and becomes more than
itself. As discourse proliferates, there are now many Manets and correspondingly
many different views on his paintings. And Prina's series adds to this spiral. An

Exquisite Corpse was a game played by Surrealists in Paris in the 20s and 30s. One person would draw a head, cover it up and pass the paper to the next person who would draw the upper torso and so on. The result would be a fantastical, often erotically charged, monster; the product of the unconscious. Manet has drawn the head, Prina the upper torso and the viewer sees the body of work – 'completes' it – in its now relocated space as the inhabitant of a number of systems. Andrew Wilson

79 **Prognosis: Sermon, Film, Banquet** (Plummet, 1996). In provoking irritation Plummet had no equal amongst alternative spaces. Its brief life on the top floor of a high rise council block near Old Street was ended by director/ tenant William Shoebridge with the exhibition 'Euthanasia' for which 'Sermon', 'Film' and 'Banquet', as three parts of 'Prognosis', were a kind of vanguard wake. The first show I saw there was Tina Keane's trans-American train movie, a meditation on her mother's death. From the beginning there was a morbid aesthetic to the place which recalled Freud's speculation about organisms living only long enough to die in their own fashion. I'd come to recognise this as the unspoken drive behind monochrome painting's drawn out self-mortification but never recognised it as a factor in institutional decline. Shoebridge was smart to end things precipitously. That may have been his only big idea for the space but it was more critically challenging than I remember other galleries being at the time.

Visits and openings were always really uncomfortable there. It could have taken an hour and a half to cross town to this wasteland (there wasn't much else in the area then) yet Shoebridge and his mates would act as if they'd rather you hadn't bothered. Opacity and frostiness were the vehicles of communication and it didn't seem that the artists in the show were any less bewildered than the public.

For 'Sermon' a room had been set up with an installation of pews and a lectern. Exactly at 7pm a priest walked in and began his sermon which, as I remember, lasted about an hour. The room was full and more people stood in the corridor. With some knowledge of Heideggerian phenomenology I could appreciate parts of the talk, but it must have instantly alienated many in the audience. This was a speculative discussion of philosophical aesthetics in relation to theology, with non-sequiturs and misleading deviations, and no application to the immediate context in which Plummet operated. The priest never acknowledged the artificiality of the staging, never conceded any disparity between his artist audience and a typical congregation, and when he finished speaking he went straight out the door of the flat and didn't return. No one would say whether or not he was genuine.

Under a critique of aesthetic irritation these events have interesting status. In terms of successful provocation their properties include the deliberate withholding of pleasure, which would normally have derived from comprehension and a sense of resolution. Furthermore, with 'Sermon' the tacit legitimacy derived from an integrated milieu was subverted by converting one community (gallery public) into another (parishioners) with predictable alienation. It brought one institution (the church) into collision with the other (contemporary art) without discernible critical objective. And as if that wasn't enough, at the end of the gruelling address we were served cups of tea, not alchohol.

A month later 'Film' brought a similar audience together for a second unexplained group event. Plummet screened a von Sternberg movie (I can't remember which one) where a glamorous diva risks her neck to get military information to the allies. We were asked to wear 3D glasses throughout since there were several frames of the word Euthanasia – intercut as three-dimensional text – into the main film stock. This was a long movie from which it was impractical to leave and the glasses were an uncomfortable requirement for a few seconds' effect. The usual bafflement followed with no clarification offered and little on which the crowd could speculate. I was starting to feel there was something sadistic about these openings, as if in voluntarily dying Plummet was determined to take a few us along with it. After all, this was also a nicely malignant jab at the conventional ethos of group events as informative, celebratory, or intoxicating. In a converstation I had years later with John Russell he was saying that he was fed up with the inattentiveness of much of BANK's audience and that perhaps they should force visitors to read a three-page theoretical text before coming into a show. Even though their press releases did get longer things never came to such a disciplinary measure. In a sense Plummet went a step further in their last events by making the audience literally sit through hours of obfuscation and still get nothing out of it. Here was an impressive nihilism, born out of anger at the distraction of the art public and at the ineffectiveness of art to have any sort of agency. In a sense here was an anethical positioning where any purposeful end was denied simply in order to assert the implausibility of purpose.

I never went there again. I missed 'Banquet' which, from what I heard, matched its predecessors for infuriating effect—the artists were sat down to a dinner which visitors watched through a Plexiglas window in the kitchen. I almost forgot to mention it – I met the priest some time later and he confessed, after some persuading, that he was really an actor. Mark Harris

80 **Protest and Survive** (Whitechapel Art Gallery, 2000). There used to be a peeling black and red 'Protest and Survive' sticker on the grotty toilet cistern of a studio myself and some friends lived in not so long ago. It looked like the perfect prop from an early episode of *The Young Ones*. You could almost hear Rik Mayall's nasal tones pushing his housemates further into a state of apathy as he berated them for not attending his student Socialist Worker (Maoist-Trotskyite Branch) meetings. Taken from a 1980s CND booklet, the title of Matthew Higgs' and Paul Noble's survey of socially conscious and politically engaged work from the last thirty years conjured up images of dour agit-prop collages, reams of type-written text and the odd photo of Parisian barricades manned by extras from an Ed van der Elsken shoot. It could have been a dismal *Young Ones* idea of protest. Rather, what was offered was far broader and sensitive in its remit than the rather lumpen title initially suggested. Sex, race, class, politics, war, science, information, play – 'Protest and Survive' refracted a myriad of ideas surrounding an art of refusal and active engagement.

A criticism levelled against the show at the time was its air of 'political nostalgia'. That this was partly the point was overlooked. Yes, it did indeed hark back to a time when there was more faith in the efficacy of intellectual and political protest, but in a manner that came across more as an optimistic set of blueprints for future activity than a resigned closing time shrug of the shoulders. Thomas Hirschhorn's 'The Bridge', connecting the gallery café with the Freedom Press Bookshop opposite was a fantastically simple portal to a valuable alternative information resource – an example of potential rather than a document of past struggles. The show certainly wasn't humourless either. Amongst others, Tariq Alvi's tumescent library visitor, Rob Pruitt's fountain of Evian water and a fantastic *Private Eye* cartoon (depicting a factory skyline with a flat-capped northerner telling his son that "one day, all this will be art galleries") were reminders of the crucial importance of satire.

In recent years social and political utopianism seems to have been a popular subject for artists to address, or rather, glibly misappropriate. Utopian modernism, after all, looks damn cool and the Situationists had a neat turn of phrase. 'Protest and Survive' was a pre 9/11 show that – post 9/11 – does not seem cheap, and whose message to travel hopefully still rings clear. Dan Fox

81 Pyramids of Mars (The Curve, Barbican, 2001). A notorious set of photographs of the surface of Mars led a number of people to believe that pyramids existed on the Red Planet. The sightings of illusory Martian ziggurats were born of a very human desire to find systems, pattern and meaning anywhere, Forever lost in space, any connections are reassuring. The Queen, Kylie Minogue, Chairman Mao, George Harrison, various members of the art world, Miss Piggy, Claudia Schiffer, the living and the dead all appear in Aleksandra Mir's 'Hello', and somehow that's a comforting thought. Stretching the full span of the Curve's main wall, the work comprised a set of photographs featuring two or more individuals. When read either from left to right or vice versa, at least one person from the previous photo could be found in the image adjacent to it. As a demonstration of the premise that there are roughly six degrees of separation between everyone on earth, 'Hello' was dizzying. Although drawn to Sture Johanesen's hard-edged psychedelic graphic posters from the 1960s, and sidetracked for a time by Palle Nielsen's 'Model for a Qualitative Society' (images from the week the Moderna Museet became a playground for children's spontaneous creativity), the human factor in Mir's project overwhelmed any desire to search for patterns elsewhere. Dan Fox

82 Ramsay Bird New Flotex (Gimpel Fils Gallery, 1992). BABIES. BABIES. BABIES. THEY GROW UP. REMEMBER THAT. THEY ALWAYS DO. LOTS OF BABIES. And there were lots of carboard boxes. With prints of babies. Under the name Ramsay Bird. In the gallery were lots of mirror-stage prints of BABIES: "ARE YOU LOOKING AT ME?" on Flotex carpet, with texts like "HOWDY BOURGEOIS DEVIANT" (I thought it said "BONJOUR BOURGEOIS BABY!") and large prints of penguins on Flotex carpet with texts saying: "KILL THE FASCISTS" and prints of tropical fish with texts saying: "EVERYTHING IS UNDER CONTROL" and "THE PROJECT IS GOING WELL". And "WHO'S WHO IN NAZI CROYDON" (or was that another show). "ARE YOU LOOKING AT ME?" And so the baby grows up a bit and misrecognises itself as a subject and flops out of the oceanic into THE MODERN WORLD but Good and Evil have gone and only schizophrenic civil obedience remains. Which is where Travis Bickle comes in. TRAVIS BICKLE steps off a train at Charing Cross. Brown shades and a mohican. WE ARE THE PEOPLE – SUCK ON THIS Beagles and Ramsay (1999). A video of Travis Bickle on a day trip to London. Coming to check out his democratic rights – except there aren't any. All that's left is the protocol and procedures and so he proceeds along these lines. Smiling and taking pills. Walking around the palaces and castles, which are now the Palaces of the people but there's nothing left. Travis Bickle is a good citizen. He has principles and he wants to PUT OUT THE TRASH and ELIMINATE THE SCUM. He hands in a letter to 10 Downing Street which says: "WE ARE THE PEOPLE". It could be the end or A WHOLE NEW BEGINNING. John Russell

83 Bridget Riley Paintings from the 1960s and 70s (Serpentine Gallery, 1999). Even though the mid-1960s marked the ascendance of full colour in the interconnected worlds of art, fashion and design, it also saw the elaboration of the most impressive argument yet in favour of the two somewhat basic colours, black and white. Bridget Riley had her first solo exhibition in New York at Richard Feigen Gallery, timed to accompany her inclusion in MoMA's 'The Responsive Eye'. And Truman Capote threw his lavish Black and White Ball at the Plaza, to which he invited notables ranging from Babe Paley to Andy Warhol, who was just coming out of his own black and white cycle. Each guest had to adhere strictly to the duochrome dress code imposed by the host.

Now while Riley may not have been attracted to Capote's deviously ornate jabber, he certainly was entranced by the sinuous elegance of her paintings. Cecil Beaton snapped a photograph of Capote standing in front of Riley's 'Fission' wearing an elated expression on his face, surely a response to the way Riley makes over a regular polka-dot pattern with such mischievous cartoonery. To this end, 'Fission' injects perspective, previously a device specific to figurative painting, into abstraction. 'Shift', also from 1963, is premised on quite a different compositional schema. The painting's completely regulated pattern, formed by the interlocked triangles that nudge and budge each other, occasions an overall motion. And even though perspective has been eschewed in favour of flat pattern the painting is more difficult to get a hold on – the beholder can't quite tell what is making its patterns jump and jiggle so. Over the next few years Riley continued to run these two compositional strategies parallel. To complicate things even further, in 1964 she introduced another element into both – the colour grey.

While in the one series the effect was to exaggerate perspective, in the other it was to work against it. 'Turn' co-ordinates both strategies to the extent that tonal variance warps flat pattern. Everything experienced thus far fades upon encountering the resplendent sparkles that emanate from 'Arrest 2'. The painting marks Riley's first subtle attempts at colour, before the full-blown embrace of 1967. Executed in 1965, it is one of the first paintings to introduce colour into the grey end of the palette while simultaneously reducing tonal contrast. The outcome is something like a set of highly buffed metallic bars rotating in front of a white background. Pattern delicately converges in parts of 'Arrest 2' and lightly undulates in others as vertiginous optics is replaced by a serene mirage.

Despite these paintings being design catalysts for the late 60s, Riley draws her ideological line discretely before then. She is more late 50s/early 60s in terms of sensibility, a subtlety that contemporary artists and critics revisiting the period often choose to overlook. The outcome means everyone enraptured by Riley is drawn to the reception of her work in the popular culture of the mid-to-late 60s for reference points: think of Jim Lambie as just the tip of the iceberg. Not that there is anything wrong with privileging the late 60s: but why can't a few artists go for the turn into the 60s instead? Often the transition between periods yields the more interesting moment.

A fine example of such a moment came in 1965 when a dress manufacturer affiliated with MoMA presented Riley with a mass-produced textile version of one of her delicately nuanced paintings. Riley was mortified. The age of discretion to which she was attached was over; the swinging 60s were, well, starting to swing. Layouts for *Tatler* and *Vogue* were already composed and the shop windows of Madison Avenue were teeming with Op dresses. To Riley's credit, it was not that she couldn't conceive of this expanded role for her patterns, it was more the iniquitous way they were lifted and the inept way they were applied that irked her. But still it is interesting to note that as soon as the ideological consequences of having a romance with design became sticky, Riley enlisted the services of a lawyer – Barnett Newman's to be exact – to clean things up, in true 50s style. Herewith confirming the old adage that interdisciplinarity always breaks down when one discipline goes legal.

By continuously sublimating the connections to fashion and design, Riley and her commentators have always closed down possible readings of the paintings. This has affected their future to such an extent that the bulk of the currently available discourse pertaining to the paintings insists on consummating Riley's relation to the Old Masters. The paintings are consequently made to feel more secure while all that is destabilising about them is taken away. The same principle is also carried over into her writings, throughout which she deliberates over the work with a moral tone inherited from her illustrious forebear, John Ruskin. Even when going this far back in time to look for a methodology there is another option though. Following on from one of Ruskin's most devoted yet disobedient students, Oscar Wilde, it develops a fresh methodology. One flexible enough to deal with the paintings' relation to fashion and design while being able to retain the cunning that is necessary to tell a good painting from a bad one. For the artwriting to come must permit new methodologies and fields to percolate through the faculty of judgement rather than being barred by it. Wilde knew this over a hundred years ago, when, with a whisk of the quill, a spatter of ink, he talked up the choice examples from Whistler's black, white and grey portraits through the dress codes of the fashionable gentlemen parading around Green Park. Alex Coles

84 **Rites of Passage: Art for the End of the Century** (Tate Gallery, 1995).

'Rites of Passage: Art for the End of the Century' gets mixed up every time with art at the end of the passage, or even art at the end of the back passage. But anyway, Stuart Morgan wanted to transmit a different atmosphere. He said that he wanted people to cry. He and Frances Morris, who co-curated it, worked with a good range of European artists. The show was to do with the body, rather than jolly Pop life, with death even, with subtlety rather than everything else going on at that time: a chance to represent serious European and British artists who need to be seen properly.

The old Tate used to have a shaky relationship with the contemporary and this was really its first mixed contemporary show. It felt serious and dark. It was dark, in fact, with long passages. It had a labyrinthine feel to it, looping round and round and coming out for air in strongly-lit clearings, usually for some figurative reference. Jana Sterbak with meaty clothing and a hoop of a dress hung with lights. Miroslaw Balka with a stony exterior but reputed warmth inside. John Copelan all tied up, upside-down, and nowhere to go. Poor Hamad Butt, who had died when young after showing at Milch probably just once, was present here with suspended glass containers, a giant executive toy.

Pepe Espaliu uses leather and figures that come out from the wall to show symbolic, sexual work with a different touch and Mona Hatoum's own passages are to be journeyed down, for real. All merging mind and matter on a higher plane, work that many people call GOOD. Sacha Craddock

85 **Sensation: Young British Artists from the Saatchi Collection** (Royal Academy, 1997 (Hamburger Bahnhof, Berlin, 1998 Brooklyn Museum of Art, New York, 1999)). The Sensation exhibition shown first in London in 1997 at the Royal Academy then at the Hamburger Bahnhof in Berlin and subsequently in New York at the Brooklyn Museum of Art, drew different responses in all three venues. It is in the everyday life of a community that that community's culture is embodied and reproduced. Societies come with their own forms of inherited and reactionary traditions and this was made apparent in all three cities.

Marcus Harvey's monumental painting 'Myra' (1995) of mass child-murderer Myra Hindley drew an outraged reaction from the British audience. This icon of evil was reproduced using children's handprints and brought back all the horror of her crimes. It would be a startling and beautiful painting were it not for its moral qualities, and it had Academicians howling and resigning in protest. Daubed in red ink by a demonstrator the painting was hastily restored over-night and then guarded by day.

In Berlin the painting was admired for its power and technique, Hindley being unknown to them. Damien Hirst's 'A Thousand Years' (1990) is a vitrine containing a decaying cow's head lying in a pool of blood beset by flies which once airborne would be zapped by the insecticutor above them. The artist tackles life and death with mordant humour. Deep concern for 'die Flieden' had animal rights protestors in serried ranks waving placards at the entrance to the gallery. When more flies were called for they could not be supplied locally, a suitcase full of maggots was hastily flown over from a supplier of fishing bait in England.

When Sensation got to New York a year later, it was Chris Ofili's 'The Holy Virgin Mary' (1996) that caused affront. A cartoon rendering of a black madonna, the painting is extravagantly covered in glitter and coloured pins surrounded by countless scattered cut-outs of grossly pornographic close-up photographs of female genitalia. It had the American audience in shock and the mayor on the point of closing the museum. Yards of column inches and television slots were devoted to this perceived offence to Catholic taste. Was it a coincidence that on the opening night it was announced that the nearest subway station would be closed for routine maintenance? After an attempt to vandalise this work too, a heavy double-glazed glass screen was placed in front of it and two New York cops made it impossible to see the work close-up. People of nervous dispostion and children were asked to pass by the alcove in which it hung. A later show by Ofili up-town had queues around the block.

Defining moments in art's history have always been scandalous, art has always shocked, but a universal grasp of contemporary art is as yet, incomplete. It was mooted that the exhibition would continue to Australia. Might they have objected to Damien Hirst's 'The Physical Impossibility of Death in the Mind of Someone Living.' (1991), the 'shark in a tank', now a protected species (though not then) with strict laws prohibiting its removal from the sea? Penny Govett

86 **Serious Games** (Barbican Gallery, 1997). The mid nineties may turn out to have been the highpoint of electronic art, where everyone interested congregated at the ISEA symposiums, Ars Electronica in Linz, or at Siggraph in the USA. Never quite an art movement – too international and fluid for that – and making little impact in Britain, nevertheless these were the defining events where the prototype art forms engineered for the twenty-first century were launched. If there really was to be a 'new' art driven by technology, this was the cutting-edge. 'ISEA Montreal 95' was one defining moment, where Char Davies' 'Osmose', a VR dip into wispy cyberspace – and the most substantial piece in 'Serious Games' – was premiered. It sharply divided the audience: new-age high-tech utopians one side, gritty sceptics on the other. Coming out of these exhibitions you imagined a road ahead where come 2000 all art forms would be vaporised, transformed into a luminous aura – the global consciousness of the world wide web, then a delightfully new and esoteric domain. Art would become a heightened consciousness, not wall furniture; the viewer would be enveloped, drive the content from within; be not a spectator but an active partner, would … interact.

The serious point – the theory – behind 'Serious Games' was that people mattered: so it was a show of interactive art which was both fun and not fun, tech and not tech. You were supposed to play the 'games' – make music with magic squares – but keep in mind that this was an art experience with a difference: it was an interactive experience.

'Serious Games' had two big problems to overcome: first it had to introduce the new ideas of electronic art to a London public that had not heard of any of the artists, nor seen nor read much about this hugely expanded field of electronic art. The last show had been 'Cybernetic Serendipity' at the ICA in 1968! Second, how on earth could you condense so much material, argument, and contradiction without trivialising it. The games idea followed the hunch that the key factor in the use of computers in art would be viewer feedback.

Did it work? Not in the sense that traditional artist felt challenged to get interactive, and I don't think people flocked to the exhibition to play the 'serious games' because these were a step ahead of regular and unserious video games. The title was off-putting. I recall one of the organizers, an art historian, who enjoyed pressing the buttons but was unaware of the clunkiness of 'art' installations. He had never heard of PlayStation. 'Osmose' was in fact sponsored, and something of a demo for Soft Image software (used for *Jurassic Park*). Was it a technology show or an art show? 'Interactivity' was a vague idea – you could say any art that involves a spectator, a reader, or a listener is interactive – and pundits are now no longer quite as mesmerised by the promises of a 'new' art. In retrospect the show did catch a segment of electronic art at its most optimistic, self-deluded, and confused, but it is a pity it labelled it as 'game therapy'. There were works here by significant figures – Harwood, Iwai, Seaman – who deserve to be treated as artists in a more open discussion. Since then VR has lost much of its magic, and web art is where the museum 'experts' hang around. Meanwhile the odder corners of the field – the extraordinary works of Perry Hoberman, Stelarc, Verostko, Rejane Sptz, Kac, Mignonneau and Sommerer among others – remain unsurveyed, along with all the subtle hybrids where the digital and the non-digital are interwoven. James Faure Walker

87 Johnnie Shand Kydd True Brits (Independent Art Space, 1997). Wankers. I have to admit that was my first thought upon entering the old IAS just off the Kings Road. I was on my way back from working at an archive of Black and Asian artists at Chelsea Art School just further on down the road and I thought I'd pop my head in. The gallery was filled with smallish, black and white (I think) snapshot type photos of various members of the YBa scene. The Starrs and Bullochs of the age. At first glance, it seemed that most of the images were taken whilst they were at play – at restaurants, openings and so forth. The type of thing that, frankly,

I wasn't getting any invites for, and as a consequence, was feeling extraordinarily bitter about. After looking at a few, I think I decided to take a more positive attitude and stop feeling so twisted about the fact that I had been working in dusty archives instead of sipping quality white wine around various top parties. Whatever, at some point I decided to hunt around for the photo of Tom Gidley – listed on the A4 print-out of works. I found him and I felt oddly pleased – a few years previously I had been an intern for *frieze*, which Tom co-founded and designed under a pseudonym. Not that Tom and I had got on or anything – in fact, he usually ignored me or shot me a withering glance or two – but here, at least, was someone I could have claimed once having talked to. I think at this point I turned around and was about to leave the gallery – but at some point between Tom and the door I can clearly remember seeing two photos. Each was of three people – Jay Jopling, Angus Fairhurst and another bloke. The first was of them intently watching England play Germany in *Euro '96*. The second was of them leaping around wildly at some event during the game – presumably a goal. And I can remember noticing one thing – whilst it looked like Fairhurst knew what was going on, Jopling looked as if he'd discovered football about 3 days beforehand. His body language was all over the place. Years later when *The Fast Show* did that skit of the recently converted Arsenal supporter in the pub who knows nothing about football, I'd remember Jopling's crazed poses and smile. Niru Ratnam

88 **John Smith** (Pearl, 2002). "I first noticed it in spring last year – it must have been early April. I remember it well – it was a Saturday morning and I'd been to the corner shop to buy some food for a fried breakfast. For some reason the shop was closed so I decided to cut through a back-street to the supermarket on the high road. It was a bright morning but most of the street was still in shadow – I found myself walking very close to the front walls and hedges in order to expose my face to the thin strip of warm sunlight that ran the length of the street. It was from here that I first saw it, its crest protruding over the roofs on the other side of the road. Surprised that I hadn't noticed it before, I wondered what it was and then forgot about it for several weeks."

I wonder if a sizeable proportion of younger artists working with film and video have had the same reaction to John Smith's work as the protagonist of his film 'The Black Tower' had to the malevolent, mobile monolith pursuing him across London. Surprised they never noticed it before. Wondered what it was. Then forgot about it. It strikes me as odd that some of Britain's most consistently inventive experimental filmmakers remain unfamiliar to many. Despite the recent efforts of certain institutions and individuals to rescreen the work of The London Filmmaker's Co Op and other practitioners operating around the same time, names such as John Smith, Peter Gidal, William Raban, Liz Rhodes or Malcolm LeGrice still seem to draw blanks when mentioned in conversations with artists of a certain age. Pearl's screenings of work by John Smith was a small but perfectly executed attempt to bring to a wider audience his deft blend of linguistic acrobatics, literary nous and filmic game-playing. In addition to 'The Black Tower', Pearl's programme included 'The Girl Chewing Gum', in which an authoritative voice-over appears to direct the activity of passers-by on the street, when in fact he's only describing events before him; 'The Waste Land', an interpretation of T.S. Eliot's work from the vantage point of a pub toilet, and 'Om', a study of a Bhuddist boot-boy.

Smith's work explores the armatures of fictional and documentary genres with the deadpan humour and reserve characteristic of filmmakers such as Patrick Keiller. Along the way they zone out into darker terrain — states of paranoia, uneasy speculations on methods of control, systems for control, perhaps the point at which language can slip out of gear and the mind out of control. They seem borne of an era when certain filmmakers were attempting to side-step the message of their medium, but don't seem dated by undue emphasis on formal and structural codes. Narrative simplicity belies a laser-guided directness in the execution of the ideas at play, but Smith is never afraid to laugh at himself or his audience. The borderline neurotic world he evokes is one in which if you can't laugh, you might as well cry. Dan Fox

89 **Some Went Mad, Some Ran Away...** (Serpentine Gallery, 1994). There haven't been many good shows in London in the last 15 years. One of which was a big group show organised by Damien Hirst called 'Some Went Mad, Some Ran Away...' (1994) at the Serpentine (a pattern is beginning to form). Damien Hirst is a force and of that there is no doubt. He didn't whoop up a storm with this show, which was good of him in many respects, but it had a couple of things in it that I liked. I sound like I have subtly put myself at the centre of a vast and tumultuous universe in that last passage, a kind of 'eye of the storm'. But I just meant to tactfully step aside and simply say that there were two pieces in the show I liked. No inverted grandiosity meant. And, by stepping aside, I do not

reserve for myself a sense of survival like those who videoed the tornado while stuffing themselves in a cranny of a road bridge. I stepped aside. I didn't stuff myself in any cranny with a video camera. Now I have stepped aside I will say that the first piece was a painting by Alexis Rockman. The ecological message gets me down, but it was a stunning painting of trash and a fish pond in great detail, with LA looming like the City of the Daleks in the background, "Exterminate! Exterminate!" emanating from the oily pigment. The other was a bicycle with lots of bags loaded on it. David Mollin

90 **Space International** (2–6 Battlebridge Rd, 1992). This was not BANK's first show – that had already taken place in a former bank in Brockley, South East London, from which they had derived their name. But I believe it was as a result of this show, that BANK emerged with a self-defensive sense of the absurd which would later enable them to create a position for themselves in the 1990s London art world.

In a vast semi-derelict space open to the elements behind Kings Cross – a completely disparate group of British and Spanish artists, recent graduates mostly, mounted an exhibition. It was the kind of formless, theme-less group show that appears simply to be a vehicle for showing some recent work (no harm in that? After all, isn't that what an exhibition is really for?). It also had one of those rather more tiresome international exchanges/link-ups based upon someone in London making friends with someone from elsewhere and deciding to collaborate, and assuming that this would be a 'good thing'.

However many of the above assumptions that I have credited to the curators, were clearly already ways of thinking that they themselves were starting to question. The exhibition had, according to the 'catalogue' – a *Snappy Snaps* ring binder effort – no rationale. The exhibition turned out to be a huge exercise in not meeting expectations: even the credits page in the catalogue is photographed surrounded by so much rubbish and so many strategically placed Embassy packets that you can't read some of the names of the participating artists. The anonymous interview in the catalogue goes on to question the need for a rationale, and questions the notion of 'rationale', also getting in a swipe at the Arts Council for not funding the project.

Clearly the professionalism of exhibitions such as 'Modern Medicine' at Building One (1991), featuring Damien Hirst et al was something that every subsequent artist-organized show had to square up to. 'Space International' was an attempt at a challenge to this – it was a loose and inept exhibition, which made little or no attempt to make the space look anything other than a huge empty shed. So the show acted as an antidote to the glossy presentational strategies that became the norm in the 90s. BANK claimed the right to do something free-form, just to see what happened. Perhaps this laissez faire attitude was a case of making a virtue of necessity – BANK had neither the funds nor the inclination to ape the Saatchi look, and so they chose the low road instead. 'Space International' was therefore allowed to be a non-event, leaving vast areas of concrete completely untouched by art or artist. But perhaps this question of the space, and the getting of it was more important than the show itself? For young artists, wasn't there a huge thrill in grabbing such a large central London site? Thanks to the property slump of the early 90s, space all over London was available – artists played at being tycoons and landlords for a few days, indulged with space that no one else wanted. Emma Dexter

91 **Sam Taylor-Wood Killing Time** (The Showroom, 1994). Thinking now about Sam Taylor-Wood's 'Killing Time' is a strange experience. Of course her production values have risen since then; over the last eight years she has become a successful artist and we would expect nothing less. However, set amongst the noise and hoopla framing her work now, 'Killing Time' is still a jolt to the system. On the one hand the installation took on film history, not in terms of specific reference to specific film moments, but in respect of an undermining (or is that emphasising?) of film time as against real time: duration. On the other hand, in the midst of *fortissimo* opera, the work is about dislocation (spatially, in the gallery where the four projections could not be taken-in at once; in a filmic sense, between the soundtrack and the actors' desultory miming; psychologically – or is that in the script?), detachment and silence. All of this is in the title before you even see the work, film-time, life-time and staged time is being killed.

The work as it was shown at The Showroom consists of four projections each showing one person miming to a long soundtrack loop (about an hour) of opera. Two projections were in the front room of the gallery and two in the even more wedge-shaped back room. The actors exhibit the boredom of the disengaged, one swigs from a bottle of water; the music seems to mean as much as life to them, not very much. There is no connection, staged or otherwise, between the actors except for the music, the projection is both interrupted frieze and four separate portraits (the camera is static throughout). The work makes the four actors into a group. The same year, 1994, saw a number of artists make multi-part video works, two of which stand comparison with 'Killing Time'. Mark Wallinger's four-part 'Royal Ascot 'and Jaki Irvine's five-part 'Margaret Again'. Both play with time and a relationship to both the subject of film and the depicted subjects in the film. However, where Wallinger and Irvine present their work as narrative through the multipart form (Wallinger's serialisation of actual staged repetitions forms the beginnings of his critical narrative, Irvine's narrative has to be excavated from the gaps and overlapping looping between the five film elements), 'Killing Time' shows no narrative other than the purely filmic – a narrative that is underpinned by the use of the soundtrack. These people in her work do nothing other than mime and act. They are mute. Andrew Wilson

92 **These Epic Islands** (Vilma Gold, 2000). Sculpture that you can walk around has become a bit of a joke. It should be in a corner, provide a whole context like a hut, be part of the floor, transient, leading out of the space, impermanent… all these things but up to this point sculpture had been unable to insist on its own independent existence. It had become almost invisible, the physical equivalent of 'seen and not heard'; maybe heard and not seen, or heard, seen and then turned off at night. The title of this show tells you how to think. 'These Epic Islands' refers obviously to the circular, round-about possibility of sculpture. Free-standing in playland, or *Toy Town*, shifting up and down in imaginative scale but never really big because this is Vilma Gold after all. Brian Griffiths invited his friends, mainly, to make a series of places, to produce aisles, of a sort, down which to walk. Griffiths' astronaut monkey gestures dramatically from a cardboard-box plinth. Illusion has been brought by all out of rough, ready material but Keith Wilson's elegant fence, trapped in a bound base, draws a tenuous association out of the material through the activity of winding, layering, or just whittling. Jeremy Deadman's fine, thin white plinth supports an apple which makes a munching noise, the sculptural equivalent of the plaque that displays the singing sea-bass. Sacha Craddock

93 Padraig Timoney (Milch, 1992). Milch's second manifestation in a spectacular Bloomsbury townhouse was host to two of the best shows held in London during the 90s: the still under-rated Nayland Blake's first – and only – UK solo exhibition and Padraig Timoney's gloriously loopy show – made prior to his subsequent and equally strange series of shows for Laure Genillard. An unlikely graduate of Goldsmiths, Timoney's work has continued to defy and resist easy categorization. Timoney's work often communicates through sly, conceptual 'nods' and 'winks'. For his Milch show a mural-sized, spray painted version of a Renaissance masterpiece shared space with a meticulous ink drawing of a landscape rendered on the flip-side of a fast-food carton, downstairs a vast single-slide projection of a red pepper being singed atop a gas-flamed stove stoically went about its business. Like Martin Kippenberger's show at Karsten Schubert Timoney's Milch show was strangely coherent, and as such, inspired a degree of confidence amongst its slightly bemused audience, that the artist at least – if no-one else – knew what was going on. Matthew Higgs

94 Rosemarie Trockel (Whitechapel Art Gallery, 1998). Throughout the 80s, Rosemarie Trockel's practice demonstrated how traditional forms of artistic materiality (mostly printed textiles and craft based objects) could activate complex layers of critical and political signification, while also reflecting an exciting renewal of post feminist art practice. The Whitechapel retrospective announced itself as a long overdue investigation into the practice of one of the most collected German artists of the post 60s generation. Over the years, her work has gone on to explore issues as varied as gender and technology, art's love-hate relationship to craft, and the impact technological modes of production has had on the western definition of the beautiful.

But, when it came to it, the exhibition was set upon, both by mainstream newspapers and the art press, for lacking formal sophistication and conceptual coherence. It was reported as a most obscure visual experience, in which the display of blunt objects was being compensated for by badly edited video works amongst a hodge-podge of literary references, a context in which even the best known works such as the 'Balaclavas' series of 1986–90, (adorned with various patterns and logos such as *Woolmark*, the hammer and sickle, swastikas or *Playboy* bunnies) could not be redeemed. To top it all, Trockel's most recent work (1993 onwards) featuring the much discussed 'Egg-Space Installation' resulted in her being diagnosed with a near pathological concern with metaphors of fertility or, if in doubt, infertility.

What had gone wrong? It seems the UK timing of the retrospective had back-fired badly, pushing the reception of Trockel's show beyond the pale of the over-hermetic 'foreign' art category. It might take a gross parallel here to measure the enormity of the case: no one's ever reproached Broodthaers for overdoing it with the mussels, or the egg-shells, come to think of it. His quasi obsessive recourse to rather language specific puns and bon-mots (mussel/moule/mould), and the occasional metaphorical hermetism have never got in the way.

Not so for Trockel. Of course the critics had a role to play in this. And possibly something of a cultural-specific response was also being played out here. Since Trockel's works last appearance in the UK (ICA group show, 1988), a certain idea of intertextual feminist art practice had been supplanted by the very cultural-specific YBas' arty chicks' attitude. Given that Trockel's work has always ad-dressed the cultural myths of feminine glamour and beauty, engineered jointly by patriarchy and the media machine, her take on the matter couldn't possibly have partaken of the trendy affectation for 'Girl Power.' But more to the point, how could Trockel's work be penalised for being "over culturally specific" (read unintelligibly opaque) when the very cultural specificity of the YBa phenomenon has done so much for its local success (hence the known cases of resistance to and semi-failure of YBa show-case exhibitions outside the UK).

In the wake of the post 80s disenchantment with theoretically grounded art, hasn't the punter become increasingly accustomed to a lazy modality of viewing, with what there is to be 'got' is spelled out in a press release? If Trockel's work can appear of an other time, a time when having one's art made to industrial finish sparked-off heated debates in British art schools and when, following on from American feminist practices, technologically produced art objects were placed at the service of critique, a few lessons in the art of poetic juxtaposition (ready-made meets minimalism meets narrative) would not be superfluous, especially when one considers some of the vapid objects churned out during one decade of YBa-mania.

On closer inspection, ironically, Trockel's work since the late 70s has con-sistently provided the kind of art based subversive genealogy from which the works of Tracey Emin and Sarah Lucas have borrowed. Emin's recourse to story telling is not complete without its reliance on her 'labour of love' approach to making, as exemplified by the appliqués works 'Everyone I have ever slept with 1963-95' (1995) and 'Psycho-slut'(1999). Often, Emin restages a form of practice in which craft-based repetitive gestures become central to her hybrid aesthetic. Sarah Lucas' re-appropriation of the gendered ready made, as in 'Two Fried Eggs and a Kebab'(1992) or 'Bitch'(1995) also shares a legacy with Trockel's 'stove' sculpture pieces of the late 80s while Lucas' more recent *Marlboro* Reds covered objects suggest a cunning resemblance to Trockel's unbroken chain of object-specific installation. Given the unequivocally enthusiastic reception of such works, one wonders what else but the lack of spectacle (through deliberate self-effacement) got in the way of Trockel's work. Not only did Trockel's topical address of the 'bad girl' author-function, through her 'Brigitte Bardot' series, get lost in the poor reception of this show but so did the scope of Trockel's ongoing critical reflection on possible strategies for the practice of visual art.

Unless this practice of prioritizing critically 'lite' and culturally familiar forms of work over more demanding forms of contemporary art is addressed, we are in danger of seeing key European artists like Rosemarie Trockel relegated to all-women retrospectives, packed with catalogue-essays discussing the visibility of 'women's time' and the legacy of Simone de Beauvoir. If Trockel overlooked the necessity to explain herself (and since when are artists under the obligation to provide a complete post-rationalisation of their work, the how and the why of each piece?) what seemed more concerning here was the general consensus of bad will, the refusal to engage with the materiality of the works on show, complaining instead, that there were too many eggshells and not enough translations.
Alexia Defert

95 **Markus Vater** (Vilma Gold, 2002). I suspect Markus Vater has secret ambitions to be a master of disguise. Three elements remain in mind. A rough piece of chipboard lying as casually on the floor as a rough piece of chipboard in a hip East End gallery can, depicts an ape – a pretty savvy, cool looking ape – pointing towards a small monitor in an adjacent space. Propped up against a wall to one side of the monitor is perhaps one of the most extraordinarily ugly paintings in Christendom. The ape is beautifully rendered in pencil, the chipboard giving the creature's pelt the curious characteristic of camouflage. The painting is huge – too tall for the gallery, too wide for any wall. A goat's head soup of floating heads and lurid daubs, its obdurate presence makes it almost impossible to

concentrate on the animations quietly playing out their hilarious, dirty, beautiful and whimsical narratives on the monitor behind. A woman out walking her dog mutates into her dog and it into her. She shits on the floor then runs off, chased by her dog. A man walking towards a chest of drawers starts to shrink as he crosses the room. By a law of literally diminishing returns, he realises he'll never make it. The ape is trying to hide. People change. Individuals conceal their identities. Still the monolithic paint splurge sits there. We may grow but the song remains the same. Dan Fox

96 **Wall to Wall** (Serpentine Gallery, 1994 (curated by Maureen Paley)). 'Wall to Wall' was about each artist having a place. It happened concurrently in Southampton and Leeds and the Serpentine, which sounds almost like a Premiership fixture. I only saw the show at the Serpentine Gallery. Barbara Kruger installed an emphatic patch, completely strong and not conducive to reverie. Lawrence Weiner put up some lettering. Niele Toroni made delicate claims touching the walls, but the most exciting was Lothar Baumgarten's piece. In the central area, the high domed middle part of the Serpentine, in which it was impossible to speak without an echo, he set up a light three dimensional play of poetry. He somehow made something out of nothing, planting a relationship between patches of lettering and colouring on the wall. The names of countries set up a flight path flow chart – almost a 1990s symbol of imaginative flexibility across the interior space. Baumgarten capped this with coloured patches in the very top of the cupola, a final detail that was too romantic for words. Sacha Craddock

97 **Watergate a single-screen video installation by Victor Burgin** (Matt's Gallery, 2002). 'Watergate', is an important word in the U.S. It's so important it's spawned several offspring: 'Monica-gate', 'Iran/Contra-gate', and for any number of politically, or otherwise sensationally scandalous news items needing a little saucing up by an inspired investigative reporter 'Whatever-gate'. The question in the original Watergate was one of a burglary, or rather, the questions, at first unasked about the burglary at that hotel/office/apartment complex. Eventually, through the helpful gravelly-voiced citizen in the car park with the porno *nomme de informant*, the right questions (at least the most interesting) began to be asked by Woodward and Bernstein. Nixon was up to rather bad things, and didn't want anyone to find out. He hid the facts, in the form of audiotapes, and

prevented anyone hearing what they had to say. Today, one can visit (as a qualified scholar) the Library of Congress in Washington D.C. or the Nixon Presidential Library in California, and listen to these historical documents. Importantly, at some point in the recordings, Nixon gave the go-ahead for G. Gordon Liddy and the other 'Plumbers' to check out the Democrats the Watergate Hotel. And so begins the story of a routine burglary.

'Watergate', the single-screen video installation, is an intended object. It has three parts in time. The first two are continuous pans of digitally produced panoramic images of two different rooms. This produces an effect not entirely unlike what is visible to a person standing in the middle of a room and rotating to look about the room. Only there is a slight strangeness to the apparent rotation because it's actually a computer animation produced from a still, flat image. Shifting wonky geometries sliding across the 2D screen make for an unfamiliar experience of looking. In addition, origination from single central points within the rooms, means – in effect, that the recording device, a still camera, leaves no trace in the image, except the trace of an attempt to present objectivity by obscuring the machine of production.

The first room is the nineteenth century 'American Romantic Painting and Sculpture Gallery' at the Corcoran (for which the piece was commissioned). We see 15 paintings mostly from the Hudson River School accompanied by a couple of sculptures contemporary to the paintings. Paintings by Albert Bierstadt, Thomas Cole, Frederick Edwin Church and others are slowly passed over. In Burgin's installation history and iconography are emphasised, as signs of the brush are not reproduced. The propagandistic aspect of the paintings is of particular importance here, i.e. these works propagandized the Manifest Destiny and other ideas regarding the classical and the democratic. This is the popularly accepted academic version of how these paintings are written into American history, and this information is germane to the role in which Burgin casts them.

The second room is a room with a view. First, you see a painting over a sofa, which looks like one (of a waterfall) in the first room but smaller, then you see a chair, window (onto another building and some trees), an indoor plant. Then a television screen, then the back of the room (lamp, door, etc.) then repeat. According to the press release, this image was recorded within the Watergate complex.

Over both of these scanning views is the voice of a woman talking about meeting someone she knows in a café. Or rather, more importantly, looking for that person, but recognizing that that person is not there. In a beautiful, almost poetic rumination, she describes what it's like to look about a space but not find who or what you're looking for. Everything in the narrator's field is subjected to the classically aesthetic test of being what one is looking for. The voice-over concludes that that "nothingness which slides as a nothing on the surface of the ground" is the foundation for a conclusion that the person she expected to meet is not there. I read in the press release that this text is from Sartre, the nothingness here is the Existential nothing, or the gap in experience burned into the present by the subject's conception of her absent friend. Not finding is not a nothingness but is instead a very specific human experience recollected in 'Being and Nothingness'.

The problem in using Sartre's description is that intention/construction is attributed to something unstructured and unintended (i.e. the scene of a café). The process of constructing the nothingness out of the experience is, at best, apathetic, and at worst, pathetic. An alternative is to conceive of the café as structured by the surveyor herself, not a will-driven orientation or organization of things, but simply the experience of the human ability to process 'sense data'. Even in this case the construct of nothingness remains useless. Burgin's figure of the absent person echoes the no-show of the Watergate scandal.

The last of the parts is a black screen which presents, in white letters, the details of almost all of the American artists' works in the Corcoran room shown with title, date, name of artist, and last, nationality; each word or words fades in then out, centered, not unlike film credits. Significantly Burgin has chosen to leave five small paintings unrepresented. The credits, as a return to, and re-representation using textual means, foreground historicism. Burgin's choice to use this curated group of objects indicates his attention to the specified ethos.

In this darkened space, a slow, melodic aria written by Handel plays over the succession of titles, dates, names, and places. The severely protestant one-sentence lyrics are repeatedly sung by a woman in Italian: "Inflict punishment on a faithless body".

The one thing represented throughout each of the three sections is the painting 'Niagara' (1857) by Thomas Cole. First as the original in the Corcoran, second, as the reproduction, mimetic down to the frame on a smaller scale, and lastly as text in the list of works. The presence of the reproduction of Church's 'Niagara' in the second part of the video locates the site of the most massive flow of water – returning to the title 'Watergate". Burgin uses the water as a metaphor for the monumental, of course, absent, representation of the Watergate event. The title introduces the video in this way, yet it's absent from the work otherwise. Like submitting a writ of *habeas corpus,* and as an analogue to the Sartre story, Burgin produces a demand to have the body presented. There is hardly a nothingness associated with this absence.

By conjuring the spectre of a scandal, representing visual art, music, and philosophical writing with built-in historical sense. By associating metaphor for flow and stoppage, the absent body and the aesthetics of searching, by engaging the attenuated piety of the Calvinist composer in relation to a contemporary politics, Burgin makes an elegant argument for art with social agency. But, what about this missing body? It shouldn't be Watergate or Clinton, as they're both found in this text. It could be Sartre (he's not credited in the work), or the five small missing paintings. Maybe it's the 'corpus' of the exhibition if that includes the press release which helped reconstruct Burgin's complex video. Burgin or his practice are possible suspects, just as 'Deep-Throat' could be Mark Felt. Inscribing guesses serves to demonstrate that only speculation could fill this kind of vacuum. I look for the body because, at once, I've become interested and it's a pleasurable experience. My attempted explicit description a stab at not being an historian. Turn discourse against the mortifying effect of reviewing from the present moment as if it were the intersection point of Renaissance perspective. Reincorporate a tangle of errors. Leave the corpse alone but watch it rot; that sort of thing. The deployment of history, in particular history manifest in the intended objects of others, is more than anything else, a sign of the body that desires power, and as Burgin's earlier work has shown – there's much more compelling stuff to do than that. Dustin Ericksen

98 **White Trash** (Lost in Space, 1995 (curated by Martin Maloney)). This was the ur living space show. Maloney laid himself bare when he installed artworks by friends and peers in his chaotic flat above a shop in Brixton – doing 5 shows over a period of 8 months. We were used to people living in galleries with white walls and clean grey floors who looked as if they had no possessions. But Maloney hadn't tidied up at all, and this created a charming *melange* of his personal clutter, studio mess and an exhibition stuffed with other people. This sort of informality is what the British are so good at – alongside dirty dishes in the sink we

saw Maloney's own version of newly gentrified skip art. In Maloney's hands there was none of the macho or worthy abstraction normally associated with skip-art; instead Maloney had used found materials to joyfully create functional and beautiful objects. There were flower paintings on scraps of carpet and table lamps made from mayonnaise buckets and sticky-backed plastic, with ketchup bottles for a base. These were decorated with friezes of figures in Maloney's signature style. There were also tables made with ridiculously wobbly legs, all made from salvaged materials. Domesticity and beauty were the themes of the show.

Elsewhere in the flat, in a series of small rooms, the exhibition unfolded with a savage energy: a Peter Davies painting, a Richard Reynolds wall drawing, Clare Woods' paintings of hands, Jun Hasegawa's cut outs. There were many other artists and yet it was one of those 'experience' exhibitions where the atmosphere, the location, and the conversation with the resident curator and caretaker were as much a part of it as the works on display. Has any city ever done this better than London? Surely this is a key London contribution to art of the 90s – honest, impromptu and intimate.

In these and subsequent exhibitions such as 'Die Yuppy Scum' at Karsten Schubert and 'Die Young Stay Pretty' at the ICA, Martin Maloney identified a new sensibility in British art. Turning his back on the semantically clever and ironically leaden works that had dominated Goldsmiths during the late 1980s and 1990s, Maloney identified a new breed of artist, (most notably Michael Raedecker, David Thorpe, Peter Davies, Dexter Dalwood) concerned with a return to suburban subjects, exploiting a desire for authenticity, craft, and the decorative. Emma Dexter

99 **Yukinori Yanagi Wandering Position** (Chisenhale, 1997). I'd heard of Yanagi before – possibly in *frieze* or perhaps *Artforum*. And boy did he ring my postcolonial bell with his crossing borders, erasing identities and wandering around in a nomad-like style. It was like Homi Bhabha had re-emerged as a Japanese artist who used ants. I was raring to go. So much so that I invited my girlfriend (who is not big on contemporary art) to accompany me down to the Chisenhale. When I got there, I was very excited. There was a big drawing on the floor and it was made up of lots of squiggly, red lines. And looking closer, you realised that the line was just one big line squiggled around. To create the installation Yanagi had traced the movements of an ant around the floor of the Chisenhale for a few days. It was all about migration and border-crossing I

excitedly explained to my girlfriend. She said it was okay, but basically it was a big doodle. To trump that caustic observation, I remember showing her the accompanying video piece which I think actually showed Yanagi following the ant and tracing the little blighter's scurrying motions. The ant could be a migrant worker, or an exile, or even a tourist I explained. My girlfriend said that following the ant around with a big marker pen was cruel and they probably used more than one ant as successive ant stars were killed by Yanagi's feet or simply exhaustion. Niru Ratnam

100 **Zombie Golf** (Bankspace, 1995). An old woman in a headscarf and a blue dress lies slumped, barefoot on the floor. Behind her a man in a cap and striped shirt with his right arm missing at the elbow hides behind a pillar. His head is slumped to one side as if his neck is broken. At the other end of the gallery a tall man in a suit pulls violently at the outstretched arm of a woman bent double, as his accomplice holds her from behind. The tall man appears to be about to fall over with the exertion. In front of this group another man kneels with a piece of raw human flesh between his legs. Close by a bloodied and eyeless corpse lies on a patch of golf course green, the fingers of his right – and only – hand outstretched in horror. BANK's 'Zombie Golf', was a show that produced a swerve in how people believed things should be done and how they should be thought about. It seems strange to say this now, after the demise of the original group, and the dissipation of the critical energies that brought the work into being, but Zombie Golf, was one those shows where dissidence and disaffirmation as means of stock-taking counted for something. That is, it connected with what other people were thinking and doing, or wanted to do, and therefore made not just some kind of cultural sense but cognitive sense. The show highlighted two things: what could be made from collective and collaborative activity that didn't look like a clerisy or a sect, and what could be made from popular modes of attention that didn't look like Pop art or the mass cultural image-as-simulacrum of the 1980s. It wasn't so much the theatricality of the curation or the horror-content, then, which carried the show – these things were hardly novel for art of the early 1990s – but the forms of recalcitrance and irritability that they imposed on the viewer. The zombies in the gallery, interfered with, or hindered, the untroubled viewing of the art on the walls and hanging from the ceiling (Dave Beech, Adam Chodzko, Maria Cook, Martin Creed, Peter Doig, Matthew Higgs, Sivan

Lewin, John Stezaker). Indeed, the zombies and their bloody activities dominated the space, reducing the art on the walls to a side-show or a curious remnant from a previous exhibit. But, of course, this recalcitrance wasn't that much of a hardship. The pleasure lay in seeing the zombies do their fiendish deeds, and not being frustrated in getting to the art.

This conflation of installation with curation was something that was gathering pace in the artworld in the early 1990s. Yet BANK gave it an expanded content and a corrosive twist. The zombies were themselves 'stand-ins' for BANK. The painted wax figures were based on the features of the group and their artist friends. This provides a suggestive range of motives for the zombie's heinous crimes. Were the zombies/BANK in the process of attacking the art they had curated and/or disrupting a private view – a kind of anti-art vanguardism – or were they, as the title of the show implied, simply the indiscriminate killers of golfers? The first claim is perhaps more auspicious, given the theme of cultural violence which underwrote the tension between the installation and the art on the walls. By functioning as artist-surrogates the zombies physical violence became a form of symbolic violence. That is, the zombies appetitive disregard of others and their iconoclasm becomes the art-lover's worst nightmare: the aesthetically desensitized spectator. In other words the zombie's lack of subjectivity stands in for a notion of the would-be uncultured. BANK's zombies are the spectre of the culturally excluded. But the show was not a kind of grim anti-art gesturalism, a Bourdiean debunking of art as cultural capital. BANK's zombies unveiled a world of logical complexities, that produced a more exacting encounter between art and anti-art, the cultured and 'uncultured'.

Zombies supposedly do not have powers of self-reflection, their agency is preprogrammed. To have them stand in as artists, therefore, is, to both derogate the artist-as-thinker, and, obviously to overinflate the intellectual capacities of zombies. Daniel Dennett in a dismissal of the scientific possibility of zombies, calls the imaginary category of zombies-with-powers-of self-reflection 'zimbies'. So maybe really BANK's zombies-as-artists are actually zimbies. Or zimbies pretending to be zombies. And maybe this is what artists have to be now, at some level, in a world where the relations between art and anti-art are necessarily intertwined: smart zimbies. In this 'Zombie Golf' was able to foreground some of the pressing problems which faced artists in the 1990s, specifically, thinking the place of art beyond both the critique of the spectacle and the critique of the critique of the spectacle. Artists, in the 1990s, were much more amenable to using the 'popular' as a deflationary and non-popular tactic. In Zombie Golf and other self-curated shows at the time, BANK were perhaps more adept at this than most. John Roberts

**REVIEWS OF UK
SHOWS 1987–2002**

Maggie Smith

A–Z (including Adam Chodzko, Martin Creed, Jeremy Deller, Richard Hamilton, Emma Kay, Paul Noble, curated by Matthew Higgs), The Approach, London 1998

O'Kane, Paul. 'A–Z', *AN magazine*, July 1998.

Musgrave, David. 'A–Z' *Art Monthly*, no. 216, May 1998, pp. 29–30.

About Vision: New British Painting in the 1990s (including Ian Davenport, Gary Hume, Lisa Milroy, Chris Ofili, Fiona Rae), Museum of Modern Art, Oxford 1996/Fruitmarket Gallery, Edinburgh 1997

Dimitrakaki, Angela. 'About di/vision/s', *Third Text*, no. 38, September 1997, pp. 99–104.

Feaver, William. 'Crooked style', *The Observer*, 17 November 1996.

Packer, William. 'A talent for the derivative', *Financial Times*, 12 November 1996.

Shone, Richard. 'About Vision', *Burlington Magazine*, vol.139, no.1128, March 1997, pp. 208–209.

Wilson, Andrew. 'The vision thing', *Art Monthly*, no. 202, December/January 1996/7, pp. 7–9.

Abracadabra: International Contemporary Art (including Maurizio Cattelan, Patrick Corillon, Emma Kay, Paul Noble, Momoyo Torimitsu), Tate Gallery, London 1999

Gisbourne, Mark. 'Abracadabra', *NU: The Nordic Art Review*, issue 2, October 1999, p. 83.

Heinzelmann, Susan. 'Is the Tate flogging a dead horse?', *Basildon Evening Echo*, 21 July 1999.

Holmes, Brian. 'Abracadabra', *Parachute*, no. 97, January–March 2000, pp. 36–37.

Hunt, Ian. 'Ever felt had?', *Art Monthly*, no. 229, September 1999, pp. 7–10.

Mollin, David. 'Abracadabra', *100 Reviews*, 1999.

Sewell, Brian. 'Don't roll up for the sad little freak show', *Evening Standard*, 23 July 1999, pp. 32–33.

Acting Out (including Vito Acconci, Matthew Barney, Cheryl Donegan, John Lindell, Steve McQueen), Royal College of Art, London 1994

Freedman, Carl. 'Acting Out/Remote Control', *frieze*, issue 16, May 1994, pp. 53–54.

Eija-Liisa Ahtila: real characters, invented worlds, Tate Modern, London 2002

Cumming, Laura. 'One Finn leads to another', *The Observer*, 19 May 2002, p.11.

Ellis, Samantha. 'Eija-Lisa Ahtila', *Make*, no. 92, 2002, pp. 48–50.

Searle, Adrian. 'The never-ending story', *The Guardian*, 30 April 2002, p.12.

Smyth, Cherry. 'Eija-Liisa Ahtila', *Art Monthly*, no. 257, June 2002, pp. 32–33.

Doug Aitken, New Ocean, Serpentine Gallery, London 2001

Bishop, Claire. 'Pretty vacuous?', *Untitled*, no. 26, Autumn/Winter 2001, pp. 4–5.

Morton, Tom. 'Doug Aitken', *Modern Painters*, Winter 2001, pp.102–103.

Searle, Adrian. 'Attention all shipping', *The Guardian*, 16 October 2001, p.12.

Wilsher, Mark. 'Doug Aitken', *Art Monthly*, no. 251, November 2001, pp. 28–29.

the americans. new art. (including Brian Calvin, Liz Craft, Rachel Feinstein, Kara Walker, Pae White, curated by Mark Sladen), Barbican Art Gallery, London 2001

Charlesworth, JJ. 'The Americans at Barbican Gallery', *Contemporary*, February 2002.

Corris, Michael. 'The Americans New Art', *Art Monthly*, no. 252, December/January 2001/2, pp. 30–33.

Farquharson, Alex. 'The Americans. New Art', *Artforum*, vol. 40, no. 7, March 2002, p. 136.

Gellatly, Andrew. 'the americans. new art', *frieze*, issue 64, January/February 2002, pp. 99–100.

Mac Giolla Léith, Caoimhin. 'the americans.new art', *Modern Painters*, Winter 2001, vol. 14, no. 3, pp. 100–102.

Myers, Terry R. 'the americans.new art', *Art & Text*, Spring 2002, pp. 80–81.

Carl Andre, Sadie Coles HQ, London 2001

Hunt, Ian. 'Carl Andre', *Art Monthly*, no. 253, February 2002, pp. 37–38.

Carl Andre, Whitechapel Art Gallery, London 2000

Diehl, Carol. 'Carl Andre at Whitechapel & Paula Cooper', *Art in America*, vol.89, no. 2, February 2001, p. 151.

Musgrave, David. 'Carl Andre', *Art Monthly*, no. 239, September 2000, pp. 136–137.

Potts, Alex. 'Carl Andre', *Burlington Magazine*, vol. 142, no. 1170, September 2000, pp. 582–584.

Searle, Adrian. 'Space oddities', *The Guardian*, 11 July 2000, p. 13.

Andrea & Philippe, Independent Art Space, London 1997

Barrett, David. 'Andrea & Philippe', *Art Monthly*, no. 206, May 1997, pp. 30–33.

Glover, Izi. 'Andrea & Philippe', *frieze*, issue 35, June/July/August 1997, pp. 83–84.

Andrea & Philippe, The Showroom, London 1999

Buck, Louisa. 'UK Q&A: Andrea & Philippe', *The Art Newspaper*, vol. 10, no. 96, October 1999

Ant Noises Part I & II (including Damien Hirst, Ron Mueck, Jenny Saville, Jake & Dinos Chapman), Saatchi Gallery, London 2000

Darwent, Charles. 'Jenny Saville', *Modern Painters*, vol. 13, no. 2, Summer 2000, pp. 108–109.

Feaver, William. 'Ant Noises', *ARTnews*, vol. 99, no. 9, October 2000, p. 188.

Shone, Richard. 'Ant Noises and Out There', *Burlington Magazine*, vol. 142, no. 1168, July 2000, pp. 455–456.

Wilson, Michael. 'Shop Front', *Art Monthly*, no. 237, June 2000, pp. 7–10.

Apocalypse: Beauty and Horror in Contemporary Art (including Maurizio Cattelan, Jake & Dinos Chapman, Chris Cunningham, Angus Fairhurst, Jeff Koons, Tim Noble & Sue Webster, curated by Norman Rosenthal and Max Wigram), Royal Academy of Arts, London 2000

Gellatly, Andrew. 'Apocalypse', *frieze*, issue 57, March 2001, pp. 95–96.

Searle, Adrian. 'The end of the world as we know it', *The Guardian*, 21 September 2000, p. 12.

Schmitz, Edgar. 'Apocalypse: Beauty and Horror in Contemporary Art', *Kunstforum International*, no. 153, January-March 2001, pp. 413–415.

Wilson, Michael. 'Woops apocalypse!', *Art Monthly*, no. 241, November 2000, pp. 1–5.

(Bishop, Claire. 'Angus Fairhurst: picking at a scab', *Art & Text*, no. 72, February-April 2001, pp. 56–59.)

Ida Applebroog, Cubitt Street Gallery, London 1993

Archer, Michael. 'What's in a Prefix' (with Bad Girls/ Anya Gallaccio), *Art Monthly*, no. 173, February 1994, pp. 3–5.

Rasheed Araeen, To whom it may concern, Serpentine Lawn, London 1996

Cubitt, Sean. 'Rasheed Araeen', *Art Monthly*, no. 201, November 1996, pp. 30–31.

Liz Arnold, Lotta Hammer, London 1999

Jones, Jonathan. 'Liz Arnold', *frieze*, issue 50, January/February 2000, p. 93.

Art Crazy Nation Show (including Gilbert & George, Colin Lowe & Roddy Thomson, Sarah Lucas, John McLean, Geoff Rigden), Milton Keynes Gallery, Milton Keynes 2002

Charlesworth, JJ. 'On the breezy road to parochial nowhere' (in conversation with Matthew Collings), *Untitled*, no. 27, Spring 2002, pp. 7–9.

Art & Language, Institute of Contemporary Arts, London 1991

Cohen, David. 'Art & Language', *Galleries*, March 1991.

Corris, Michael. 'Art & Language', *Artforum,* May 1991.

Renton, Andrew. 'Art & Language', *Flash Art*, no. 143, May/June 1991.

Wilson, Andrew. 'Art & Language', *Forum International*, no. 8, May/June 1991, p. 75.

(Archer, Michael. 'Hello, Terry Speaking', *Art Monthly*, no. 146, May 1991, pp. 3–9.)

Art & Language, Lisson Gallery, London 1994

Holert, Tom. 'Art & Language Painting by Mouth', *Flash Art*, March-April 1994, pp. 79–82.

Searle, Adrian. 'Art and Language', *Time Out*, 22-29 June 1994.

Art & Language, Lisson Gallery, London 1988

Archer, Michael. 'Art & Language', *Artscribe*, no. 72, November/December 1988, p. 74.

Art Now: Fiona Banner, Tate Gallery, London 1998

Ellis, Michael. 'Art Now: Fiona Banner', *Art Monthly*, no. 220, October 1998, pp. 30–32.

Art Now: Graham Gussin, Tate Gallery, London 1998

Tozer, John. 'Graham Gussin', *Art Monthly*, no. 215, April 1998, pp. 23–24.

Art Now: Cerith Wyn Evans, Tate Britain, London 2000

Adian, Rose. 'Homage to Blake in the sparkle of a mirrorball', *Independent on Sunday*, 19 November 2000, p. 4.

Kent, Sarah. 'Cerith Wyn Evans', *Time Out*, no. 1579, 22–29 November 2000, p. 51.

artranspennine98 (including Christine Borland, Mark Dion, Anya Gallaccio, Felix Gonzalez-Torres, curated by Lewis Biggs, Robert Hopper) Liverpool, Manchester, Leeds, Hull 1998

Faure Walker, Caryn. 'artranspennine98', *Art Monthly*, no. 218, July/August 1998, pp. 42–45.

Atelier van Lieshout, Camden Arts Centre, London 2002

Bullivant, Lucy. 'Free associations', *Blueprint*, May 2002, pp. 80–83.

Herbert, Martin. 'Atelier van Lieshout', *Tema Celeste*, issue 92, July/August 2002, pp. 84–85.

Wilkinson, Dan. 'Atelier van Lieshout', *frieze*, issue 69, September 2002, p. 119.

Conrad Atkinson, Bluecoat Gallery, Liverpool 1999

Harris, Mark. 'Conrad Atkinson', *Art Monthly*, no. 233, February 2000, pp. 24–25.

B.OPEN (Tatsumi Orimoto, Chris Burden, Jane & Louise Wilson, James Plensa, Julian Opie), Baltic, Gateshead 2002

Falconer, Morgan. 'B.Open', *Modern Painters*, Autumn 2002, p. 142.

Searle, Adrian. 'Joined-up thinking', *The Guardian*, 16 July 2002, p. 12.

Usherwood, Paul. 'B.Opened', *Art Monthly*, no. 259, September 2002, pp. 1–4.

Bad Girls (Helen Chadwick, Dorothy Cross, Nicole Eisenman, Rachel Evans, Nan Goldin, Sue Williams), Institute of Contemporary Arts, London 1993/ Centre for Contemporary Arts, Glasgow 1994

Archer, Michael. 'What's in a Prefix', *Art Monthly*, no. 173, February 1994, pp. 3–5.

Corris, Michael. Avgikos, Jan. Weissman, Benjamin. 'Bad girl blues', *Artforum*, vol. 32, no. 9, May 1994, pp. 86–89.

Hall, Charles. 'Best of Bad Girls', *Art Review*, vol. 45, December/January 1993/4, pp. 54–55.

Stallabrass, Julian. 'The Flesh is Weak' (with Elective Affinities/Tate Liverpool), *Art Monthly*, no. 172, December/January 1993/4, pp. 27–29.

'Who's Bad?', including Iwona Blazwick, Helen Chadwick, Laura Cottingham, Suzanne Moore, *frieze*, issue 15, March/April 1994, pp. 26–29.

BANK, Anthony Wilkinson Gallery, London 2002

Tan, Eugene. 'BANK', *Contemporary*, June–August 2002.

Williams, Gilda. 'BANK', *Art Monthly*, no. 256, May 2002, pp. 35–36.

BANK, Chapman Fine Arts, London 2001

Farquharson, Alex. 'BANK', *100 Reviews (Again)*, 2001.

Claire Barclay, The Showroom, London 2000

Gellatly, Andrew. 'Claire Barclay', *frieze*, issue 53, June/July/August 2000, pp. 123–124.

Kyriacou, Sotiris. 'Claire Barclay', *Art Monthly*, no. 236, May 2000, pp. 50–51.

McLaren, Duncan. 'Claire Barclay', *Independent on Sunday*, 16 April 2000.

O'Kane, Paul. 'Claire Barclay', *Untitled*, no. 22, Summer 2000.

Claire Barclay, Transmission, Glasgow 1994

McArther, Euan. 'Claire Barclay', *Art Monthly*, no. 180, October 1994, pp. 29–30.

The Bart Wells Gang (Sam Basu, Luke Gottelier, Mick Mee, Harry Pye and his friends, Francis Upritchard), Bart Wells Institute, London 2001

Seymour, Benedict. 'The Bart Wells Gang', *frieze*, issue 66, April 2002, p. 93.

David Batchelor, Electric Colour Tower, Sadler's Wells, London 2000

Coles, Alex. 'Electric Colour Tower', *Art in America*, March 2001.

Haynes, Kathy. 'Electric Colour Tower', *Public Art Journal*, March 2001.

Jones, Jonathan. 'Rainbow Warrior', *The Guardian*, 5 September 2000, pp. 12–13.

Mead, Andrew. 'Fear and Loathing in EC1', *The Architects' Journal*, September 2000, p. 51.

David Batchelor, 38 Langham Street, London 2002

Coles, Alex. 'David Batchelor', *Art & Text*, no. 78, Autumn 2002, pp. 82–83.

Beagles & Ramsay, Goodnite! Goodnite!, Collective Gallery, Edinburgh 1997

Burrows, David. 'It's Goodnight from Me and It's Goodnight from Him, Goodnite,Goodnite', *Art Monthly*, no. 213, February 1998, p. 23.

Burrows, David. 'Correspondences: Olympic Village. Beagles & Ramsay', *Art Monthly*, no. 216, May 1998, pp. 23–26.

Beck's Futures 1, Institute of Contemporary Arts, London 2000

Smyth, Cherry. 'Beck's Futures', *Art Monthly*, no. 236, May 2000, pp. 45–47.

Beck's Futures 2, Institute of Contemporary Arts, London 2001

Coomer, Martin. 'Mind Your Becks', *Time Out*, 28 March – 4 April 2001.

Farquharson, Alex. 'Beck's Futures 2', *100 Reviews (Again)*, 2001.

Harris, Mark. 'Beck's Futures', *NY Arts*, May 2001.

Searle, Adrian. 'Been there, done that', *The Guardian*, 3 April 2001, p. 12.

Beck's Futures 3, Institute of Contemporary Arts, London 2002

Johnson, Holly. 'Reading the Stars', *Modern Painters*, vol. 15, no. 2, Summer 2002, pp. 96–97.

Searle, Adrian. 'I have seen the future, and it sucks', *The Guardian*, 26 March 2002, p. 12.

Beck's New Contemporaries, Cornerhouse, Manchester 1997

Barrett, David. 'Beck's New Contemporaries', *Art Monthly*, no. 208, April 1997, pp. 37–39.

Vanessa Beecroft, FB43, Gagosian Gallery, London 2000

Smyth, Cherry. 'Vanessa Beecroft', *Art Monthly*, no. 240, October 2000, pp. 33–34.

Between Cinema and a Hard Place (including Miroslaw Balka, Janet Cardiff, James Coleman, Mona Hatoum, Gary Hill, Julian Opie), Tate Modern, London 2000

Heartney, Eleanor. 'A turbo-powered Tate', *Art in America*, vol. 88, no. 95, 2000, pp. 98–103.

Big Blue (including Mark Dean, Sean Dower, Peter Fillingham, Mark Harris, David Mollin, Elizabeth Price, curated by Peter Lewis), Coins Coffee Shop, London 1997

Bernard, Kate. 'Galleries Choice: Big Blue', *Evening Standard*, 1 May 1997, p. 50.

Prasad, Raekha. 'Dawn of new blue period, Big Blue', *The Independent*, 30 April 1997.

Richard Billingham, Anthony Reynolds Gallery, London 1996

Sladen, Mark. 'A family affair', *frieze*, issue 28, May 1996, pp. 50–51.

Williams, Gilda. 'Richard Billingham', *Art Monthly*, no. 199, September 1996, pp. 31–32.

Pierre Bismuth, The Showroom, London 1998

Cruz, Juan. 'Pierre Bismuth', *Art Monthly*, no. 215, April 1998, p. 22.

Herbert, Martin. 'Pierre Bismuth', *Time Out*, 25 March 1998, no. 1440.

Nayland Blake, Milch, London 1992

Wilson, Andrew. 'Nayland Blake', *Forum International*, September/October 1992, p. 101.

Ross Bleckner, Maureen Paley Interim Art, London 2000

Coles, Alex. 'Ross Bleckner', *Art Monthly*, no. 242, December/January 2000/1, pp. 31–33.

Ross Bleckner, Waddington Galleries, London, 1988

Archer, Michael. 'Ross Bleckner', *Art Monthly*, no. 118, July/August 1988, pp. 17–18.

Rut Blees Luxemburg, Liebeslied, Laurent Delaye Gallery, London 2000

Walsh, Maria. 'Rut Blees Luxemburg', *Art Monthly*, no. 242, December/January 2000/1, pp. 51–51.

Henry Bond, The Cult of the Street, Emily Tsingou Gallery, London 1998

Barrett, David. 'Henry Bond', *Art Monthly*, no. 217, June 1998, pp. 33–34.

Henry Bond, Emily Tsingou Gallery and 2&6 Shorrold's Way, London 2000

Seymour, Benedict. 'Henry Bond', *frieze*, issue 54, September/October 2000, p. 118.

Christine Borland, From Life, Tramway, Glasgow 1994

Morgan, Stuart. 'Christine Borland', *frieze*, issue 20, January/February 1995, p. 50.

Wilson, Andrew. 'Christine Borland', *Art Monthly*, no. 181, November 1994, pp. 36–37.

(Hunt, Ian. 'Chrisitine Borland', *frieze*, issue 26, January/February 1996, pp. 42–45.)

Louise Bourgeois, Tate Modern, London 2000

Madoff, Steven Henry. 'Towers of London: Louise Bourgeois', *Artforum*, vol. 38, no. 10, Summer 2000, p. 162.

Leigh Bowery, Anthony d'Offay Gallery, London 1988

Carpenter, Merlin. 'Leigh Bowery', *Artscribe*, no. 73, January/February 1989, p. 8.

Ian Breakwell, De la Warr Pavillion, Bexhill-on-Sea 2002

McFarland, Dale. 'Ian Breakwell', *frieze*, issue 67, May 2002, p. 104.

British Abstract Painting 2001 (including Gillian Ayres, Jane Bustin, Mikey Cuddihy, Geoff Rigden, Trevor Sutton, curated by Matthew Collings), Flowers East, London

Coomer, Martin. 'British Abstract Painting', *Time Out*, 22–29 August 2001.

Gayford, Martin. 'Crtitics' Choice: British Abstract Painting', *The Sunday Telegraph*, 26 August 2001.

Packer, William. 'Alive and Abstract', *Financial Times*, 25 August 2001.

The British Art Show (3), (including Ian Davenport, Grenville Davey, Bethan Huws, Gary Hume, Julian Opie, Fiona Rae, Caroline Russell), McLellan Galleries, Glasgow/ Leeds City Art Gallery/ Hayward, London 1990

Batchelor, David. 'Show Business', New Statesman and Society, vol. 3, no. 86, 2 Feb 1990.

Bernard, Bruce. 'The British Art Show', The Independent Magazine, 2 June 1990.

Bush, Kate. 'The British Art Show', Artscribe, no. 81, May/June 1990, pp. 71–72.

Collier, Caroline. 'The British Art Show', Women's Art Magazine, September 1990.

Gillick, Liam. 'Critical Dementia: The British Art Show', Art Monthly, no. 134, March 1990, pp. 14–16.

Morgan, Stuart. 'Complaints Department', Artscribe, no. 81, May/June 1990.

Watkins, Jonathan. 'British Art Show', Art International, Winter 1990.

The British Art Show (4), (including Christine Borland, Mat Collishaw, Douglas Gordon, Damien Hirst, Gillian Wearing), Manchester, Edinburgh and Cardiff 1995

Corrigan, Susan. 'Get the Picture, British Art's Next Superstars', i-D magazine, December 1995.

Garnett, Robert. 'British Art Show 4', Art Monthly, no. 192, December/January 1995/6, pp. 27–29.

Hall, James. 'Butterfly Ball', The Guardian, 14 November 1995.

Hall, James. 'The British Art Show 4', Artforum, March 1996, p. 111.

Searle, Adrian. 'British Art with Attitude', The Independent, 14 November 1995.

The British Art Show (5) (including Martin Creed, Tracey Emin, Paul Graham, Paul Noble, John Stezaker, Keith Tyson), Edinburgh, Southampton, Cardiff, Birmingham 2000

Grant, Simon. 'British Art Show 5', The World of Interiors, April 2000, p. 181.

Morley, Simon. 'What is British Art?', Art Review, vol. 52, October 2000, pp. 70.

Stallabrass, Julian. 'Looking at the New', RA Magazine, no. 68, Autumn 2000, p. 27.

British Rubbish, Tim Noble and Sue Webster, Independent Art Space, London 1996

Brown, Neal. 'Tim Noble and Sue Webster', frieze, issue 30, September/October 1996, pp. 84–85.

Burrows, David. 'British Rubbish' (with Banana Republic, Yerself is Steam), Art Monthly, no. 199, September 1996, p. 45–48.

British Wildlife, Tim Noble and Sue Webster, Modern Art, London 2000

Callow, Claire. 'Tim Noble and Sue Webster', Contemporary Visual Arts, December/January 2000/1, p. 76.

Herbert, Martin. 'Tim Noble & Sue Webster', Time Out, 4–11 October 2000, p. 52.

Broken English (Angela Bulloch, Ian Davenport, Anya Gallaccio, Damien Hirst, Gary Hume, Michael Landy, Sarah Staton, Rachel Whiteread), Serpentine Gallery, London 1991

Collings, Matthew. 'Broken English' (with New Contemporaries/ICA), City Limits, no. 515, 15–22 August 1991, p. 18.

Gale, Ian. 'Broken English', The Independent, 13 August 1991, p. 13.

Kent, Sarah. 'Broken Ground', Time Out, no. 1095, 14–21 August 1991, p. 39.

Brown (including Mark Leckey, Steven Gontarski, Jason Meadows, Mark Titchner, curated by Gary Webb), The Approach, London 2001

Clark, Paul. 'Brown: Going Out', Evening Standard, 4 July 2001.

Herbert, Martin. 'Brown by Gary Webb', Camera Austria, September 2001.

(Archer, Michael. 'Virile Logic', Untitled, no. 26, Autumn/Winter 2001, p. 12–13.)

Roderick Buchanan, Inside out, Lisson Gallery, London 2001

Armitstead, Claire. 'Pass the Remote Control', The Guardian, 13 October 2001.

Buck, Louisa. 'Pitching and catching at Lisson', The Art Newspaper, September 2001, p. 73.

Cork, Richard. 'Roderick Buchanan', *The Times*, 6 October 2001.

McLaren, Duncan. 'Roderick Buchanan', *Independent on Sunday*, 14 October 2001.

Roderick Buchanan, Players, Dundee Contemporary Arts, Dundee 2000

Bell, Gavin. 'Cutting to the Chase', *The Scotsman*, S2, 21 November 2000, pp. 10–11.

Bird, Nicky. 'Roderick Buchanan', *Art Monthly*, no. 243, February 2001, pp. 37–38.

Mahoney, Elizabeth. 'Players/ Roderick Buchanan', *The Guardian*, 5 December 2000, p. 22.

Angela Bulloch, Insititue of Visual Culture, Cambridge 2002

Farquharson, Alex. 'Angela Bulloch', *frieze*, issue 71, November 2002.

Angela Bulloch, Magnani, London 2001.

–. 'Blurring the boundaries and escaping the cubes', *Independent on Sunday*, 10 June 2001.

Currah, Mark. 'Angela Bulloch', *Time Out*, 20–27 June 2001, p. 58.

Angela Bulloch, Robert Prime, London 1996

Bussel, David. 'Angela Bulloch', *frieze*, issue 35, June/July/August 1997, p. 85.

Cross, Andrew. 'Angela Bulloch', *Art Monthly*, no. 202, December/January 1996/7, pp. 25–26.

Harris, Mark. 'Angela Bulloch', *Art in America*, May 1997.

Tsingou, Emily. 'Angela Bulloch', *Flash Art*, no. 193, March/April 1997.

Chris Burden, London Projects, London 1996

Harris, Mark. 'Chris Burden', *Art Monthly*, no. 200, October 1996, pp. 52–53.

Victor Burgin, Listen to Britain, Arnolfini, Bristol 2002

Durden, Mark. 'Victor Burgin', *Portfolio*, no. 36, 2002.

Herbert, Martin. 'Victor Burgin', *Art Review*, November 2002.

Victor Burgin, Watergate, Matt's Gallery, London 2002

Slyce, John. 'Victor Burgin' (with Victor Burgin/ Arnolfini), *Art Monthly*, no. 261, November 2002.

David Burrows, fa projects, London 2002

Beech, Dave. 'David Burrows', *Art Monthly*, no. 253, February 2002, pp. 45–46.

Jean-Marc Bustamante, Timothy Taylor Gallery, London 2001

Buck, Louisa. *The Art Newspaper*, vol. 12, no. 114, May 2001.

Darwent, Charles. 'Soft Edges Conceal Hard Truths', *Independent on Sunday*, 22 April 2001.

Green, Alison. 'Jean-Marc Bustamante', *Art Monthly*, no. 247, June 2001, pp. 34–35.

Hamad Butt, Familiars, Milch, London 1994

Morgan, Stuart. 'Hamad Butt', *frieze*, issue 16, May 1994, p. 58.

Brian Calvin, Corvi-Mora, London 2001

Gleeson, David. 'Brian Calvin', *Time Out*, no. 1609, 2001, p. 59.

Higgie, Jennifer. 'Brian Calvin', *frieze*, issue 61, September 2001, p. 96.

Candyman II (including Matthew Arnatt, Matthew Collings, Justine Daf, Sher Rajah, Giorgio Sadotti, Elizabeth Wright), Building C, London 1994

Guha, Tania. 'Candyman II', *Time Out*, no. 1245, 29 June – 6 July 1994, p. 50.

(Stallabrass, Julian. 'Candyman II', *Art Monthly*, no. 182, December/January 1994/5, pp. 3–6.)

Care and Control (including Jordan Baseman, Jason Coburn, Derek Jarman, Donald Rodney, Jo Spence), Rear Window at Hackney Hospital, London 1995

Sladen, Mark. 'Care and Control', *Art Monthly*, no. 189, July/August 1995, pp. 13–15.

Maurizio Cattelan, Laure Genillard Gallery, London 1994

Grant, Simon. 'Maurizio Cattelan', *Art Monthly*, no. 174, March 1994, p. 22.

The Cauldron (Christine Borland, Angela Bulloch, Jake & Dinos Chapman, Steven Pippin, Georgina Starr, Gillian Wearing, curated by Maureen Paley), The Henry Moore Studio, Dean Clough, Halifax 1996

Garner, Lesley. 'Cops on top in the Cauldron', *Daily Express*, 2 August 1996, p. 40.

Usherwood, Paul. 'The Cauldron', *Art Monthly*, no. 198, July/August 1996, pp. 30–31.

Patrick Caulfield, Hayward Gallery, London 1999/ Yale Center of British Art, New Haven, Connecticut, USA 1999.

Bussel, David. 'Happy Hour', *frieze*, issue 45, March/April 1999, pp. 69–73.

Cumming, Laura. 'Quiche Terrain', *The Observer*, 7 February 1999.

Hall, James. 'Contours of a crime scene', *Times Literary Supplement*, 5 March 1999.

Levy, Paul. 'Portraits of Missing Persons', *Wall Street Journal (Europe)*, 5 February 1999, p. 13.

Lubbock, Tom. 'Cool, calm, disconnected', *The Independent*, 9 February 1999.

Musgrave, David. 'Patrick Caulfield', *Art Monthly*, no. 225, April 1999, pp. 33–34.

Schwabsky, Barry. 'The not-so-happy hours of Patrick Caulfield', *Art in America*, vol. 87, no. 11, November 1999, pp. 128–133.

Vija Celmins, Anthony d'Offay Gallery, London 1999

Smyth, Cherry. 'Vija Celmins', *Art Monthly*, no. 229, September 1999, pp. 40–41.

Vija Celmins, Institute of Contemporary Arts, London 1996

Feldman, Melissa E. 'Vija Celmins', *Art Monthly*, no. 202, December/January 1996/7, pp. 32–33.

Century City, Art and Culture in the Modern Metropolis, Tate Modern, London 2001

Beech, Dave. 'Century City', *Untitled*, Spring 2001.

Garlake, Margaret. 'Art in the City', *Art Monthly*, no. 245, April 2001, pp. 1–4.

Grant, Simon. 'City snapshots', *Art Review*, no. 53, April 2001, pp. 72–73.

Mollin, David. 'Century City', *100 Reviews (Again)*, 2001.

Turner, Chris. 'Century City', *frieze*, issue 60, June/July/August 2001, p. 113.

Dinos and Jake Chapman, Bring Me the Head of Franco Toselli!, Ridinghouse Editions, London 1995

Roberts, James. 'Jake and Dinos Chapman', *frieze*, issue 24, September/October 1995, pp. 68–69.

(Morgan, Stuart. 'Rude awakening', *frieze*, issue 19, November/December 1994, pp. 28–33.)

Dinos and Jake Chapman, Chapmanworld, Institute of Contemporary Arts, London 1996

Burrows, David. Smithard, Paula. 'Representing desire in postmodernity', *Variant*, vol. 2, no. 2, Spring 1997, pp. 14–15.

Harris, Mark. 'Jake and Dinos Chapman', *Art in America*, October 1996.

Rosenblum, Robert. 'Dinos & Jake Chapman, ICA, London', *Artforum*, September 1996, pp. 100–101.

Searle, Adrian. 'Morbid, mutant dummies...', *The Guardian*, 11 May 1996.

Dinos and Jake Chapman, The Disasters of War, Victoria Miro Gallery, London 1993

Corris, Michael. 'The Disasters of War', *Artforum*, vol. 31, no. 10, Summer 1993, pp. 121–122.

Freedman, Carl. 'Dinos and Jake Chapman', *frieze,* issue 11, Summer 1993, p. 50–51.

Dinos and Jake Chapman, Disasters of War, White Cube, London 1999

Jones, Jonathan. 'Jake and Dinos Chapman', *frieze*, issue 47, June/July/August 1999, pp. 104–105.

Searle, Adrian. 'Objects' (with David Shrigley/ Stephen Friedman), *The Guardian*, 23 March 1999, p. 9.

Dinos and Jake Chapman, Great Deeds Against the Dead, Victoria Miro Gallery, London 1994

Worsdale, Godfrey. 'Dinos and Jake Chapman', *Art Monthly*, no. 180, October 1994, pp. 36–37.

**Dinos and Jake Chapman, Zygotic accelera-
tion, biogenetic, de-sublimated libidinal
model (enlarged x 1000), Victoria Miro
Gallery, London 1995**

Maloney, Martin. 'The Champman Bros. When will
I be famous?', *Flash Art*, no. 186, February 1996,
pp. 64–67.

(Sladen, Mark. 'The Body in Question', *Art
Monthly*, no. 191, November 1995, pp. 3–5.)

**The Charge of the Light Brigade (BANK,
John Cussans & Colin Lane, Matthew Higgs,
Orphan.drift>, Ingrid Pollard, Bob & Roberta
Smith), BANKspace, London 1995**

Garnett, Robert. 'The Charge of the Light Brigade',
Art Monthly, no. 191, November 1995, pp. 26–28.

Guha, Tania. 'Bank, Charge of the Light Brigade',
Time Out, 11–18 October 1995.

**Adam Chodzko, Camden Arts Centre at O2
Centre, London 2000**

Jones, Jonathan. 'Adam Chodzko', *frieze,* issue 52,
May 2000, p. 95.

**Adam Chodzko, Ikon Gallery, Birmingham
1999**

Barrett, David. 'Adam Chodzko', *Art Monthly*,
no. 229, September 1999, pp. 29–31.

Adam Chodzko, Lotta Hammer, London 1996

Burrows, David. 'Adam Chodzko', *Art Monthly*,
no. 198, July/August 1996, pp. 28–29.

Roberts, James. 'Adult Fun', *frieze*, issue 31,
November/December 1996, pp. 62–67.

**Citigroup Private Bank Photography Prize
(Roger Ballen, Elina Brotherus, Philip-Lorca
di Corcia, Thomas Ruff, Shirana Shahbazi),
The Photographers' Gallery, London 2002**

Gillick, Liam. 'Citibank', *100 Reviews(3)* 2002, p. 28.

**City Racing 1988–1998: A partial account
(including John Burgess, Keith Coventry,
Robert Ellis, Matt Hale, Mark Hosking,
Imprint93, Peter Owen, Christina Mackie,
Paul Noble, Jemima Stehli), Institute of
Contemporary Arts, London 2001**

McLaren, Duncan. 'The favourite retires', *Art
Review*, vol. 53, March 2001, p. 67.

Withers, Rachel. 'City Racing 1988–1998:
A Partial Account', *Artforum*, January 2001.

**Larry Clark & Bruce Weber, Corvi-Mora,
London 2000**

–. 'Larry Clark & Bruce Weber', *Metro Life*,
3 February 2000, p. 17.

**Cocaine Orgasm (including Liz Arnold,
BANK, Simon Bill, David Burrows, John
Cussans, Chris Ofili, John Stezaker, Michael
Stubbs, Jessica Voorsanger, Rebecca Warren,
Max Wigram), BANKspace, London 1995**

Guha, Tania. 'Cocaine Orgasm', *Time Out*, 11–18
October 1995.

James Coleman, Lisson Gallery, London 1991

Gillick, Liam. 'Time Flies', *Artscribe*, no. 88,
September 1991, p. 85.

**Mat Collishaw, duty free spirits, Lisson
Gallery, London 1997**

Hall, James. 'Mat Collishaw', *Artforum*, vol. 36,
no. 5, January 1998, pp. 111–112.

**Mat Collishaw, Karsten Schubert Ltd,
London 1991**

–. 'Mat Collishaw', *Nikkei Art,* March 1991.

Lloyd-Jacobs, Clio. 'Mat Collishaw', *Artscribe*,
no. 86, March/April 1991, p. 64.

Stallabrass, Julian. 'Mat Collishaw', *Art Monthly*,
no. 143, February 1991, pp. 17–18.

**Mat Collishaw, Ridinghouse Editions,
London 1997**

Freedman, Carl. 'Mat Collishaw', *frieze,* issue 34,
November/December 1997, p. 79.

**Comedie (Samuel Beckett / Marin Karmitz),
Anthony Reynolds Gallery, London 2000**

Chesher, Andrew. 'Samuel Beckett', *Untitled*,
no. 26, Autumn/Winter 2001, p37.

Downey, Anthony. 'Samuel Beckett / Marin Karmitz',
Contemporary Visual Arts, issue 33, 2001, p. 66.

**Common Culture (David Campbell, Mark
Durden, Paul Rooney), Cornerhouse,
Manchester 1999**

Bracewell, Michael. 'Common Culture', *frieze,*
issue 47, June/July/August 1999, p. 106.

Common Culture (David Campbell, Mark Durden, Paul Rooney), Gasworks, London 2001

Charlesworth, JJ. 'Common Culture', *Art Monthly*, no. 242, December/January 2000/1, pp. 42–43.

The Communications Department (including Artclub 2000, Matthew Arnatt, Jeremy Deller, Liam Gillick, Jeff Koons, Carey Young, curated by Alex Farquharson), Anthony Wilkinson Gallery, London 2001

Beech, Dave. 'The Communications Department', *Art Monthly*, no. 249, September 2001, pp. 33–35.

Wilson, Rob. 'The Communications Department', *Untitled*, no. 26, Autumn/Winter 2001, pp. 38–39.

Couldn't Get Ahead (Andrea Bowers, Sam Durant, Robert Gunderman, Bob & Roberta Smith, Georgina Starr), Independent Art Space, London 1995

Barrett, David. 'Couldn't Get Ahead', *frieze*, issue 23, July/August 1995.

Melanie Counsell, Matt's Gallery, London 1989

Currah, Mark. 'Melanie Counsell', *City Limits*, 30 November–6 December 1989.

(Bush, Kate. 'Melanie Counsell', *Artscribe*, no. 80, March/April 1990, p. 58.)

Keith Coventry, Emily Tsingou Gallery, London 2000

Burrows, David. 'Keith Coventry', *Art Monthly*, no. 240, October 2000, p. 37.

Keith Coventry, The Showroom, London 1997

Currah, Mark. 'Keith Coventry', *Time Out*, no. 1420, 5–12 November 1997.

Craddock, Sacha. 'London Exhibitions', *The Times*, 21 October 1997.

Feldman, Melissa. 'Keith Coventry at The Showroom', *Art in America*, April 1998.

Herbert, Martin. 'Keith Coventry' (interview with KC), *Dazed and Confused*, no. 44, July 1998, pp. 126–129.

Keith Coventry, Spacex, Exeter 1997

Freedman, Carl. 'Keith Coventry', *frieze*, issue 35, June/July/August 1997, pp. 95–96.

Tony Cragg, Whitechapel Art Gallery, London 1997

Reiser, Jesse. 'Latent tectonics in work of Tony Cragg', *Art & Design*, no. 55, July/August 1997, pp. 76–83.

Wollheim, Richard. 'Tony Cragg at forty-seven at the Whitechapel', *Modern Painters*, vol. 10, no. 1, Spring 1997, pp. 42–45.

Michael Craig-Martin, Whitechapel Art Gallery, London 1989

Batchelor, David. 'A Fig Leaf: Michael Craig-Martin', *New Statesman and Society*, vol. 2, no. 76, 1989.

Collings, Matthew. 'Diary. Britain is Best', *Modern Painters*, vol. 3, no. 1, Spring 1990, pp. 90–91.

Gillick, Liam. 'Michael Craig-Martin', *Art Monthly*, no. 132, December/January 1989/90, pp. 21–23.

Godfrey, Tony. 'London: Michael Craig-Martin at the Whitechapel', *Art in America*, March 1990, p. 211.

Graham-Dixon, Andrew. 'Seeing is Believing', *The Independent Magazine*, 4 November 1989.

Hatton, Brian. 'Michael Craig-Martin', *Artscribe*, no. 80, March/April 1990, p. 76.

Joyce, Conor. 'Michael Craig-Martin', *Artforum*, February 1990, p. 154.

Shone, Richard. 'From a glass of water do mighty oak trees grow', *The Observer*, 5 November 1989.

Crash! (including Beagles & Ramsay, Christian Jankowski, Mark Leckey, Carey Young, Szupergallery), Institute of Contemporary Arts, London 1999

–. 'Crash!', *Sleazenation*, December 1999.

Charlesworth, JJ. 'Crash!', *Art Monthly*, no. 233, February 2000.

Searle, Adrian. 'Crash!', *The Guardian*, 30 November 1999.

Martin Creed, The Portico, London 1999

Beech, Dave. 'Martin Creed', *Art Monthly*, no. 226, May 1999, pp. 24–25.

Martin Creed Works, Southampton City Art Gallery/ Leeds City Art Gallery, Leeds/ Bluecoat, Liverpool/ Camden Arts Centre, London 2000–2001

Coles, Alex. 'Martin Creed Works', *Art in America*, vol. 88, no. 11, November 2000, p. 176.

Morley, Simon. 'Small epiphanies and natural histories' (with Simon Starling/Camden), *Independent on Sunday*, 19 November 2000.

Searle, Adrian. 'Is this what they call pop art? Balloons, Blu-tack and a crumpled sheet of paper', *The Guardian*, 18 January 2000, p. 14.

Critical Decor, Laughing in the Face of Tragedy, Independent Art Space, London 1996

Martin, Tim. 'Critical Decor', *frieze*, issue 32, January/February 1997, pp. 77–78.

Worsdale, Godfrey. 'Critical Decor', *Art Monthly*, no. 200, October 1996, pp. 59–60.

Juan Cruz, Portrait of a Sculptor, Matt's Gallery, London 2001

Bolton, Will. 'Juan Cruz: Portrait of a Sculptor', *AN magazine,* September 2001.

Hall, James. 'Juan Cruz: Portrait of a Sculptor', *Artforum*, November 2001.

Hunt, Andrew. 'Juan Cruz', *Untitled*, no. 26, Autumn/Winter 2001, p. 40.

Millar, Jeremy. 'Juan Cruz', *Artforum (online)*, July–September 2001.

Alan Currall, Jerwood Space, London 2002

Judd, Ben. 'Alan Currall', *Art Monthly*, no. 260, October 2002.

John Currin, Sadie Coles HQ, London 2000

Higgie, Jennifer. 'John Currin', *frieze,* issue 54, September/October 2000, p. 115.

John Cussans, Cabinet Gallery, London 1994

Guha, Tania. 'John Cussans', *Time Out*, March 1994.

Dexter Dalwood, New Paintings, Gagosian Gallery, London 2000

Archer, Michael. 'Dexter Dalwood', *Artforum*, December 2000.

Ellis, Patricia. 'Dexter Dalwood', *Flash Art*, October 2000.

Hubbard, Sue. 'Dexter Dalwood', *Independent on Sunday*, 22 October 2000.

Ian Davenport, Gary Hume, Michael Landy, Karsten Schubert Ltd, London 1988

Archer, Michael. 'Ian Davenport, Gary Hume, Michael Landy', *Artforum*, vol. 27, no. 6, February 1989, p. 147.

Shone, Richard. 'Ian Davenport, Gary Hume & Michael Landy', *Burlington Magazine*, vol. 121, no. 1030, January 1989.

Ian Davenport, Poured Paintings, Waddington Galleries, London 1996

Archer, Michael. 'Ian Davenport', *Artforum*, vol. 35, no. 3, November 1996, p. 110.

Wilson, Andrew. 'Ian Davenport', *Art Monthly*, no. 200, October 1996, pp. 55–56.

Ian Davenport, Waddington Galleries, London 1990

Beaumont, Mary Rose. 'Ian Davenport', *Art Review*, October 1990.

Graham-Dixon, Andrew. 'Leaving a mark', *The Independent*, 9 October 1990.

Hicks, Alistair. 'New star's course seems all too predictable', *The Times*, 19 October 1990.

Inter Alia (Dave Beech & Mark Hutchison). 'Ian Davenport', *Artscribe*, no. 85, January/February 1991, pp. 75–76.

Rankin-Reid, Jane. 'Painting Alone', *Artscribe*, no. 85, January/February 1991.

Renton, Andrew. 'Ian Davenport:', *Flash Art*, January/February 1991.

Shone, Richard. 'London, Davenport at Waddington', *Burlington Magazine*, vol. 132, no. 1052, November 1990.

Grenville Davey, Lisson Gallery, London 1987

Althorpe-Guyton, Marjorie. 'Grenville Davey', *Flash Art*, no.138, January/February 1988.

Archer, Michael. 'Grenville Davey', *Artforum*, January 1988.

Morgan, Stuart. 'Degree Zero: Grenville Davey', *Artscribe*, January/February 1988.

Peter Davies, The Approach, London 1998

Coomer, Martin. 'Peter Davies', *Time Out*, no.1437, 4–11 March 1998.

Maloney, Martin. 'The art of Peter Davies', *Frank*, March 1998.

(Roberts, James. 'Be There or be Square', *frieze*, issue 41, June/July/August 1998, pp. 68–69.)

Willem de Kooning, Tate Gallery, London 1995

Brown, Glenn. 'Willem de Kooning', *frieze*, issue 22, May 1995, pp. 54–55.

Lucie-Smith, Edward. 'Willem de Kooning', *Art Review*, vol. 47, February 1995, pp. 29–31.

Sylvester, David. 'The Birth of 'Woman I'', *Burlington Magazine*, vol.137, no.1105, April 1995, pp. 220–232.

Mark Dean, Laurent Delaye Gallery, London 2000

Wilson, Michael. 'Mark Dean', *Art Monthly*, no. 235, April 2000, pp. 43–44.

Tacita Dean, Recent films and other works, Tate Britain, London 2001

Campbell, Jim. 'Tacita Dean: the artist as narrator', *Contemporary Visual Arts*, no. 34, 2001, pp. 46–51.

Schmitz, Edgar. 'Tacita Dean: Recent films and other works', *Kunstforum International*, no.155, June/July 2001, pp. 436–437.

Tan, Eugene. 'Only time can tell', *Art Review*, vol. 53, May 2001, p. 66.

Walsh, Maria. 'Tacita Dean', *Art Monthly*, no. 246, May 2001, pp. 26–27.

Tacita Dean, Tate Gallery, London 1996

Feldman, Melissa. 'Tacita Dean', *Art Monthly*, no. 200, October 1996, pp. 53–54.

Death to the Fascist Insect that Preys on the Life of the People (including Dan Perfect, Kirsten Glass, Martin McGinn, Elizabeth Neal, curated by Martin Maloney), Anthony d'Offay Gallery at Haunch of Venison Yard, London 2001

Mollin, David. 'Death to the Fascist Insect…', *100 Reviews (Again)*, 2001.

Jeremy Deller, The Battle of Orgreave, Orgreave, Yorkshire 2001 (Artangel)

Barton, Lynn. 'Eerie echoes as Orgreave battle refought', *Yorkshire Post*, 18 June 2001.

Beech, Dave. 'Jeremy Deller', *Art Monthly*, no. 248, July/August 2001, pp. 37–39.

Braid, Mary. 'Miners side with the enemy as Battle of Orgreave becomes art', *The Independent*, 18 June 2001.

Dunn, David. 'Miners fight another day', *The Star*, 18 June 2001.

Farquharson, Alex. 'Jeremy Deller', *frieze*, issue 61, July/August 2001, p.108.

Lubbock, Tom. 'When history repeats itself too soon', *The Independent*, 19 June 2001, p.11.

Wainwright, Martin. 'Strikers relive battle of Orgreave', *The Guardian*, 18 June 2001, p. 3.

Jeremy Deller, Cabinet Gallery, London 1996

Currah, Mark. 'Jeremy Deller', *Time Out*, 6–13 March 1996.

Freedman, Carl. 'Jeremy Deller', *frieze*, issue 29, July/August 1996, pp. 70–71.

Worsdale, Godfrey. 'Jeremy Deller', *Art Monthly*, no.195, April 1994, pp. 31–32.

Thomas Demand, Victoria Miro Gallery, London 1995

Morgan, Stuart. 'Thomas Demand', *frieze*, issue 23, July/August 1995, pp. 70–71.

Die Young Stay Pretty (including Dexter Dalwood, Peter Davies, Steven Gontarski, David Thorpe, Gary Webb, curated by Martin Maloney), Institute of Contemporary Arts, London 1998

Garnett, Robert. 'Die Young Stay Pretty', *Art Monthly*, no. 222, December/January 1998/9, pp. 39–40.

Slyce, John. 'Die Young Stay Pretty', *Flash Art*, January/February 1999, p. 93.

Rineke Dijkstra, The Photographers' Gallery, London 1998

Higgie, Jennifer. 'Rineke Dijkstra', *frieze*, issue 39, March/April 1998, p. 81.

Mark Dion, Tate Thames Dig, London 1999

Birnbaum, Daniel. 'Mark Dion. Tate Thames Dig', *Artforum*, vol. 38, no. 3, November 1999.

Blazwick, Iwona. 'Mark Dion's Tate Thames Dig', *Oxford Art Journal*, vol. 24, no. 2, 2001, pp. 103–112.

Coles, Alex. 'Mark Dion Tate Thames Dig', *Parachute*, April–June 2000.

Craig-Martin, Michael. 'Mark Dion Tate Thames Dig', *Parachute*, April-June 2000.

Wilson, David. 'Here's Mud in Your Eye', *The Independent*, 26 July 1999, pp. 1–3.

Dinner (artists including Mark Dickinson, Peter Doig, Rachel Evans, Liam Gillick, Gavin Turk, Elizabeth Wright, guests including Patricia Bickers, Sacha Craddock, Emma Dexter, Maureen Paley, Anthony Reynolds, Isobel Johnstone, Nell Wendler, curated by Giorgio Sadotti), Cubitt Gallery, London 1996

Harvey, William. 'Dinner, Cubitt Street', *Untitled*, Summer 1996, p. 25.

Documents, Henry Bond & Liam Gillick, Karsten Schubert Ltd, London 1991.

Archer, Michael. 'Documents', *Artforum*, March 1991.

Jeffrey, Ian. 'Bond & Gillick', *Art Monthly*, no. 144, March 1991, pp. 11–12.

Jennings, Rose. 'Documents: Karsten Schubert', *City Limits*, 7–14 February 1991.

Willie Doherty, At the End of the Day, Tate Liverpool 1998

Hunt, Ian. 'Willie Doherty', *Tate magazine*, no. 16, Winter 1998, pp. 16–17.

Willie Doherty, Retraces, Matt's Gallery, London 2002

Prince, Nigel. 'Willie Doherty', *Untitled*, no. 27, Spring 2002, pp. 29–30.

Smyth, Cherry. 'Willie Doherty', *Art Monthly*, no. 254, March 2002, pp. 30–31.

Suchin, Peter. 'Willie Doherty', *frieze*, issue 66, April 2002, pp. 99–100.

Peter Doig, Freestyle, Victoria Miro Gallery, London 1996

Cruz, Juan. 'Peter Doig', *Art Monthly*, no. 194, March 1996, p. 30.

Feldman, Melissa E. 'Peter Doig', *Art in America*, September 1996.

Gisbourne, Mark. 'Peter Doig', *Untitled*, no. 10, Spring 1996.

Peter Doig, 100 Years Ago, Victoria Miro Gallery, London 2002

Higgie, Jennifer. 'Peter Doig', *frieze*, issue 68, June/July/August 2002, pp. 102–103.

Herbert, Martin. 'Peter Doig. 100 Years Ago', *Modern Painters*, vol. 15, no. 2, Summer 2002, p. 109.

Peter Doig, Whitechapel Art Gallery, London 1998

Brown, Neal. 'Peter Doig', *frieze*, issue 43, November/December 1998, p. 80.

Rita Donagh, 197419841994: Paintings and Drawings, The Irish Museum of Modern Art, Dublin, Ireland/ Cornerhouse, Manchester/ Camden Arts Centre, London 1994–1995

Warwick, Nigel. 'Rita Donagh', *frieze*, issue 23, July/August 1995, pp. 77–78.

Szulakowska, Ursula. 'Rita Donagh', *Art Monthly*, no. 182, December/January 1994/5, pp. 30–31.

Itai Doron, The Immaculate Stereoscopic Conception of Mr D/ The Secret Life and Archaic Times of Mr D, Jay Jopling at The Passmore Building, Canary Wharf and White Cube, London 1993

Freedman, Carl. 'Itai Doron', *frieze*, issue 12, September/October 1993, p. 60.

(Wilson, Andrew. 'Art for Life's Sake', *Art Monthly*, no. 168, July/August 1993, pp. 19–22.)

Doubletake: Collective Memory & Current Art (including Stephan Balkenhol, Mike Kelley, Jeff Koons, Simon Patterson, Boyd Webb), Hayward Gallery, London 1992

Barter, Ruth. 'Doubletake', *Art Monthly*, no. 155, April 1992, pp. 16–17.

Fleissig, Peter. 'Kitschy, Kitschy Koons', *City Limits*, 12–19 March 1994.

Gillick, Liam. 'Doubletake', *Art Monthly*, no. 154, March 1992, pp. 14–15.

Graham-Dixon, Andrew. 'Dismembered vision', *The Independent*, 3 March 1992.

Hilton, Tim. 'Banal, trivial – memories aren't made of this', *The Guardian*, 26 February 1992.

McEwan, John. 'The South Bank Joke Show', *The Sunday Telegraph*, 23 February 1992.

Morgan, Stuart. 'Thanks for the Memories', *frieze*, issue 4, April-May 1992, p. 6–11.

Sewell, Brian. 'Punk junk strictly for the dinosaurs', *Evening Standard*, 5 March 1992.

Whitford, Frank. 'Schlock of the new', *Sunday Times*, 23 February 1992.

Stan Douglas, Serpentine Gallery, London 2002

Morton, Tom. 'Stan Douglas', *frieze*, issue 68, June/July/August 2002, pp. 105–106.

Searle, Adrian. 'Twelve tubs of popcorn and a gallon of Coke, please', *The Guardian*, 5 March 2002, p. 10.

Wilsher, Mark. 'Stan Douglas', *Art Monthly*, no. 255, April 2002, pp. 30–32.

Sean Dower, No Room in Hell (Absent Qualia), Matt's Gallery, London 1998

Brown, Neal. 'Sean Dower', *frieze*, issue 39, March/April 1998, pp. 92–93.

Dub'L inTROOder (including Beagles & Ramsay, Daiziel & Scullion, Ecole de Burrows et Bob Smith, Paul McCarthy & Mike Kelley), Transmission Gallery, Glasgow 2001

Jeffery, Moira. 'When solo artists meet their match', *The Herald* (Glasgow), 12 March 2001.

Lowndes, Sarah. 'Dub'L inTROOder', *The List*, March 2001.

Mahoney, Elizabeth. 'Dub'L inTROOder', *The Guardian*, 14 March 2001.

Mulholland, Neil. 'Dub'L inTROOder', *frieze*, issue 60, June 2001.

Early One Morning (Shahin Afrassiabi, Claire Barclay, Jim Lambie, Eva Rothschild, Gary Webb), Whitechapel Art Gallery, London 2002

Charlesworth, JJ. 'Not Neo but New',(with Tra-la-la: British Sculpture in the Sixties/Tate Britain, Shimmering Substances/ Arnolfini), *Art Monthly*, no. 259, September 2002, pp. 7–12.

Dorment, Richard. 'Better than Brit Art', *The Daily Telegraph*, 17 July 2002.

Hackworth, Nick. 'Early One Morning', *Evening Standard*, 9 July 2002.

Herbert, Martin. 'Early One Morning/Tra-la-la', *Modern Painters*, Autumn 2002, p. 139.

Januszczak, Waldemar. 'A new movement for British Art ...', *Sunday Times*, 4 August 2002.

EAST, Norwich Gallery, Norwich Insitute of Art and Design, Norwich 1991–2002

Burrows, David. '10th EAST', *Art Monthly*, no. 239, September 2000, pp. 32–34.

Durden, Mark. 'EAST', *Art Monthly*, no. 189, September 1995, pp. 39–40.

Durden, Mark. 'EAST', *Art Monthly*, no. 199, September 1996, pp. 38–40.

Hilton, Tim. 'The truly East of England show', *Independent on Sunday*, 27 July 1997.

Slyce, John. 'EAST', *Art Monthly*, no. 259, September 2002, pp. 33–35

East Country Yard Show (Henry Bond, Anya Gallaccio, Gary Hume, Michael Landy, Sarah Lucas, Virginia Nimarkoh, Peter E. Richardson, Thomas Trevor, curated by Henry Bond, Sarah Lucas), East Country Yard, Surrey Docks, London 1990

Brooks, Liz. 'East Country Yard Show', *Artscribe*, no. 83, September/October 1990, p. 16.

Graham-Dixon, Andrew. 'The Midas Touch? East Country Yard Show', *The Independent*, 31 July 1990.

Hall, James. 'East Country Yard Show', *The Sunday Correspondent*, 17 July 1990.

Renton, Andrew. 'East Country Yard Show', *Flash Art*, vol. 23, no.154, October 1990, p.191.

White, Tony. 'East Country Yard Show', *Artists Newsletter*, October 1990, pp. 37–38.

('It's a Maggot Farm; The B-Boys and Fly Girls of British Art: Five Statements and a Conversation', by David Batchelor, Kate Bush, Liam Gillick, Jutta Koether, Sotiris Kyriacou, Adrian Searle, *Artscribe*, no. 84, November/December 1990).

William Eggleston, Hayward Gallery, London 2002

Green, Alison. 'William Eggleston', *Art Monthly*, no. 259, September 2002, pp. 27–28.

McClure, Richard. 'Gallery marries an odd couple', *Financial Times*, 22 July 2002.

Searle, Adrian. 'The sordid and the sublime'(with Ansel Adams), *The Guardian*, 9 July 2002, p.12.

Tracey Emin: I Need Art Like I Need God, South London Gallery, London 1997

Barrett, David. 'Tracey Emin', *Art Monthly*, no. 207, June 1997, pp. 36–37.

Dorment, Richard. 'All about Tracey Emin', *The Daily Telegraph*, 30 April 1997.

Jackson, Tina. 'Mad Tracey of Margate', *The Big Issue*, 7–13 April 1997, pp.12–15.

Morgan, Stuart. 'The Story of I' (interview with TE), *frieze*, issue 34, May 1997, pp. 56–61.

Searle, Adrian. 'Me,me,me,me', *The Guardian*, 22 April 1997.

Thomas, Lesley. 'From Margate to Monument Valley', *The Express*, 10 April 1997.

Tracey Emin Museum, 221 Waterloo Rd, London 1995–1998

Brown, Neal. 'Tracey Emin', *frieze*, issue 26, January/February 1996, pp. 81–82.

Windsor, John. 'A different kind of bond', *The Independent*, 25 January 1997.

The Epic and the Everyday: Contemporary Photographic Art (including Bernd and Hilla Becher, Andreas Gursky, Robert Smithson, Thomas Struth, Jeff Wall, curated by James Lingwood), Hayward Gallery, London 1994

Cork, Richard. 'An eye fixed firmly on the future', *The Times*, 19 July 1994.

Frangenberg, Thomas. 'The Epic and the Everyday', *Art Monthly*, no.179, September 1994, pp. 40–41.

Hall, James. 'Monoliths from life's monotony', *The Guardian*, 27 June 1994.

Jeffrey, Ian. 'The Epic and the Everyday', *Creative Camera*, October 1994.

Muir, Gregor. 'The Epic & The Everyday', *Flash Art*, vol. 27, no.178, October 1994, p. 93.

Stallabrass, Julian. 'The epic of the Everyday', *Art Monthly*, no.179, September 1994, pp. 8–11.

(Bickers, Patricia. 'Wall Pieces', *Art Monthly*, no.179, September 1994, pp. 3–7.)

Examining Pictures: Exhibiting Paintings (including Philip Guston, Richard Hamilton, Joanne Greenbaum, Laura Owens, Elizabeth Peyton, curated by Francesco Bonami, Judith Nesbitt), Whitechapel Art Gallery, London 1999

Ebner, John. 'Der Zustand des Tafelbildes', *Kunstforum International*, no.128, December/January 1999/2000, pp. 389–390.

(Grabner, Michelle. 'Examining Pictures: Exhibiting Paintings' (at Museum of Cont. Art, Chicago), *frieze*, issue 49, November/December 1999, pp.108–109.

Exchange (including Henry Coleman, Peter Fillingham, Roger Hiorns, David Musgrave, Rupert Norfolk, Mark Titchner), Richard Salmon Gallery, London 2002

Charlesworth, JJ. 'Exchange', *Contemporary*, April 2002.

Charlesworth, JJ. 'Exchange', *100 Reviews (3)*, 2002, pp. 35–36.

O'Reilly, Sally. 'Exchange', *frieze*, issue 67, May 2002, pp. 96–97.

Angus Fairhurst, All Evidence of Man Removed, Karsten Schubert Ltd, London 1993.

Archer, Michael. 'Angus Fairhurst', *Artforum*, December 1993.

Angus Fairhurst, Low Lower Lowest, White Cube, London 1996

Harris, Mark. 'Angus Fairhurst', *Art Monthly*, no. 202, December/January 1996/7, pp. 24–25.

Angus Fairhurst, More or Less Angus Fairhurst, Sadie Coles HQ, London 2001

Hackworth, Nick. 'Less is Less – More or Less', *Evening Standard*, 23 March 2001.

Herbert, Martin. 'Angus Fairhurst', *Time Out*, no. 1597, 28 March-4 April 2001, p. 51.

Angus Fairhurst, 71 Hartham Rd, London 1994

Muir, Gregor. 'Angus Fairhurst', *frieze*, issue 17, June/July/August 1994, pp. 60–61.

David Falconer, Chapman Fine Arts, London 1998

Brown, Neal. 'David Falconer', *frieze*, issue 40, May 1998, p. 78.

Keith Farquhar, Anthony Reynolds Gallery, London 1998

Judd, Ben. 'Keith Farquhar', *Art Monthly*, no. 221, November 1998, pp. 29–30.

Keith Farquhar, Anthony Reynolds Gallery, London 2002

Morton, Tom. 'Keith Farquhar', *frieze*, issue 65, March 2002, p. 83.

Keith Farquhar and Gary Webb, Nouveau Riche, The Approach, London 2000

Fox, Dan. 'Keith Farquhar and Gary Webb', *frieze*, issue 55, November/December 2000, pp. 116–117.

15/1 (including Adam Chodzko, Pauline Daly, Sean Dower, Anya Gallaccio, Andreas Ginkel, David Griffiths, Denise Hawrysio, Graham Ramsay, curated by Denise Hawrysio), Malania Basarab Gallery, London 1992

Guha, Tania. '15/1', *City Limits*, 23–30 July 1992.

Kent, Sarah. '15/1', *Time Out*, 22–29 June 1992, p. 40.

Wilson, Andrew. 'Summer round-up', *Art Monthly*, no. 159, September 1992, p. 19.

fig-1, 50 projects in 50 weeks (including Enrico David, Tacita Dean, Jeremy Deller, Gilbert & George, Richard Hamilton, Runa Islam, Bridget Riley, Will Self, Gavin Turk, Cerith Wyn Evans), Fragile House, London 2000–2001

Colomar, Christina. Stewart, Christabel. 'Focus: London', *Art Review*, vol. 52, December/January 2000/1, pp. 84–85.

'fig-1, 50 projects in 50 weeks', by Maria Walsh, Emma Smith, John Tozer, Michael Archer, Gilda Williams, Michael Wilson, David Lillington, Margaret Garlake, *Art Monthly*, no. 243, February 2001, pp. 43–45.

Fox, Dan. 'fig-1', *frieze*, issue 58, April 2001, p. 91.

Peter Fischli and David Weiss, In a Restless World, Serpentine Gallery, London 1996

Williams, Gilda. 'Fischli & Weiss', *Art Monthly*, no. 198, July/August 1996, pp. 23–25.

Flag (including Justine Daf, Luigi Gelati, Runa Islam, David Medalla, David Mollin, Sophie Rickett), Clink Wharf, London 1996

Harris, Mark. 'Flag', *Art Monthly*, no. 193, February 1996.

Ceal Floyer, City Racing, London 1997

Archer, Michael. 'Ceal Floyer', *Art Monthly*, no. 207, June 1997, pp. 32–33.

Ceal Floyer, Ikon Gallery, Birmingham 2001

Clark, Robert. 'Ceal Floyer', *The Guardian*, 12 February 2001.

Lewisohn, Cedar. 'Ceal Floyer', *Flash Art*, vol. 34, no. 217, March/April 2001, pp. 116–117.

Mac Giolla Léith, Caoimhin. 'Ceal Floyer', *Artforum*, vol. 39, no. 8, April 2001, p. 150.

Musgrave, David. 'Ceal Floyer', *Art Monthly*, no. 244, March 2001, pp. 45–46.

Safe, Emma. 'Ceal Floyer', *Contemporay Visual Arts*, issue 34, 2001, p. 64.

Freeze (Parts 1–3), (including Mat Collishaw, Ian Davenport, Angus Fairhurst, Damien Hirst, Abigail Lane, Sarah Lucas, Simon Patterson, curated by Damien Hirst), PLA Building, Surrey Docks, London 1988

Craddock, Sacha. 'Freeze: The fast Dockland train to simplicity', *The Guardian*, 13 September 1988, p.17.

Bulloch, Angela. 'Freeze', *Art & Design Magazine*, vol. 5, no. 3/4, September 1989, pp. 52–53.

Morgan, Stuart. *Artscribe*, no. 73, January/February 1989, p.10.

From Here (including Glenn Brown, Alan Charlton, Keith Coventry, Peter Davis, Mark Francis, Callum Innes, Zebedee Jones, Jason Martin, Fiona Rae, Bridget Riley), Waddington Galleries and Karsten Schubert, London 1995

Archer, Michael. 'Licensed to Paint', *Art Monthly*, no.186, May 1995, pp. 8–10.

Coomer, Martin. 'From Here', *Time Out*, 19–26 April 1995, p. 46.

Searle, Adrian. 'Any Colour You Like as Long as It's a Joke', *The Independent*, 4 April 1995, p. 21.

Future Perfect (including Liam Gillick, Paul Noble, Simon Starling, David Thorpe), Centre for Visual Arts, Cardiff 2000

Higgie, Jennifer. 'Future Perfect', *frieze*, issue 55, November/ December 2000, p.104.

Green, Alison. 'Future Perfect', *Art Monthly*, no. 239, September 2000, pp. 41–43.

Anya Gallaccio, Glaschu, Tramway at Cortinthian Gallery, Glasgow 1999.

Mahoney, Elizabeth. 'Anya Gallaccio, Glaschu', *Art Monthly*, no. 226, May 1999, pp. 31–33.

Anya Gallaccio, Intensities and Surfaces, Wapping Pumping Station, London 1996

Bickers, Patricia. 'Meltdown: Anya Gallaccio interviewed', *Art Monthly*, no.195, April 1996, pp. 3–8.

Cork, Richard. 'Meltdown at the cube station', *The Times*, 20 February 1996.

Gayford, Martin. 'A big chill in Wapping', *The Daily Telegraph*, 6 March 1996, p.18.

Jong, Kim. 'No pretentions to monumental solidity or minimal love', *Make*, no. 76, June/July 1997, pp. 6–7.

Lee, David. 'Anya Gallaccio', *Art Review*, vol. 48, April 1996, pp.10–12.

Anya Gallaccio, Karsten Schubert Ltd, London 1991

Santacatterina, Stella. 'Anya Gallaccio', *Tema Celeste*, January 1992, no. 34, p.12.

Anya Gallaccio, Stroke, Karsten Schubert Ltd, London 1994

Alberge, Dalya. 'Tasty Art Exhibit Doomed to Rot', *The Independent*, 13 January 1994, p.11.

Archer, Michael. 'What's in a prefix (with Bad Girls/ICA, Applebroog/Cubitt)', *Art Monthly*, no.173, February 1994, pp. 3–5,

Chapman, Jake. Falconer, David. 'Anya Gallaccio', *frieze*, issue 15, March/April 1994, pp. 53–54.

Collings, Matthew. 'Please taste the art', *Daily Express*, 21 January 1994, pp. 4–5.

Herbert, Susannah. 'And all because the lady loves a room full of chocolate', *The Independent*, 13 Janaury 1994.

Gambler (including Dominic Dennis, Angus Fairhurst, Tim Head, Damien Hirst, curated by Carl Freedman, Billee Sellman), Building One, London 1990

Craddock, Sacha. 'Dropping like flies for art's sake', *The Guardian*, 1 August 1990.

Gillick, Liam. 'It's a Maggot Farm', (interview with Damien Hirst) *Artscribe*, no. 84, November/December 1990.

Kent, Sarah. 'Gambler', *Time Out*, July 1990.

Morgan, Stuart. 'Gambler', *Art Monthly*, no.139, September 1990, p.15.

General Idea, Robert Prime & Camden Arts Centre, London 1998

Ellis, Michael. 'General Idea', *Art Monthly*, no. 218, July/August 1998, p. 27.

Kent, Sarah. 'General Idea', *Time Out*, 24 June – 1 July 1998, p. 52.

Gilbert & George, The Naked Shit Pictures, South London Gallery, London 1995

Sylvester, David. 'Two Just Men', *The Guardian*, 8 September 1995.

Gilbert & George, The Rudimentary Pictures, Milton Keynes Art Gallery 1999

Collings, Matthew. 'Right up their street', *Independent on Sunday*, 10 October 1999.

Glancey, Jonathan. 'Rude boys enter virgin territory', *The Guardian*, 21 October 1999.

Jahn, Wolf. 'Blood, toil, tears and sweat', *Independent on Sunday, Review Magazine*, 3 October 1999.

Wilson, Andrew. 'Gilbert & George', *Art Monthly*, no. 231, November 1999, pp. 26–27.

Liam Gillick, Corvi-Mora, London 2001

Bussel, David, 'Inbetweener', *i-D magazine*, May 2001, p.186.

Clark, Paul. 'Liam Gillick', *Evening Standard*, 17 April 2001.

Liam Gillick, Renovation filter: recent past and near future, Arnolfini, Bristol 2000

Andrews, Max. 'Liam Gillick', *Contemporary Visual Arts*, issue 32, December/January 2000/1, p. 73.

Musgrave, David. 'Liam Gillick', *Art Monthly*, no. 241, November 2000, pp. 33–34.

Liam Gillick, Robert Prime, London 1996

Herbert, Martin. 'Liam Gillick', *Time Out*, no.1343, 15–22 May 1996.

Higgie, Jennifer. 'Liam Gillick', *frieze*, issue 30, September/October 1996, pp. 77–78.

Lovatt, Estelle. 'Liam Gillick', *Southern Cross*, issue 395, 15 May 1996.

Williams, Gilda. 'Liam Gillick', *Art & Text* , issue 55, October 1996.

Worsdale, Godfrey. 'Liam Gillick', *Art Monthly*, no.197, June 1996, pp. 29–31.

Liam Gillick, The Wood Way, Whitechapel Art Gallery, London 2002

Campbell-Johnston, Rachel. 'Liam Gillick and Hélio Oiticica', *The Times*, 18 May 2002, p. 23.

Dawson, Mike. 'Liam Gillick', *FLUX*, August/September 2002, pp. 62–65.

Harris, Mark. 'Liam Gillick/Hélio Oiticica', *Art Monthly*, no. 257, June 2002, p. 24–26.

Herbert, Martin. 'Liam Gillick', *Art Review*, May 2002, pp. 52–53.

Loyer, Béatrice. 'Parallel scenarios', *Techniques & Architecture*, August/September 2002, pp. 74–77.

Mac Giolla Léith, Caoimhin. 'Liam Gillick', *Artforum*, vol. XLI, no. 2, October 2002, p.169.

McLaren, Duncan. 'The Artist as Builder', *Contemporary*, September 2002, pp. 46–49.

Give & Take (including Hans Haacke, Jeff Koons, Lisa Lou, Marc Quinn, Hiroshi Sugimoto, Andreas Serrano, Yinka Shonibare), Serpentine Gallery and Victoria and Albert Musuem, London 2001

Cork, Richard. 'What would happen if the V & A and the Serpentine swapped works for a while?', *The Times*, 24 January 2001.

Farquharson, Alex. 'Give and Take/Hans Haacke', *frieze*, issue 59, May 2001.

Higgs, Matthew. 'Politics of Presentation' (interview with HH), *Tate magazine*, no. 24, Summer 2001, pp. 56–59.

Pamela Golden, Gimpel Fils Gallery, London 1993

Archer, Michael. 'Pamela Golden', *frieze*, issue 14, January/February 1994, pp. 59–60.

Nan Goldin, Devil's Playground, Whitechapel Art Gallery, London 2002

Bickers, Patricia. 'Nan Goldin', *100 Reviews (3)*, 2002, p. 41.

Farquharson, Alex. 'Nan Goldin', *frieze,* issue 67, May 2002, pp. 90–91.

Lowndes, Sarah. 'Nan Goldin', *Untitled*, no. 27, Spring 2002, pp. 28–29.

Searle, Adrian. 'Walk on the wild side', *The Guardian*, 29 January 2002, p.10.

Walsh, Maria. 'Nan Goldin', *Art Monthly*, no. 254, March 2002, pp.19–20.

Dominique Gonzalez-Foerster, Robert Prime, London 1996

Craddock, Sacha. 'Gallery round-up', *The Times*, 19 April 1996.

Currah, Mark. 'Dominique Gonzalez-Foerster', *Time Out*, April 1996.

Douglas Gordon, Feature Film (with James Conlon), Atlantis, London 1999 (Artangel)

Bishop, Claire. 'Douglas Gordon: are you looking at him?' *Flash Art*, vol. 32, no. 207, Summer 1999, pp. 103–104.

Cork, Richard. 'Hitching a dizzy ride, *The Times*, 7 April 1999.

Higgie, Jennifer. 'Douglas Gordon', *frieze*, issue 48, September/October 1999, p. 97.

Searle, Adrian. 'Hitchcock's finest hour', *The Guardian*, 3 April 1999.

Sladen, Mark. 'The Hitchcock that fell to earth', *The Independent*, 11 April 1999, p. 7.

Douglas Gordon, Lisson Gallery, London, 1994

Blazwick, Iwona. 'Douglas Gordon', *Art Monthly*, no. 183, February 1995, pp. 35–36.

Kingston, Angela. 'Douglas Gordon', *frieze*, issue 21, March/April 1995, pp. 60–61.

Douglas Gordon, 24 Hour Psycho, Tramway, Glasgow 1993

Renton, Andrew. 'Douglas Gordon', *FlashArt*, vol. 26, no. 172, October 1993

Sinclair, Ross. 'Douglas Gordon', *Art Monthly*, no. 167, June 1993, pp. 22–23.

Villiers, Sarah. 'Psycho with surreal touch', *Glasgow Herald*, May 1993.

Luke Gottelier, Kill the Young, One in the Other, London 2001

Bussel, David. 'Off the wall', *i-D magazine*, May 2001, p. 185.

Clark, Paul. 'Last Chance: Luke Gottelier', *Evening Standard*, 14 May 2001, p. 60.

Coomer, Martin. 'Luke Gottelier', *Time Out*, 1–8 May 2001, p. 59.

Dan Graham, Camden Arts Centre, London 1997

Higgs, Matthew. 'Dan Graham' (with DG/ Architectural Association), *Art Monthly*, no. 207, June 1997, pp. 28–29.

Dan Graham, Pavilion Sculptures and Photographs, Lisson Gallery, London 1991

Hatton, Brian. 'Dan Graham: Present Continuous', *Artscribe*, no. 89, 1991, pp. 64–71.

Thomson, Mark. 'Dan Graham' (interview with DG), *Art Monthly*, no. 162, January 1993, pp. 3–7.

Paul Graham, Anthony Reynolds Gallery, London 1994

Guha, Tania. 'Paul Graham', *Time Out*, 2–9 November 1994.

Craddock, Sacha. 'Paul Graham', *The Times*, 14 November 1994.

Durden, Mark. 'Paul Graham', *frieze*, issue 20, January/February 1995, p. 58.

Paul Graham, Hypermetropia, Tate Gallery, London 1996

–. 'Hypermetropia', *The Architects' Journal*, 27 June 1996

Feaver, William. 'Paul Graham', *The Observer Review*, 5 May 1996.

Januszczak, Waldemar. 'Tokyo in High Definition', *The Sunday Times*, 5 May 1996.

Jenkins, Rupert. 'Strangers in Strange Lands', *See*, May 1996.

Patten, Sally. 'Images of an Empty Heaven', *Asia Times*, 29 May 1996.

Rodney Graham, Lisson Gallery, London 1996

Archer, Michael. 'Rodney Graham', *Artforum*, vol. 35, no. 7, March 1997, pp. 26–27.

Rodney Graham, Whitechapel Art Gallery, London 2002

Coomer, Martin. 'Mental as anything', *Time Out*, 16–23 October 2002, p. 53.

Cumming, Laura. 'Watch carefully... oh you missed it? I'll do it again', *The Observer*, 29 September 2002.

Gayford, Martin. 'Here we go again', *The Daily Telegraph*, 25 September 2002.

Lubbock, Tom. 'Out of the loop', *The Independent*, 1 October 2002.

Searle, Adrian. 'Weird and wonderful', *The Guardian*, 24 September 2002, pp. 12–13.

Gravity and Grace: the changing condition of sculpture 1965–1975 (including Marcel Broodthaers, Giuseppe Penone, Richard Long, Bruce Nauman, Robert Smithson, curated by Jon Thompson), Hayward Gallery, London 1993

Archer, Michael. 'Gravity and Grace: Too much grace?', *Art Monthly*, no. 164, March 1993, pp. 13–15.

Araeen, Rasheed. 'Gravity & (Dis)Grace', *Third Text*, no. 22, Spring 1993, pp. 93–97.

Batchelor, David. 'The Wonder Years', *frieze*, issue 9, March/April 1993, pp. 10–13.

Corris, Michael. 'London. Gravity and Grace', *Artforum*, April 1993, pp. 109–110.

Feaver, William. 'Green frills from a lettuce sacrifice', *The Observer*, 24 January 1993.

Hall, James. '1968 and all that', *The Independent*, 26 January 1993.

Harper, Madeleine. 'Hayward parrot ruffles RSPCA feathers', *Evening Standard*, 22 January 1993.

Hopper, Robert. 'Gravity and Grace', *Burlington Magazine*, April 1993.

Januszczak, Waldemar. 'Grins and grimaces', *The Guardian*, 25 January 1993.

Renton, Andrew. 'Gravity and Grace', *Flash Art*, vol. 26, no. 169, March/April 1993, p. 75.

Joanne Greenbaum and Mary Heilmann, greengrassi, London 2001

Harris, Mark. 'Mary Heilmann' (with Mary Heilmann/ Camden Arts Centre), *Art Monthly*, no. 246, May 2001, pp. 29–30.

The Greenhouse Effect (including Anya Gallaccio, Tom Friedman, Cerith Wyn Evans), Serpentine Gallery, London 2000

Searle, Adrian. 'Stuck in the woods', *The Guardian*, 4 April 2000, p. 14.

Staple, Polly. 'The Greenhouse Effect', *Art Monthly*, no. 236, May 2000, pp. 38–40.

Graham Gussin, Ikon Gallery, Birmingham 2002

Slyce, John. 'Graham Gussin', *Art Monthly*, no. 257, June 2002, pp. 37–38.

Vincent, David. 'Graham Gussin', *Modern Painters*, vol. 15, no. 2, Summer 2002, p. 112.

Graham Gussin, Lotta Hammer, London 1996

Cruz, Juan. 'Graham Gussin', *Art Monthly*, no. 196, May 1996.

Hans Haacke, Victoria Miro Gallery, London 1988

Batchelor, David. 'Hans Haacke', *Artscribe*, no. 68, 1988.

Peter Halley, Recent Paintings, Institute of Contemporary Arts, London 1989

Batchelor, David. 'A Man in a Sombrero Frying an Egg' (with a review of Peter Halley: Collected Essays), *Artscribe*, no. 76, 1989

Peter Halley, Waddington Galleries, London 1999

Coles, Alex. 'Peter Halley at Waddington Galleries', *Art & Text*, no. 67, November–January 1999/2000, p. 82.

Haswell, Russel. 'Peter Halley', *frieze*, issue 48, September/October 1999, p. 96.

Tozer, John. 'Peter Halley', *Art Monthly*, no. 227, July/August 1999, pp. 42–43.

Richard Hamilton, Anthony d'Offay Gallery, London 1991

Whitford, Frank. 'Veneer All Through', *Art Monthly*, no. 149, September 1991, pp. 3–5.

Richard Hamilton, Fruitmarket Gallery, Edinburgh 1988

Wood, Paul. 'Richard Hamilton', *Artscribe*, no. 72, November/December 1988, pp. 77–78.

Siobhán Hapaska, Institute of Contemporary Arts, London 1995

Collings, Matthew. 'Siobhán Hapaska', *frieze*, issue 27, March/April 1995, pp. 73–74.

Cruz, Juan. 'Siobhán Hapaska', *Art Monthly*, no. 193, February 1995, p. 37.

Hardcore Part 2 (including Don Brown, Mat Collishaw, Gary Hume, Gavin Turk), Factual Nonsense, London 1995

Guha, Tania. 'Hardcore Part 2', *Time Out*, no. 1314, 25 October–1 November 1995, p. 48.

Heart & Soul (including Dexter Dalwood, Keith Farquhar, Roger Hiorns, Gary Webb), 60 Long Lane, London 1999

Archer, Michael. 'Heart and Soul', *Artforum*, vol. 38, no. 3, November 1999, p. 153.

Williams, Gilda. 'Heart and Soul', *Art Monthly*, no. 229, September 1999, pp. 23–25.

Mary Heilmann, Camden Arts Centre, London 2001

Harris, Mark. 'Mary Heilmann' (with Joanne Greenbaum, Mary Heilmann/greengrassi), *Art Monthly*, no. 246, May 2001, pp. 29–30.

Higgie, Jennifer. 'Mary Heilmann', *frieze*, issue 60, June/July/August 2001, p. 106.

Searle, Adrian. 'Excess all areas', *The Guardian*, 10 April 2001, pp. 12–13.

Henry VIII's Wives, Tramway, Glasgow 2002

Bang Larsen, Lars. 'Henry VIII's Wives', *Artforum*, vol. XLI, no. 1, September 2002, pp. 215–216.

Lowndes, Sarah. 'Henry VIII's Wives', *frieze*, issue 69, September 2002, pp. 105–106.

Georg Herold, Paley Wright, London 1991

Myerson, Clifford. 'Georg Herold', *Art Monthly*, no. 152, December/January 1991/2, pp. 18–19.

Wilson, Andrew. 'Georg Herold', *Forum International*, January/February 1992, p. 82.

Patrick Heron, Tate Gallery, London 1998

Anfam, David. 'Patrick Heron', *Artforum*, vol. 37, no. 3, November 1998, p. 106.

Cork, Richard. 'Colourful career of a Cornish crusader', *The Times*, 30 June 1998, p. 18.

Garlake, Margaret. 'Patrick Heron', *Art Monthly*, no. 219, September 1998, pp. 38–39.

Lubbock, Tom. 'The art of decoration and the colour of pleasure', *The Independent*, 30 June 1998.

Searle, Adrian. 'Better than sex', *The Guardian*, 30 June 1998, pp. 10–11.

Whitford, Frank. 'Colours you can eat', *The Sunday Times*, 28 June 1998, p. 8.

Susan Hiller, The Freud Museum, London 1994

Bush, Kate. 'Susan Hiller', *Untitled*, Summer 1994.

Susan Hiller, Gimpel Fils Gallery, London 1994

Archer, Michael. 'Susan Hiller: Freud Museum/ Gimpel Fils', *Artforum*, vol. 32, no. 10, Summer 1994, pp. 103–104.

Faure Walker, Caryn. 'Susan Hiller: Gimpel Fils/ Freud Museum', *Art Monthly*, no. 177, June 1994.

Susan Hiller, Witness, The Chapel, 92 Golborne Road, London 2000 (Artangel)

Bishop, Claire. 'Susan Hiller: Witness', *Make*, issue 89, September-November 2000.

Dorment, Richard. 'Close encounters of the aural kind', *The Daily Telegraph*, 31 May 2000, p. 19.

Grant, Simon. 'Testing our faith with tales of aliens', *Evening Standard*, 24 May 2000, p. 57.

Lubbock, Tom. 'Close encounters of the transcendental kind', *The Independent*, 23 May 2000.

Roger Hiorns, Corvi-Mora, London 2001

Archer, Michael. 'Roger Hiorns', *Artforum*, vol. 40, no. 4, December 2001, p. 131.

Falconer, Morgan. 'Roger Hiorns' (with David Musgrave at greengrassi), *Untitled*, no. 26, Autumn/Winter 2001 p. 32.

Wilsher, Mark. 'Roger Hiorns', *What's On*, 3 October 2001, pp. 24–25.

(Charlesworth, JJ. 'Secret Secretions', *Art Monthly*, no. 249, September 2001, pp. 20–21.)

Thomas Hirschhorn, Laundrette, Stephen Friedman Gallery, London 2001

Manchester, Clare. 'Thomas Hirschhorn', *Art Monthly*, no. 248, July/August 2001, pp. 36–37.

Morton, Tom. 'Thomas Hirschhorn', *frieze*, issue 62, September/October 2001, p. 90.

Searle, Adrian. 'My ugly launderette', *The Guardian*, 3 July 2001.

Damien Hirst, In & Out of Love, Woodstock St, London 1991

Craddock, Sacha. 'Dead or Alive', *The Guardian*, 16 July 1991.

Graham-Dixon, Andrew. 'Hatching a Scheme', *The Independent*, 16 July 1991.

Morgan, Stuart. 'Life and Death', *frieze*, pilot issue, Summer 1991.

Searle, Adrian. 'Love in a Cold Climate', *Artscribe*, no. 88, September 1991, p. 84.

(Morgan, Stuart. 'Damien Hirst: The Butterfly Effect' 1991 first published in 'What the Butler Saw. Selected Writings of Stuart Morgan', Durian Publications, London 1996)

Damien Hirst, Internal Affairs, Institute of Contemporary Arts, London 1991

Althorpe-Guyton, Marjorie. 'Cry Wolf', *Artscribe*, no. 89, October 1991, pp. 60–65.

Francis, Mary Anne. 'Damien Hirst', *Art Monthly*, no. 153, February 1992, p. 18.

Shone, Richard. 'Damien Hirst: ICA', *Burlington Magazine*, March 1992.

(Gillick, Liam. (in conversation with DH), *Artscribe*, no. 84, November/December 1990, pp. 61–62)

Damien Hirst, Still, White Cube, London 1995

Batchelor, David. 'Damien Hirst: White Cube', *Artforum*, vol. 34, no. 7, September 1995, pp. 101–102.

Barrett, David. 'Damien Hirst: White Cube', *Art Monthly*, no. 188, July/August 1995, pp. 37–38.

Kent, Sarah. 'White Cube: Damien Hirst', *Time Out*, 31 May-7 June, 1995.

David Hockney, Portraits and Still Lifes, Annely Juda Fine Art, London 1999

Moir, Jan. 'It is odd to be an orphan at my age', *The Daily Telegraph*, 12 June 1999.

Packer, William. 'The draftsman's special friend', *Financial Times*, 3 July 1999.

(Hockney, David. 'Did Ingres use a camera?', *The Independent*, 25 June 1999.)

Stewart Home, Vermeer II, workfortheeye-todo, London 1996

Burrows, David. 'Stewart Home', *Art Monthly*, no. 200, October 1996, pp. 58–59.

Homeless Project (including Lothar Götz, Volker Eichelmann, Denise Hawrysio, Stewart Home, curated by David Goldenberg), Mota, London 1998

–. 'Homeless – developing new models of the exhibition event', *Infection magazine for art and public spaces*, no. 2, June 1999.

Buck, Louisa. 'Homeless art finds a home in the Old Kent Road', *The Art Newspaper*, February 1999.

Herbert, Martin. 'Homeless Project', *Time Out*, no. 1484, 27 January-3 February 1999, p. 47.

O'Rorke, Imogen & Burns, Anna. 'Homeless Project', *Scene Magazine*, April/May 1999, p. 27.

Host (including Rod Dickinson, Peter Fillingham, Imprint93, Derek Ogbourne, Donald Parsnips, Jessica Voorsanger, curated by Peter Lewis), The Tramway, Glasgow 1998

Cooper, Neil. 'Host', *The List*, 16–30 April 1998.

Mahoney, Elisabeth. 'Host', *Contemporary Visual Art*, issue 19, 1998, pp. 64–65.

Mulholland, Neil. 'Host', *Art Monthly*, no. 217, June 1998, pp. 26–28.

White, Nicola. 'All Together Now', *The Herald*, 4 April 1998, p. 24.

Douglas Huebler, Camden Arts Centre, London 2002

Green, Alison. 'Duration, Duration, Duration', *Art Monthly*, no. 255, April 2002, pp. 6–10.

Lubbock, Tom. 'How conceptual art went mainstream', *The Independent*, 19 March 2002, p. 10.

Sundell, Margaret. 'Douglas Huebler', *Artforum*, vol. XLI, no. 1, September 2002, p. 200.

Tan, Eugene. 'Douglas Huebler', *Contemporary*, February 2002, p. 109.

Wilsher, Mark. 'Douglas Huebler', *Untitled*, no. 27, Spring 2002, pp. 32–33.

Gary Hume, The Dolphin Paintings, Karsten Schubert Ltd, London 1991

Morgan, Stuart. 'Gary Hume', *Artscribe*, no. 89, October 1991, p. 98.

Wilson, Andrew. 'Gary Hume', *Forum International*, November/December 1991, p. 83.

Gary Hume, Recent Works, Karsten Schubert Ltd, London 1989

Carpenter, Merlin. 'Gary Hume', *Artscribe*, no. 78, November/December 1989, pp. 74–75.

Dannatt, Adrian. 'Gary Hume', *Flash Art*, October 1989.

Roberts, James. 'Gary Hume', *Artefactum*, November/December 1989.

Gary Hume, Whitechapel Art Gallery, London/Dean Gallery, National Galleries of Scotland, Edinburgh 1999

Hall, James. 'Gary Hume', *Artforum*, vol. 38, no. 6, February 2000, p.129.

Myers, Terry R. 'Gary Hume', *Art & Text*, no. 69, May-July 2000, p. 82.

Tozer, John. 'Gary Hume', *Contemporary Visual Arts*, issue 28, 2000, p. 62.

Gary Hume, White Cube, London 1995

Muir, Gregor. 'Vague: interview- Gary Hume', *Art & Text*, no. 51, May 1995, pp. 38–43.

Bethan Huws & The Bistritsa Babi – A work for the North Sea, on the coast near Alnwick 1993 (Artangel)

Archer, Michael. 'Bethan Huws & The Bistritsa Babi', *Art Monthly*, no.169, September 1993, pp. 20–21.

Hewison, Robert. 'On a different wavelength', *Sunday Times*, 1 August 1993.

Lubbock, Tom. 'Between the devil and the deep blue sea', *The Independent*, 27 July 1993.

Muir, Gregor. 'Bethan Huws', *frieze*, no.12, September/October 1993, pp. 58–59.

Bethan Huws, Oriel Mostyn, Llanduddno 1999

Farquharson, Alex. 'Bethan Huws', *frieze*, issue 48, September/October 1999.

Godfrey, Tony. 'Bethan Huws' (with White 3), *Art Monthly*, no. 227, June 1999, p. 26.

Bethan Huws, Riverside Studios, London 1989

Batchelor, David. 'Bethan Huws', *Artscribe*, no. 79, January/February 1990, p. 72.

Gillick, Liam. 'Bethan Huws', *Art Monthly*, no.130, October 1989, pp.18–19.

I am a camera (including Richard Billingham, Thomas Demand, Duane Hanson, Tierney Gearon, Sarah Lucas, Andy Warhol), Saatchi Gallery, London 2001

Lydiate, Henry. 'I am a camera: an inspector calls', *Art Monthly*, no. 245, April 2001, pp. 48–49.

Lydiate, Henry. 'Unfinished business: an inspector calls again', *Art Monthly*, no. 248, July/August 2001, p. 57.

Toynbee, Polly. 'For Shame! The arts versus the plod'(Tierney Gearon), *Modern Painters*, vol.14, no. 2, Summer 2001, pp.18–20.

I am making art (Vito Acconci, Joan Jonas, John Baldessari, Paul McCarthy, Bruce Nauman), Anthony Wilkinson Gallery, London 2001

Downey, Anthony. 'I am making art', *Contemporary Visual Arts*, issue 34, 2001, p. 71.

Jones, Jonathan. 'I am making art', *The Guardian*, 10 March 2001.

McLaren, Duncan. 'I am making art', *Independent on Sunday*, 18 March 2001.

Wilson, Andrew. 'I am making art', *Art Monthly*, no. 245, April 2001, pp. 20–22.

Ideal Standard Summer Time (including Pierre Bismuth, Jacqueline Donachie, Liam Gillick, Lucy Gunning, John Hilliard, Mark Hosking, John Latham, Anna Mossman, Jonathan Monk, Stephen Willats), Lisson Gallery, London 1995

Brown, Neal. 'Ideal Standard Summer Time/ Postscript', *frieze*, issue 26, January/February 1996, pp. 79–80.

Cork, Richard. 'Summer brings cold comfort', *The Times*, 13 August 1995, p. 35.

Sanderson, Philip.'Ideal Standard Summer Time', *Art Monthly*, no.189, September 1995, pp. 37–38.

The Impossible Document: Photography and Conceptual Art in Britain 1966–1976 (including Keith Arnatt, Art & Language, Victor Burgin, John Hilliard, Alexis Hunter), Camerawork Gallery, London 1997

Green, David. 'Everyday icons', *Creative Camera*, no. 347, August/September 1997, pp.12–15.

Hatton, Brian. 'Paraphotography', *Art Monthly*, no. 207, June 1997, pp.1–5.

Info Centre (Henriette Heise, Jakob Jakobsen), London 1998

Glover, Izi. 'Info Centre', *frieze*, issue 44, January/February 1999, p. 92

(Heise, Henriette. Jakobsen, Jacob. 'Info Centre', *Manedsskrift for kunst og kunstrelateret materiale* (Denmark), no. 52, 1999.)

Inside the Visible (including Claude Cahun, Mona Hatoum, Yayoi Kusama, Martha Rosler), Whitechapel Art Gallery, London 1996

del Renzio, Toni. 'Inside the Visible', *Art Monthly*, no. 202, December/January 1996/7, pp. 41–43.

The Institute of Cultural Anxiety, Works from the Collection (including Henry Bond, Christine Borland, Mat Collishaw, Peter Fillingham, Thomas Gidley, Liam Gillick, Michael Joo, Craig Richardson, curated by Jeremy Millar), Institute of Contemporary Arts, London 1994

Dorment, Richard. 'Science Fiction', *The Daily Telegraph*, 11 June 1995, p. 21.

Grant, Simon. 'The Institute of Cultural Anxiety', *Art Monthly*, no.183, February 1995, pp. 33–34.

Morgan, Stuart. 'The future is not what it used to be', *frieze*, issue 21, March/April 1995, pp. 34–37.

Intelligence: New British Art 2000 (including Jeremy Deller, Liam Gillick, Alan Kane, Julian Opie, Bob & Roberta Smith) Tate Britain, London 2000

Dunn, Justin. 'Show us yer arse, ma'am. That's the message from the Tate', *Daily Sport*, 8 August 2000.

Hall, Ed. 'Resistance against consumer culture', *Socialist Review*, September 2000, p. 29.

Miller, Keith. 'How to navigate Intelligence', *Times Literary Supplement*, 18 August 2000, p.18.

Searle, Adrian. 'Thick and thin', *The Guardian*, 8 July 2000, p. 7.

Sewell, Brian. 'How the Tate failed a simple intelligence test', *Evening Standard*, 14 July 2000, pp. 34–35.

Slyce, John. 'Intelligence. New British Art 2000', *Art & Text*, no. 7, November 2001–January 2002, pp. 90–91.

Stallabrass, Julian. 'Clever Clogs', *New Statesman*, 18 September 2000, pp. 47–48.

Wilson, Michael 'New British Art 2000: Intelligence', *Art Monthly*, no. 239, September 2000, pp. 43–46.

Withers, Rachel. 'Intelligence: New British Art 2000' (with BA5), *Artforum*, vol. 39, no. 2, October 2000, p.143.

In the Midst of Things (including Martin Boyce, Cornford & Cross, Jacqueline Donachie, Gary Perkins, Darren Lago, Kathrin Böhm, Nina Saunders, Richard Wright, curated by Nigel Prince, Gavin Wade), Cadbury World, Bournville, Birmingham 1999

Farquharson, Alex. 'In the Midst of Things', *frieze*, issue 49, November/December 1999.

Runa Islam, Director's Cut (Fool for Love), White Cube, London 2001

Kent, Sarah. 'Runa Islam', *Time Out*, no.1597, 28 March–4 April 2001, p. 51.

(Wilson, Michael. 'Lights, camera, action?', *Art Monthly*, no. 246, May 2001, pp. 24–25.)

Gareth Jones, Cabinet, London 2000

Cotter, Suzanne. 'Gareth Jones', *Flash Art*, vol. 33, no. 213, Summer 2000, p.117.

Fox, Dan. 'Gareth Jones', *frieze*, issue 53, June/July/August 2000, p.121.

Ilya & Emilia Kabakov, The Palace of Projects, The Roundhouse, London 1998 (Artangel)

Hunt, Ian. 'The People's Palace', *Art Monthly*, no. 216, May 1998, pp. 9–12.

Melvin, Jeremy. 'Giving a sense of secret lives', *The Architects' Journal*, April 1998.

Morgan, Stuart. 'Ilya & Emilia Kabakov', *frieze*, issue 41, June/July/August 1998, pp. 94–95.

Schwabsky, Barry. 'Ilya & Emilia Kabakov', *Art & Text*, no. 62, August-October 1998, pp. 78–79.

Searle, Adrian. 'Ministry of silly ideas', *The Guardian*, 24 March 1998, p. 10.

Anish Kapoor, Hayward Gallery, London 1998

Hensher, Philip. 'How Deep Is a Hole?', *Modern Painters*, Summer 1998, pp. 42–45.

Hilton, Tim. 'It's all in what the eye cannot see', *Independent on Sunday*, 10 May 1998

Packer, William. 'Now you see it, now you don't', *Financial Times*, 12 May 1998.

Plagens, Peter. 'Anish Kapoor', *Artforum*, vol. 37, no. 1, September 1998, p. 151.

Sewell, Brian. 'Talking up a load of spherical objects', *Evening Standard*, 14 May 1998, pp. 28–29.

Alex Katz, Small Paintings 1951–2002, Timothy Taylor Gallery, London 2002

–. 'Art Now', *Art Review*, vol. LIII, July/August 2002, p. 24.

Buck, Louisa. 'Alex Katz: Small Paintings 1951–2002', *The Art Newspaper*, no. 127, July/August 2002.

McEwen, John. 'Exuberant Colour and elephant dung: Chris Ofili, Alex Katz, The object sculpture', *The Sunday Telegraph*, 7 July 2002.

Alex Katz, Twenty Five Years of Painting, Saatchi Gallery, London 1998

Cohen, David. 'Alex Katz', *RA Magazine*, no. 58, Spring 1998, pp. 50–51.

Cohen, David. 'A scaled-up world', *Art in America*, vol. 86, no. 5, May 1998, pp. 102–109.

Planca, Elisabetta. 'Londra, porte aperte a Mr. Katz', *Arte* (Italy), no. 294, February 1998, pp. 96–101.

Emma Kay, The Future from Memory, Chisenhale Gallery, London/ Laing Gallery, Newcastle 2001

Morton, Tom. 'Emma Kay', *frieze*, issue 59, May 2001, pp. 101–102.

Prior, Lisa. 'Emma Kay', *Flash Art*, May/June 2001, p. 145.

Sumpter, Helen. 'How I rewrote the Bible', *The Big Issue*, 12–18 February 2001, p. 35.

Wilsher, Mark. 'Projecting the Future', *What's On*, 21 February 2001, p. 23.

Wilson, Michael. 'Emma Kay', *Art in America*, vol. 89, no. 12, December 2001, pp. 126–127.

Emma Kay, Shakespeare from Memory, The Approach, London 1998

McLaren, Duncan. 'Emma Kay', *Independent on Sunday*, 1 November 1998.

Moffat, Laura. 'Emma Kay', *Art Monthly*, no. 222, December 1998.

Mike Kelley, Institute of Contemporary Arts, London 1992

Gillick, Liam. 'Mike Kelley', *Art Monthly*, no. 158, August 1992, p. 20.

Anslem Kiefer, Anthony d'Offay Gallery/ The High Priestess, Riverside, London 1989

Archer, Michael. 'Anslem Kiefer', *Artscribe*, no. 78, November/December 1989, pp. 72–73.

Glaves-Smith, John. 'Anslem Kiefer', *Art Monthly*, no. 129, September 1989, pp. 17–18.

Karen Kilimnik, South London Gallery, London 2000

Jones, Jonathan. 'Karen Kilimnik', *frieze*, issue 54, September/October 2000, pp. 126–127.

Karen Kilimnik, Emily Tsingou Gallery, London 1998

Walsh, Maria. 'Karen Kilimnik', *Art Monthly*, no. 216, May 1998.

Martin Kippenberger, Hotel Drawings, London Projects, London 1997

Higgs, Matthew. 'Martin Kippenberger', *Art Monthly*, no. 208, July/August 1997, p. 27.

Martin Kippenberger, The Beginning was a Retrospective, Karsten Schubert Ltd, London 1991

Wilson, Andrew. 'Martin Kippenberger: The Beginning was a Retrospective', *Forum International*, March/April 1992, p. 89.

Yves Klein, The Leap into the Void, Hayward Gallery, London 1995

Barker, Barry. 'Sublime Klein', *Art Monthly*, no. 183, February 1995, pp. 3–6.

Cork, Richard. 'Shocking blue unfaded by time', *The Times*, 14 February 1995.

Craddock, Sacha. 'How I caught a falling star', *The Times*, 7 February 1995.

Roberts, James. 'Yves Klein', *frieze*, issue 22, May 1995, pp. 66–67.

Searle, Adrian. 'Come on baby light my fire', *The Independent*, 9 February 1995.

Sewell, Brian. 'Discoveries out of the blue', *Evening Standard*, 23 February 1995.

Jeff Koons, Made in Heaven, Anthony d'Offay Gallery, London 1991

Lotringer, Sylvere. 'Immaculate Conceptualsim', *Artscribe*, no. 89, October 1991, pp. 24–25.

Harmony Korine, The Diary of Anne Frank, Part II, Thomas Dane/Patrick Painter, London 2000

Fox, Dan. 'Harmony Korine', *frieze*, issue 54, September/October 2000, p. 103.

Tania Kovats, Laure Genillard Gallery, London 1995

Anderson, Libby. 'Virgin Territory', *Art Monthly*, no. 190, October 1995, pp. 22–23.

Sladen, Mark. 'Tania Kovats', *frieze*, issue 25, November/December 1995, pp. 72–73.

Jim Lambie, Voidoid, Transmission Gallery, Glasgow 1999

Sinclair, Ross. 'Jim Lambie', *frieze*, issue 46, May 1999, p. 84.

Jim Lambie, Zobop, The Showroom, London 1998.

Shave, Stuart. 'North Face', *i-D magazine*, no. 187, 1998.

Sean Landers, greengrassi, London 2000

Farquharson, Alex. 'Sean Landers', *Art Monthly*, no. 239, September 2000, pp. 51–55.

Kent, Sarah. 'Sean Landers', *Time Out*, 19–26 July 2000, pp. 60–61.

McLaren, Duncan. 'Sean Landers', *Independent on Sunday*, 23 July 2000.

Michael Landy, BREAK DOWN, C&A Store, 499–523 Oxford Street, London 2001 (Artangel/Times)

Beech, Dave. 'Michael Landy', *Art Monthly*, no. 244, March 2001, pp. 30–31.

Cumming, Tim. 'The happiest day of my life', *The Guardian*, 17 February 2001, p. 5.

Cumming, Tim. 'Stuff and Nonsense', *The Guardian*, 13 February 2002, p. 12.

Fox, Dan. 'Michael Landy', *frieze*, issue 60, June/July/August 2001, p. 92.

Stein, Judith E. 'London: Michael Landy at C&A Store on Oxford Street', *Art in America*, vol. 89, no. 6, June 2001, pp. 136–137.

Withers, Rachel. 'Michael Landy', *Artforum*, vol. 39, no. 9, May 2001, p. 189.

Michael Landy, Closing Down Sale, Karsten Schubert Ltd, London 1992

Myerson, Clifford. 'Michael Landy and the Great Sale', *Art Monthly*, no. 157, June 1992, p. 17.

Michael Landy, Market, Building One, London 1990

Burn, Gordon. 'Playing to the Galleries', *Sunday Times*, 30 September 1990, pp. 38–40.

Feaver, William. 'Market, Building One', *The Observer*, 7 October 1990.

Kent, Sarah. 'Market, Building One', *Time Out*, 10–17 October 1990, pp. 7,38.

Khosla, Kiron. 'Michael Landy, Building One', *Artscribe*, no. 85, January/February 1991, pp. 77–78.

McGeown, Martin. 'Michael Landy: Building One', *Art Press*, January 1991.

Shone, Richard. 'Landy at Building One', *Burlington Magazine*, vol. cxxxII, no. 1052, November 1990.

Michael Landy, Scrapheap Services, The Henry Moore Institute, Electric Press Building, Leeds/ Chisenhale Gallery, London, 1996

Pierini, Esther. 'Michael Landy', *Flash Art*, no. 191, November/December 1996, p. 108.

Wilson, Andrew. 'Bin it for Britain', *Art & Text*, no. 55, October 1996, pp. 72–77.

Abigail Lane, Institute of Contemporary Arts, London 1995

Grant, Simon. 'Abigail Lane', *Art Monthly*, no. 185, April 1995, pp. 33–34.

Abigail Lane, Karsten Schubert Ltd, London 1992

Archer, Michael. 'Abigail Lane' (with Kiki Smith/d'Offay), *Art Monthly*, no. 161, November 1992, p. 25.

Abigail Lane, Tomorrows World, Yesterdays Fever (Mental Guests Incorporated), Victoria Miro Gallery, London 2001

Morton, Tom. 'Abigail Lane', *Untitled*, no. 26, Autumn/Winter 2001, p. 39

Walsh, Maria. 'Abigail Lane', *Art Monthly*, no. 251, November 2001, pp. 22–23.

The Last Show (John Burgess, Keith Coventry, Matt Hale, Paul Noble, Peter Owen), City Racing, London 1998

Musgrave, David. 'The Last Show', *Art Monthly*, no. 222, December/January 1998/9, pp. 26–27.

John Latham, Lisson Gallery, London 1987

Batchelor, David. 'John Latham', *Artscribe*, no. 63, 1987.

Walker, John A. 'John Latham: Books for burning', *Studio International*, vol. 200, no. 1018, November 1987, pp. 26–29.

Bob Law, Kettle's Yard, Cambridge 1999

Garlake, Margaret. 'Bob Law', *Art Monthly*, no. 226, May 1999, pp. 27–28.

Lemon (Keith Arnatt, Matthew Arnatt, Justine Daf, David Mollin, Piers Wardle), 116 Commercial St, London 1993

Kent, Sarah. 'Lemon', *Time Out*, no. 1186, 1993.

Simon Linke, Lisson Gallery, London 1997

Morgan, Stewart. 'Simon Linke', *frieze*, issue 33, March/April 1997, pp. 88–89.

Want, Cristopher. 'Simon Linke', *Art Monthly*, no. 203, February 1997, pp. 24–25.

Simon Linke, Lisson Gallery, London 1987

Batchelor, David. 'Simon Linke', *Artscribe*, no. 64, 1987.

The Lisson Gallery (Matthew Arnatt, David Crawforth, David Mollin), 5 Topham St, London 1994

Grant, Simon. 'The Lisson Gallery, 5 Topham Street', *Art Monthly*, no. 176, May 1994, pp. 28–29.

Kastner, Jeffery. 'The Lisson Gallery', *Flash Art*, May 1996.

Stallabrass, Julian. 'Curating', *Art and Design*, January 1997.

Live in your head: Concept and Experiment in Britain 1965–75 (including Rasheed Araeen, Keith Arnatt, Art & Language, David Dye, Gilbert & George, David Lamelas, John Latham, Stephen Willats, curated by Clive Phillpot and Andrea Tarsia), Whitechapel Art Gallery, London 2000

Art & Language (Michael Baldwin, Mel Ramsden and Charles Harrison). 'Concept and Experiment in Britain?', *Modern Painters*, Summer 2000, pp. 23–25.

Coles, Alex. 'Live in your Head', *Parachute*, no. 99, July-September 2000, pp. 60–61.

Hunt, Ian. 'Live in Your Head', *frieze*, issue 54, September/October 2000, pp. 132–133.

Ker, Dorian. 'Britain Does Not Exist', *Third Text*, no. 50, Spring 2000, pp. 116–121.

Lubbock, Tom. 'It was the thought that counted', *The Independent*, 8 February 2000.

Meyer, James. 'Live in your head: concept and experiment in Britain 1965–1975', *Artforum*, vol. 38, no. 10, Summer 2000, p. 178.

Searle, Adrian. 'Slice of book anyone? One day they were eating paper, the next floating in offal', *The Guardian*, 8 February 2000, pp. 14–15.

Schwabsky, Barry. 'Report from London: It's All In Your Mind', *Art in America*, no. 188, no. 9, 2000, pp. 55–57.

Wilson, Andrew. 'Everything and Nothing', *Art Monthly*, no. 234, March 2000, pp. 1–5.

Hilary Lloyd, Chisenhale Gallery, London 1999

Bradley, Alexandra. 'Hilary Lloyd', *Art Monthly*, no. 231, November 1999, pp. 27–29.

Sladen, Mark. 'Hilary Lloyd', *frieze*, issue 50, January 2000.

Hilary Lloyd, Jemima Stehli, Brian Dawn Chalkley, City Racing, London 1998

Collings, Matthew. 'The Whip and the Honey', *Modern Painters*, Spring 1998.

Higgs, Matthew. 'Show 48: City Racing', *AN magazine*, March 1998.

Slyce, John. 'Show 48', *Flash Art*, May/June 1998.

Windsor, John. 'Turning the Tables on Mr Jones', *The Independent*, 18 March 1998.

Loose Threads (including Tracey Emin, Jochen Flinzer, Ernetso Neto, Michael Raedecker), Serpentine Gallery, London 1998

Archer, Michael. 'Loose Threads', *Art Monthly*, no. 220, October 1998, pp. 27–29.

Lovecraft (including Marc Chaimowicz, Vincent Fecteau, Matthew Higgs, Jim Isermann, Hilary Lloyd, curated by Martin McGeown, Toby Webster), CCA, Glasgow 1997/ South London Gallery 1998

Timoney, Padraig. 'Lovecraft', *Art Monthly*, no. 208, July/August 1997, p. 34.

Staple, Polly. 'Lovecraft', *Untitled*, no. 22, 1998.

Sarah Lucas, Beyond the Pleasure Principle, The Freud Museum, London 2000

Gleeson, David. 'Sarah Lucas', *londonart.co.uk magazine*, 24 March 2000.

MacRitchie, Lynn. 'Freud gets fleshed out', *Financial Times*, 24 March 2000.

Searle, Adrian. 'Do these pictures make you think of sex?', *The Guardian*, 28 March 2000, p. 12.

Sarah Lucas, Bunny Gets Snookered, Sadie Coles HQ, London 1997

Hunt, Ian. 'Sarah Lucas' (with The Law), *Art Monthly*, no. 207, June 1997, pp. 35–36,

Januszczak, Waldemar. 'Maybe it's because she's a Londoner' (with The Law), *Sunday Times*, 25 May 1997, pp. 8–9.

Williams, Gilda. 'Sarah Lucas', *Art & Text*, issue 59, 1997, p. 82.

(Burn, Gordon. 'Sister Sarah', *The Guardian Weekend*, 23 November 1996, pp. 26–33.)

Sarah Lucas, The Fag Show, Sadie Coles HQ, London 2000

Darwent, Charles. 'No Smoking', *New Statesman*, 20 March 2000, pp. 44–45.

Grant, Simon. 'The fag end of obsession', *Evening Standard*, February 2000.

Kent, Sarah. 'Fag hag. Cigarettes and fake breasts with Sarah Lucas', *Time Out*, 8–15 March 2000, p. 54.

McLaren, Duncan. 'The Fag Show', *Independent on Sunday*, 20 February 2000, p. 5.

(Barber, Lynn. 'Drag Queen', *The Observer Magazine*, 30 January 2000, pp. 10–16.)

Sarah Lucas, Got a Salmon On (Prawn), Anthony d'Offay Gallery, London 1994

Freedman, Carl. 'A nod's as good as a wink' (interview with SL), *frieze*, issue 17, June/July/August 1994, pp. 28–31.

Sarah Lucas, The Law, Sadie Coles HQ at St John's Lofts, London 1997

Brown, Neal. 'Sarah Lucas: St John's Lofts and Sadie Coles HQ', *frieze*, issue 36, September/October 1997, pp. 86–87.

Coomer, Martin. 'Grime passionel', *Time Out*, 14–21 May 1997, p. 44.

Harris, Mark. 'Sarah Lucas' (with Bunny), *Art in America*, January 1998.

Sarah Lucas, Penis Nailed to a Board, City Racing, London 1992

Joyce, Conor. 'Sarah Lucas' (with Five Artists at Karsten Schubert), *Art Monthly*, no. 154, March 1992, p. 16.

Christina Mackie, City Racing 1998

Higgie, Jennifer. 'Christina Mackie', *frieze*, issue 41, June/July/August 1998, p. 83.

Christina Mackie, Forcing it, Robert Prime 2000

Currah, Mark. 'Christina Mackie', *Time Out*, May 3–10, p. 46

Christina Mackie, The Showroom, London 1999

–. 'Coded Creations' *i-D magazine*, no. 185, 1999, p. 114.

Berry, Josephine. 'Promethean Homebrew', *Mute*, no. 15, 1999.

Coomer, Martin. 'Christina Mackie', *Time Out*, 14–21 April 1999.

Moffat, Laura. 'Chirstina Mackie', *Art Monthly*, no. 226, May 1999, pp. 29–30.

Made New (Barry Flanagan, Alfred Jarry, Tim Mapston, Gustav Metzger, curated by Andrew Wilson), City Racing, London 1996

Cruz, Juan. 'Made New', *Art Monthly*, no. 202, December/January 1996/7, pp. 30–31.

Piero Manzoni, Serpentine Gallery, London 1998

Barker, Barry. 'Manzoni: Being or Nothingness', *Art Montlhy*, no. 215, April 1998, pp. 1–4.

Schwabsky, Barry. 'Piero Manzoni', *Artforum*, vol. 39, no. 9, May 1998, p. 145.

Turk, Gavin. 'Piero Manzoni', *frieze*, issue 41, June/July/August 1998, p. 96.

Chirs Marker, Beaconsfield, London 1999

Hunt, Ian. 'Chris Marker', *Art Monthly*, no. 228, July/August 1999, pp. 41–43.

Martin (including Fiona Banner, Rod Dickinson, Runa Islam, Peter Lewis, Hiroko Okada, Orphan Drift, Fergal Stapleton, The White Visitation, Stephen Wong, curated by David Goldenberg), Atlantis Gallery & Commercial Gallery, London 1997/ Waygood Gallery, Newcastle Upon Tyne 1998/ Catalyst Arts, Belfast 1998

Buck, Louisa. 'Free expression', *The World of Interiors*, September 1997, p. 57.

Craddock, Sacha. 'Martin', *The Times*, 1 July 1997.

Dunne, Aidan. 'Matters of Life and Death', *Northern Ireland Times*, 25 November 1998.

Herbert, Martin. 'Martin', *Time Out*, 1–7 July 1997.

McTigue, Eoghan. 'Transgressive events', *Circa magazine*, no. 89, Autumn 1998/9, pp. 34–36.

Usherwood, Paul. 'Martin', *Art Monthly*, no. 216, May 1998, pp. 34–35.

Van Mourik Broekman, Pauline. 'Martin', *Mute*, no. 9, January 1998, pp. 62–63.

Kenneth Martin, Annely Juda Fine Art, London 1999

Garlake, Margaret. 'Kenneth Martin', *Art Monthly*, no. 224, March 1999, pp. 33–34.

Material Culture: The Object in British art of the 1980s and 90s (including Mona Hatoum, Michael Landy, Anish Kapoor, Avis Newman, Simon Patterson, Gavin Turk), Hayward Gallery, London 1997

Barrett, David. 'Material Culture', *Art & Text*, no. 58, 1997.

Batchelor, David. Freedman, Carl. 'Living in a Material World', *frieze*, issue 35, June/July/August 1997, pp. 46–49.

Cork, Richard. 'Intimations of a strange mortality', *The Times*, 8 April 1997.

Greenberg, Sarah. 'Material whirl', *The Art Newspaper*, no. 70, May 1997, p. 25.

Harris, Mark. 'Immaterial Culture', *Art Monthly*, no. 206, May 1997, pp. 6–8.

Januszczak, Waldemar. 'A true reflection of the age', *Sunday Times*, 13 April 1997.

Searle, Adrian. 'Isn't it offal?', *The Guardian*, 8 April 1997.

Slyce, John. 'Material Culture', *Flash Art*, Summer 1997, p. 75.

Stathatos, John. 'Material Culture at the Hayward', *Untitled*, no. 13, Spring 1997, p. 14.

Wilson, Andrew. 'Object Lesson', *Art Monthly*, no. 206, May 1997, pp. 1–4.

Matisse Picasso, Tate Modern, London 2002

Cork, Richard. 'Time to Take a Stand', *The Times*, 26 April 2002.

Cooper, Harry. 'Matisse Picasso', *Artforum*, vol. XLI, no. 2, October 2002, p. 147.

Dorment, Richard. The Magnificent Rivals', *The Daily Telegraph*, 8 May 2002.

Jones, Jonathan. 'Comic Strips and Cubism', *The Guardian*, 13 April 2002, p. 5.

Spurling, Hilary. 'Matisse v Picasso: the final showdown', *The Daily Telegraph*, 27 April 2002.

Searle, Adrian. 'Amomentous, tremendous exhibition', *The Guardian*, 7 May 2002, p. 12.

Sumpter, Helen. 'The Odd Couple', *The Big Issue*, 6–12 May 2002.

Wilson, Andrew. 'Rivals in Art', *Daily Mail*, 30 March 2002, pp. 19–20.

Paul McCarthy, Tate Liverpool 2001

Clark, Robert. 'In your face', *Art Review*, December/January 2001/2.

Cumming, Laura. 'An unnatural relish for ketchup', *The Observer*, 21 October 2001.

Lubbock, Tom. 'The medium is the mess', *The Independent*, 27 November 2001.

Searle, Adrian. 'Mucky devil', *The Guardian*, 10 November 2001.

John McCracken, Lisson Gallery, London 1997

Bickers, Patricia. 'UFO Technology' (interview with JMcC), *Art Monthly*, no. 240, March 1997, pp. 1–5.

Steve McQueen, Institute of Contemporary Arts, London 1999

Gellatly, Andrew. 'Steve McQueen', *frieze*, issue 46, May 1999, pp. 88–89.

Schwabsky, Barry. 'Steve McQueen', *Art & Text*, no. 66, August-October 1999, pp. 77–78.

David Medalla, 55 Gee Street, London 1995

Gooding, Mel. 'David Medalla', *Art Monthly*, no. 184, March 1995, pp. 34–36.

Steven Meisel, Four Days in LA: The Versace Pictures, White Cube², London 2001

Jones, Jonathan. *The Guardian*, 30 July 2001.

Street Porter, Janet. *Independent on Sunday*, 22 July 2001

Gustav Metzger, Museum of Modern Art, Oxford 1998

Archer, Michael. 'Gustav Metzger', *Artforum*, vol. 37, no. 6, February 1999.

Flint, Rob. 'Gustav Metzger', *Red Pepper*, December 1998.

Jones, Alison. 'Gustav Metzger', *Socialist Review*, December 1998.

O'Rourke, Imogen. 'Gustav Metzger', *The Independent*, 26 October 1998.

Wilson, Andrew. 'A Terrible Beauty' (interview with GM), *Art Monthly*, no. 222, December/January 1998/9, pp. 7–11.

Gustav Metzger, New works, documents, workfortheeyetodo, London 1995

(Walker, John A. 'Message from the Margin', *Art Monthly*, no. 190, October 1995, pp. 14–17.)

Milch Group Show (Part 4), (Hamad Butt, Lawren Maben, Nils Norman, Simon Patterson, Sarah Staton, Nicola Tyson), Milch Gallery, London 1990

Morgan, Stuart. 'Milch is good for you', *Artscribe*, no. 85, January/February 1991, pp. 13–14.

(Morgan, Stuart. 'Art au Lait!', *Art Monthly*, no. 156, April 1992, pp. 3–5.)

Lisa Milroy, Waddington Galleries, London 1993

Kastner, Jeffrey. 'Lisa Milroy', *frieze*, issue 11, Summer 1993.

Minky Manky (including Mat Collishaw, Critical Decor, Tracey Emin, Gilbert & George, Damien Hirst, Gary Hume, Sarah Lucas, Steven Pippin, curated by Carl Freedman), South London Gallery, London/ Arnolfini, Bristol 1995

Barrett, David. 'Minky Manky', *Art Monthly*, no. 196, May 1995, pp. 31–32.

Roberts, James. 'Minky Manky', *frieze*, issue 23, July/August 1995, p. 80.

Mirror's Edge (including Thomas Demand, Ceal Floyer, Steve McQueen, Yinka Shonibare, curated by Okwui Enwezor), Tramway, Glasgow 2001

Jeffrey, Moira. 'Shape of things to come', *The Sunday Herald*, 4 March 2001.

Mahoney, Elisabeth. 'Mirror's Edge', *Art Monthly*, no. 245,April 2001, pp. 39–40.

(Ericsson, Lars O. 'Mirror's Edge', *Artforum*, vol. 38, no.10, Summer 2000, p.177.)

Mise en Scène (Claude Cahun, Tacita Dean, Virginia Nimarkoh), Institute of Contemporary Art, London 1994

Hunt, Ian. 'Mise en Scène', *frieze*, issue 20, March/April 1995.

Modern Medicine (Mat Collishaw, Grannie Cullen, Dominic Dennis, Angus Fairhurst, Damien Hirst, Abigail Lane, Miriam Lloyd, Craig Wood, curated by Carl Freedman, Damien Hirst, Billee Sellman), Building One, London 1990

Archer, Michael. 'Modern Medicine', *Artscribe*, no. 82, Summer 1990.

Kent, Sarah. 'Modern Medicine', *Time Out*, 25 April 1990.

Hall, James. 'Modern Medicine', *Sunday Correspondent*, 22 April 1990.

Renton, Andrew. 'Modern Medicine', *Flash Art*, no.153, June 1990.

Stock, John. 'Modern Medicine', *The Times*, 27 March 1990.

Jonathan Monk, CCA, Glasgow 1995

Findlay, Judith. 'Jonathan Monk', *Flash Art*, vol. 28, no.181, March/April 1995, p.108.

Jonathan Monk, City Racing, London 1996

Burrows, David. 'Jonathan Monk', *Art Monthly*, no.196, May 1996, pp. 30–31.

Sarah Morris, White Cube², London 2000

Coles, Alex. 'Sarah Morris at White Cube', *Art & Text*, November-January 2000/1.

Sarah Morris, White Cube, London 1996

Kent, Sarah. 'Sarah Morris', *Time Out*, 20–27 March 1996, p. 53.

John Murphy, Lisson Gallery, London 1996

Coomer, Martin. 'Diamond dogs', *Time Out*, 15–22 May 1996, p. 47.

Wilson, Andrew. 'John Murphy', *Art Monthly*, no.197, June 1996, pp. 24–25.

David Musgrave, greengrassi, London 2001

Archer, Michael. 'David Musgrave', *Artforum*, vol. 40, no. 5, January 2002, pp.152–153.

Bussel, David. 'David Musgrave', *Art & Text*, Spring 2002, pp.86–87.

Bussel, David. 'Snoopy must die', *i-D magazine*, issue 212, 2001, pp.190–191.

Falconer, Morgan, 'David Musgrave/Roger Hiorns', *Untitled*, no. 26, Autumn/Winter 2001, p. 32.

Staple, Polly. 'David Musgrave', *frieze*, issue 64, January/February 2002, p. 94.

Bruce Nauman, Hayward Gallery, London/ Pompidou Centre, Paris 1998

Feaver, William. 'Black watch', *The Observer*, 19 July 1998.

Gayford, Maritn. 'Aesthetic mugging', *The Spectator*, 1 August 1998.

Januszczak, Waldemar. 'Without walls', *Sunday Times*, 27 July 1998.

Riley, Bridget. 'Bruce Nauman. Squaring the Circle', *Flash Art*, March/April 1999, pp. 88–91.

Searle, Adrian. 'In yer face', *The Guardian*, 21 July 1998.

Sewell, Brian. 'Master of the Mad House', *Evening Standard*, 23 July 1998.

(Collings, Matthew. 'Art's Loan Ranger', *Vogue* (London), August 1998.)

Mike Nelson, Hales Gallery, London 1995

Irvine, Jaki. 'Mike Nelson', *frieze*, issue 23, July/August 1995, pp. 68–69.

Mike Nelson, Matt's Gallery, London 2000

Beech, Dave. 'Mike Nelson', *Art Monthly*, no. 234, March 2000, pp. 36–37.

Jones, Jonathan. 'Species of Spaces', *frieze*, issue 53, July/August 2000, pp. 74–77.

Mike Nelson, Nothing is true. Everything is permitted, Institute of Contemporary Arts, London 2001

Beasley, Stephen. 'Mike Nelson', *Untitled*, no. 26, Autumn/Winter 2001, p. 41.

Mike Nelson, Trading Station AlphaCMa, Matt's Gallery, London 1996

Burrows, David. 'Mike Nelson', *Art Monthly*, no. 194, March 1996, pp. 28–29.

Mariele Neudecker, Lotta Hammer, London 1998

Barrett, David. 'Mariele Neudecker', *frieze,* issue 40, May 1998, p. 90.

Mariele Neudecker, Spike Island, Bristol 1998

Hunt, Ian. 'Mariele Neudecker', *Art Monthly*, no. 222, December 1998, pp. 43–44.

New Contemporaries 1996, Tate Liverpool/ Camden Arts Centre, London

Sanderson, Philip. 'New Contemporaries 1996', *Art Monthly*, no. 199. September 1996, pp. 40–42.

New Contemporaries 1999, Exchange Flags, Liverpool/ South London Gallery, London

Barrett, David. 'New Contemporaries 1999', *Art Monthly*, no. 231, November 1999, pp. 30–32.

New Contemporaries 2000, Milton Keynes Art Gallery, touring

Beech, Dave. 'New Contemporaries 2000', *Art Monthly*, no. 240, October 2000, pp. 25–27.

New Labour (including Enrico David, Martin Maloney, Grayson Perry, Rebecca Warren, Elizabeth Wright), Saatchi Gallery, London 2001

Darwent, Charles. 'Handmade tales of pots and porn', *Independent on Sunday*, 29 April 2001.

Januszczak, Waldemar. 'At the Saatchi Gallery, you'll find proof that New Labour really is working', *Sunday Times*, 29 April 2001.

Kent, Sarah. 'Labour intensive', *Time Out*, no. 1603, 9–16 May 2001.

Sewell, Brian. 'A touch of smut with a hand from Saatchi', *Evening Standard*, 18 May 2001.

Wilsher, Mark. 'Craftwork' (Rebecca Warren), *What's On*, 9–16 May 2001.

New Neurotic Realism Part 1 (including Steven Gontarski, Tomoko Takahashi, Martin Maloney), Saatchi Gallery, London 1999

Cork, Richard. 'Last orders in the waste land', *The Times*, 12 January 1999.

Hall, James. 'Neurotic Realism Part 1', *Artforum*, vol. 38, no. 2, October 1999, pp. 155–156.

Lubbock, Tom. 'The Trouble with Saatchi', *The Independent*, 19 January 1999

Kent, Sarah. 'Boy's Zone', *Time Out*, 13–20 January 1999.

Searle, Adrian. 'New kids in the dock', *The Guardian*, 16 January 1999.

New Neurotic Realism Part 2 (including Dexter Dalwood, Peter Davies, David Falconer, Mark Hosking, Tom Hunter), Saatchi Gallery, London 1999

Charelsworth, JJ. 'New Neurotic Realism Part II', *Art Monthly,* no. 230, October 1999, pp. 30–32.

Cork, Richard. 'A Case of Less Matter, More Rat', *The Times*, 15 Spetember 1999.

Cumming, Laura. 'Gags to Riches', *The Observer Review*, 19 September 1999.

De Cruz, Gemma. 'Neurotic Realism', *Flash Art*, November/December 1999.

Hall, James. 'Neurotic Realism Part 2', *Artforum*, vol. 38, no. 2, October 1999, pp. 155–156.

Kent, Sarah. 'Of Mice and Men', *Time Out*, 8–15 September 1999.

Paul Noble, acumulus noblitatus, Maureen Paley Interim Art, London 2001

O'Reilly, Sally. 'Paul Noble', *Time Out*, no. 1631, 21–28 November 2001.

Williams, Gilda. 'Paul Noble', *Art Monthly*, no. 252, December/January 2001/2, pp. 39–40.

(Morton, Tom. 'Bleak houses', *frieze,* issue 65, March 2002.)

Paul Noble, NOBSON, Chisenhale Gallery, London 1998

Archer, Michael. 'Paul Noble', *Artforum,* vol. 36, no.10, Summer 1998.

Beech, Dave. 'Paul Noble', *Art Monthly,* no. 215, April 1998, pp. 24–25.

Brown, Neal. 'Paul Noble', *frieze,* issue 41, June/July/August 1998, p. 89.

Coomer, Martin. 'Paul Noble', *Time Out,* no.1439, 18–25 March 1998.

Sumpter, Helen. 'Art with nobs on', *The Big Issue,* no. 271, 16–22 February 1998.

Paul Noble, Welcome to Nobpark, Maureen Paley Interim Art, London 1998

Bishop, Claire. 'Paul Noble', *Flash Art,* vol. 32, no. 206, May/June 1999.

Jones, Jonathan. 'Paul Nobel', *The Observer Review,* 20 December 1998.

McLaren, Duncan. 'Last train to nobsville' (with PN/Chisenhale), *Contemporary Visual Arts,* issue 23, 1999.

Shave, Stuart. 'Nob's town', *i-D magazine,* January/Febraury 1999.

Tim Noble and Sue Webster, 20 Rivington Street, London 1998

Chapman, Jake. 'Tim Noble and Sue Webster', *frieze,* issue 39, March/April 1998, pp. 94–95.

Harris, Mark. '20 Rivington Street', *Art in America,* July 1998.

Lucia Nogueira, Camden Arts Centre, London/Ikon, Birmingham 1994

Blazwick, Iwona. 'Lucia Nogueira', *Art Monthly,* no.177, June 1994, p. 33.

The Object Sculpture (including Thomas Schütte, Philippe Parreno, Paul Thek, Olafur Eliasson), Henry Moore Insitute, Leeds 2002

Dezeuze, Anne. 'The Object Sculpture', *Art Monthly,* no. 258, July/August 2002, pp. 35–37.

Morton, Tom. 'The Object Sculpture', *frieze,* no. 69, September 2002, p.103.

Chris Ofili, Freedom One Day, Victoria Miro Gallery, London 2002

Cumming, Laura. 'The Eden Project', *The Observer,* 7 July 2002, pp. 4–8.

Lubbock, Tom. 'Monkey business', *The Independent (Review),* 9 July 2000, pp.16–17.

Miller, Alicia. 'Chris Ofili', *Flash Art,* vol. 34, no. 226, October 2002, pp.105–106.

Schwabsky, Barry. 'Chris Ofili', *Artforum,* vol. XLI, no. 2, October 2002, p.168.

Searle, Adrian. 'Monkey Magic ...', *The Guardian,* 25 June 2002, p.10.

Offside! Contemporary Artists and Football (including Roderick Buchanan, Lucy Gunning, Natalie Turner, Mark Wallinger), Manchester City Art Gallery, touring 1996/7

Buck, Louisa. 'The Beautiful Game', *GQ Magazine,* August 1996, p. 48.

Collins, Michael. 'Games people play', *The Daily Telegraph,* 11 June 1996.

Cross, Andrew. 'Offside', *Art Monthly,* no.198, July/August 1996, pp. 37–39.

Garnett, Robert. 'A frame of two halves', *Tate magazine,* issue 9, Summer 1996, pp. 42–44.

Pryke, Sam. 'Offside: contemporary artists and football', *Third Text,* no. 36, Autumn 1996, pp.102–104.

Yoko Ono, Have you seen the horizon lately? Museum of Modern Art, Oxford 1997

Lery, Paul. *Wall Street Journal Europe,* 12–13 December 1997.

Millard, Rosie. 'Yoko Ono', *Art Review,* April 1998.

Withers, Rachel. *The Guardian,* 9 December 1997.

('Yoko Ono, Have you seen the horizon lately?', including Logsdail, Nicholas. Metzger, Gustav, *Art Monthly,* no. 212, December/January1997/8, pp.1–7.)

Julian Opie, Hayward Gallery, London 1993,

Cork, Richard. 'Landmarks and Roads to Nowhere', *The Times,* 12 November 1993.

Gillick, Liam. 'Julian Opie', *Art Monthly*, no. 172, December/January 1993/4, p. 26.

Renton, Andrew. 'Julian Opie: Hayward Gallery', *Flash Art*, vol. 26, no. 174, January/February 1994.

Julian Opie, Lisson Gallery, London 1991

Archer, Michael. 'I was not making a monument, I was not making an object', *Art Monthly*, no. 144, March 1991, pp. 3–5.

Khosla, Kiron. 'Julian Opie', *Artscribe*, no. 86, March/April 1991, p. 65.

Renton, Andrew. 'Julian Opie', *Flash Art*, no. 157, March/April 1991.

Gabriel Orozco, Empty Club, 50 St. James's Street, London 1996 (Artangel/Beck's)

Gale, Ian. 'Mexican makes waves on the club scene', *The Independent*, 2 July 1996

Gee, Maggie. 'What the butler never saw', *New Statesman*, 19 July 1996, p. 40.

Hewison, Robert. 'Games of enchantment', *Sunday Times*, 30 June 1996, p. 18.

Gabriel Orozco, Institute of Contemporary Arts, London 1996

Grant, Simon. 'Gabriel Orozco' (ICA and Empty Club), *Art Monthly*, no. 199, September 1996, pp. 33–34.

Searle, Adrian. 'The long and short of it', *The Guardian*, 20 July 1996, p. 8.

Tony Oursler, The Influence Machine, Soho Square, London 2000 (Artangel/Beck's)

Buck, Louisa. 'Ghosts of Soho Square', *The World of Interiors*, November 2000, pp. 23–24.

Burnett, Craig. 'Tony Oursler: The Influence Machine', *Modern Painters*, Winter 2000, pp. 3–4.

Collings, Matthew. 'Diary. The Great Truths of Our Time', *Modern Painters*, Winter 2000, p. 80

Grant, Simon. 'A face coming to a place near you', *Evening Standard*, 25 October 2000, p. 36.

Out of Sight, Out of Mind (including Bas Jan Ader, Giovanni Anselmo, Jan Dibbets, Barry Flanagan, Christine Kozlov, Mario Mertz, John Murphy, Richard Serra), Lisson Gallery, London 1993

Hall, James. 'The Total Concept', *The Guardian*, 15 February 1993.

Kent, Sarah. 'Trivial pursuit' (with Gravity and Grace), *Time Out*, 24 February 1993.

Packer, William. 'Minimal to the invisible' (with Ryman/Tate), *Financial Times*, 23 February 1993.

Wilson, Andrew. 'Out of Sight, Out of Mind/ Lawrence Weiner', *Art Monthly*, no. 165, April 1993, pp. 19–20.

Peter Owen, Kerry Stewart, Ana Genoves, City Racing, London 1995

Barrett, David. 'Kerry Stewart, Peter Owen', *Art Monthly*, no. 187, June 1995, pp. 33–34.

Gina Pane, John Hansard Gallery, Southampton 2001/Arnolfini, Bristol 2002

Grant, Catherine. 'Gina Pane', *Art Monthly*, no. 253, February 2002, pp. 41–43.

MacRitchie, Lynn. 'Gina Pane', *Financial Times*, 9 March 2002.

Janette Parris, Copyright, City Racing, London 1998

Guha, Tania. 'Janette Parris', *Time Out*, no. 1439, 18–25 March 1998, p. 51.

Windsor, John. 'Janette Parris', *The Independent*, 26 March 1998, p. 4.

Simon Patterson, Lisson Gallery, London 1996

Higgie, Jennifer. 'Simon Patterson', *frieze*, issue 29, July/August 1996, pp. 67–68.

Harris, Mark. 'Simon Patterson', *Art in America*, July 1996.

Hunt, Ian. 'Simon Patterson', *Art Monthly*, no. 195, April 1996, pp. 29–30.

Raymond Pettibon, Whitechapel Art Gallery, London 2001

Comer, Stuart. 'Raymond Pettibon', *Untitled*, no. 26, Autumn/Winter 2001, pp. 35–36.

Manchester, Clare. 'Raymond Pettibon', *Art Monthly*, no. 250, October 2001, pp. 33–34.

Elizabeth Peyton, The Prince Albert Pub, Brixton, London 1995

Muir, Gregor. 'Elizabeth Peyton', *frieze,* issue 24, September/October 1995, pp. 70–71.

Sigmar Polke, Join the Dots, Tate Liverpool 1995

Barker, Barry. 'Polke Dots', *Art Monthly,* no.184, March 1995, pp. 3–5.

Hall, James. 'Polke Dots', *The Guardian*, 30 January 1995, pp. 6–7.

Searle, Adrian. 'Polke Dotty', *The Independent Magazine*, 21 January 1995, pp. 24–29.

Popocultural (including John Cussans, Dan Graham, Chris Ofili, Simon Periton, Jason Fox, Jeffrey Vallance, curated by Martin McGeown, Andrew Wheatley), South London Gallery, London 1996

Burrows, David. 'Popocultural', *Art Monthly,* no. 202, December/January 1996/7, pp. 33–34.

Freedman, Carl. 'Popoculture', *frieze,* issue 34, May 1997, pp. 75–76.

Press Release, BANK, Gallerie Poo Poo, London/ Rupert Goldsworthy Gallery, New York 1999

–. 'Artists Laughing at Other Artists', *The Guardian*, 13 March 1999.

(Kino, Carol. 'BANK. Press Release', *Time Out,* New York, 7–14 October 1999.)

Protest and Survive (including Jeremy Deller, Gilbert & George, Paul Graham, Thomas Hirschhorn, Jo Spence, Wolfgang Tillmans, curated by Matthew Higgs, Paul Noble), Whitechapel Art Gallery, London 2000

Jones, Jonathan. 'Protest and Survive', *The Guardian*, 19 September 2000.

Mac Giolla Léith, Caoimhin. 'Protest and Survive', *Artforum,* vol. 39, no. 5, January 2001, p.135.

Sladen, Mark. 'Protest and Survive', *frieze,* issue 57, March 2001, pp. 96–97.

Schmitz, Edgar. 'Protest and Survive', *Kunstforum International*, no.153, January-March 2001, pp. 411–413.

Pyramids of Mars (including Sture Johanesen, Aleksandra Mir, Palle Nielson, curated by Lars Bang Larsen), The Curve, Barbican, London 2001

Farquharson, Alex. 'Pyramids of Mars', *Art Monthly,* no. 244, March 2001, pp. 33–35.

Jones, Jonathan. 'Pyramids of Mars', *frieze,* issue 60, June/July/August 2001, p. 90.

Marc Quinn, South London Gallery, London 1998

Gisbourne, Mark. 'Marc Quinn', *Contemporary Visual Arts*, issue 19, Summer 1998, p. 77.

Hall, James. 'Marc Quinn. South London Gallery', *Artforum,* May 1998.

Marc Quinn, Tate Liverpool 2002

Cork, Richard. 'Pool splashes out' (with George Romney/Walker Art Gallery), *The Times*, 5 February 2002.

Cumming, Laura. 'Out of body experiences', *The Observer Review*, 3 February 2002

Darwent, Charles. 'Keeping Time', *Modern Painters*, Spring 2002, pp. 50–53.

Hickling, Alfred. 'Marc Quinn', *The Guardian*, 1 February 2002.

(Gisbourne, Mark. 'The self and others', *Contemporary*, February 2002, pp. 52–57.)

Fiona Rae, Institute of Contemporary Arts, London 1993

Morley, Simon. 'Fiona Rae', *Art Monthly,* no.173, February 1994, pp. 23–24.

Michael Raedecker, The Approach, London 2000

Grant, Simon. 'Material success', *Evening Standard*, 16 May 2000.

O'Kane, Paul. 'Michael Raedecker', *zingmagazine*, issue 13, Autumn 2000.

(Bush, Kate. 'Flatland', *frieze,* issue 54, September/October 2000, pp. 90–93.)

Ramsay Bird, New Flotex (Graham Ramsay and Gavin Bird), Gimpel Fils Gallery, London 1992

Archer, Michael. 'Ramsay Bird', *Artforum*, March 1992.

Collings, Matthew. 'Ramsay Bird', *City Limits*, February 1992.

Hall, James. 'Ramsay Bird', *Tema Celeste*, April/May 1992.

Norman, Geraldine. 'Ramsay Bird', *The Independent*, 3 February 1992.

Renton, Andrew. 'Ramsay Bird', *Flash Art*, March/April 1992.

(–. 'Total Destruction' (interview), *G SPOT*, July 1992.)

Real Art: A New Modernism: British Reflexive Painters in the 1990s (Torie Begg, Clem Crosby, Ian Davenport, Peter Davis, Zebedee Jones, Jason Martin), Southampton City Art Gallery 1995

Muller, Brian. 'Real Art: A New Modernism. British Reflexive Pianters in the Ninties', *Art Press* (France), May 1995.

Rebecca (Tony Benn, Dexter Dalwood, Rozalind Drummond, Gerald Hemsworth, Dez Lawrence, Michael Raedecker, Mike Silva), SaliGia, London 1999

Currah, Mark. 'Rebecca', *Time Out*, 1–8 September 1999

(Arnatt, Matthew. 'Strangely Thrilling', *Manedsskrift for kunst og kunstrelateret materiale* (Denmark), no. 52, 1999.)

(Rushton, Steve. 'Mr Kaplan', *everything*, 1999.)

Rewind (Carsten Höller, Pierre Huyghe, Philippe Parreno, Rirkrit Tiravanija), City Racing, London 1995

Willaims, Gilda. 'Rewind', *Art Monthly*, no. 191, November 1995, pp. 25–26.

Gerhard Richter, 18.Oktober 1977, Institute of Contemporary Arts, London 1989

Craddock, Sacha. 'Voices from the gray', *The Guardian*, 30 August 1989, p. 37.

Graham-Dixon, Andrew. 'Solemn history into art', *The Independent*, 29 August 1989.

Hilty, Greg. '18.October 1977. Gerhard Richter', *Art Monthly*, no. 131, November 1989, pp. 27–28.

Kent, Sarah. 'Richter Scale', *Time Out*, 30 August – 6 September 1989, pp. 14–15.

Gerhard Richter, Tate Gallery, London 1991

Collings, Matthew. 'Blurred vision', *The Independent*, 5 November 1991, p. 16.

Joyce, Conor. 'Gerhard Richter', *Art Monthly*, no. 152, December/January 1991/2, pp. 3–5.

Koch, Gertrud. 'The Richter-Scale of Blur', *October* (USA), no. 62, Fall 1992, pp. 133–142.

Sewell, Brian. 'Smear tactics', *Evening Standard*, 21 November 1991, p. 30.

Sophie Rickett, Dundee Contemporary Arts, Dundee 2001

Glover, Izi. 'Sophie Rickett', *frieze*, issue 60, June/July/August 2001, p. 121.

Bridget Riley, According to Sensation: Paintings 1982–92, Hayward Gallery, London 1992

Bumpus, Judith. 'Bridget Riley', *Contemporary Art Magazine*, vol. 1, no. 2, Winter 1992, pp. 33–36.

Roberts, James. 'Visual Fabric' (interview with BR), *frieze*, no. 6, September 1992, pp. 20–23.

Bridget Riley, Paintings from the 1960s and 70s, Serpentine Gallery, London 1999

Cork, Richard. 'Dazzled by the Life of Riley', *The Times*, 23 June 1999.

Farquharson, Alex. 'Bridget Riley', *Art Monthly*, no. 229, September 1999, pp. 35–37.

Morely, Simon. 'Bridget Riley', *Burlington Magazine*, vol. 141, no. 1158, September 1999, pp. 561–563.

Packer, William. 'The Subtle Charm of Optical Illusion', *Financial Times*, 26–27 June 1999, p. 6.

Searle, Adrian. 'Eyes Wide Open', *The Guardian*, 22 June 1999, pp. 10–11.

Spurling, John. 'In My Own Way, Yes', *Modern Painters*, September 1999, pp. 34–38.

Withers, Rachel. 'Bridget Riley', *Artforum*, vol. 38, no. 3, November 1999, p. 139.

Bridget Riley, Waddington Galleries, London 2000

Coles, Alex. 'Bridget Riley at Waddington Galleries', *Art in America*, October 2000.

Rites of Passage: Art for the End of the Century (including Miroslaw Balka, Joseph Beuys, Louise Bourgeois, Robert Gober, Susan Hiller, Jana Sterbak, curated by Stuart Morgan, Frances Morris), Tate Gallery, London 1995

Collings, Matthew. 'Art of the moment', *Modern Painters*, vol. 8, no. 3, Autumn 1995, pp. 64–67.

Garnett, Robert. 'Rites of Passage: Art for the End of the Century', *Art Monthly*, no.188, July/August 1995, pp. 28–29.

Searle, Adrian. 'Rites of Passage', *frieze*, no. 24, September/October 1995, pp. 40–43.

Eva Rothschild, The Showroom, London 2001

Ratnam, Niru. 'What Lies Beneath', *The Face*, April 2001, p.162

Shave, Stuart. 'Dream Weaver', *i-D magazine*, no. 209, 2001

(Higgie, Jennifer. 'Paint it Black', *frieze*, issue 55, November/December 2000, pp. 78–79.)

Thomas Ruff, Essor Gallery, London 2001

Morton, Tom. 'Thomas Ruff', *frieze*, issue 64, January/February 2002, p. 91.

John Russell, The Collagist, The Trade Apartment, London 2002

Smith, Dan. 'John Russell', *Art Monthly*, no. 258, July/August 2002.

Robert Ryman, Tate Gallery, London 1993

Batchelor, David. 'On painting and pictures' (interview with RR), *frieze*, issue 10, May 1993, pp. 42–49.

Wilson, Andrew. 'Robert Ryman', *Forum International*, May-August 1993, p.136.

Wood, Christopher S. 'Ryman's poetics', *Art in America*, vol. 82, no.1, January 1994.

Giorgio Sadotti, Be Me, Maureen Paley Interim Art, London 1996

Williams, Gilda. 'Be Me' (Gilda Williams aka Giorgio Sadotti), *Art Monthly*, no. 201, November 1996, pp. 27–28.

Nina Saunders, The Kiosk Project, London 2002

Gleeson, David. 'Nina Saunders', *frieze*, issue 66, April 2002, p.102.

Gregor Schneider, Sadie Coles HQ, London 1998

Higgs, Matthew. 'Gregor Schneider', *Art Monthly*, no. 213, February 1998, pp. 21–22.

Sensation: Young British Artists from the Saatchi Collection (including Glenn Brown, Jake and Dinos Chapman, Keith Coventry, Marcus Harvey, Damien Hirst, Gary Hume, Sarah Lucas, Chris Ofili, Marc Quinn, Mark Wallinger, Rachel Whiteread), Royal Academy of Arts, London 1997

–. 'Exhibited by the Royal Academy in the So-Called Name of Art, Defaced by the People in the Name of Common Decency', *The Mirror*, 19 September, front page.

–. 'The Royal Academy of Porn', *Daily Mail*, 16 September 1997, front page.

Alberge, Dalya. 'Shocking? Not us, say artists as Academy issues a taste warning', *The Times*, 20 August 1997.

Barrett, David. 'Sensation: Royal Academy of Arts, London', *Art & Text*, no. 60, February–April 1998, pp. 93–94.

Bickers, Patricia. 'Sense and Sensation', *Art Monthly*, no. 211, November 1997, pp.1–6.

Burn, Gordon. 'The hand that rocked the Academy', *The Guardian*, 6 September 1997.

Cawer, Patrick. '2,800 a day visit RA's Myra Show', *Evening Standard*, 30 December 1997.

Collings, Matthew. 'Sensation', *Artforum*, vol. 36, no. 5, January 1998, pp. 94–95.

Collings, Matthew. 'The New Establishment', *Independent on Sunday*, 31 August 1997.

Daniels, Anthony. 'The Royal Academy Is Degrading Us All. It Should Not Forget That Many Talented Artists Served Adolf Hitler', *Daily Mail,* 17 September 1997.

Dorment, Richard. 'Sensation? What Sensation?', *The Daily Telegraph,* 17 September 1997.

Ellen, Barbara. 'Hindley and the Appeal of the Cynical', *The Observer,* 14 September 1997.

Elliot, Christopher. 'Withdraw Portrait of Me, Urges Hidley', *The Observer,* 14 September 1997.

Feaver, William. 'Myra, Myra on the wall...', *The Observer,* 14 September 1997.

Hauser, Kitty. 'Sensation:Young British Artists from the Saatchi Collection', *New Left Review,* no. 227, January/February 1998, pp.154–160.

Honigsbaum, Mark. Blackhurst, Chris. 'Royal Academy Warned of Acting as a Dealer for Saatchi', *Independent on Sunday,* 14 September 1997.

Januszczak, Waldemar. 'Facing the Scary Art of Our Time', *Sunday Times Magazine,* 21 September 1997.

Jardine, Liz. 'One Man Decides What is Good for Art', *The Daily Telegraph,* 18 September 1997.

Johnson, Paul. 'An Obscene Picture and the Questions: Will Decency or Decadence Triumph in British Life', *Daily Mail,* 20 September 1997.

Jury, Louise. 'Sensation' Proves Shockingly Popular', *The Independent,* 30 December 1997.

Kent, Sarah. 'It's a Sensation! But is it art? Everything you need to know about the London art scene but were afraid to ask.' *Time Out Special Supplement,* no.1412, 18–25 September 1997.

Norris, David. 'The Royal Academy of Porn', *Daily Mail,* 16 September 1997.

MacRitchie, Lynn. 'Rude Britannia', *Art in America,* vol. 86, no. 4, April 1998, pp. 36–39.

Packer, William. 'What Sensation?', *Financial Times,* 20 September 1997.

Searle, Adrian. 'Feeling Frenzy', *The Guardian Weekly,* 28 September 1997.

Self, Will. 'The Royal Academy is Casting its Mantle upon Saatchi's Brit Kids. Middle England is Shocked and Enjoying Every Minute of it', *New Statesman,* 19 September 1997, pp. 38–39.

Sewell, Brian. 'Inflated Playthings for the Shallow Mind', *Evening Standard,* 18 September 1997.

Sladen, Mark. 'Brit Pack', *RA Magazine,* no. 56, Autumn 1997, pp. 38–45.

Slyce, John. 'Sensation', *Flash Art,* vol. 30, no.197, November/December 1997, pp.106–107.

Stallabrass, Julian. 'High Art Lite at the Royal Academy', *Third Text,* no. 42, Spring 1998, pp. 79–84.

Stringer, Robin. 'Vice Squad Gives the All Clear to Sensation Show', *Evening Standard,* 18 September 1997.

Suchin, Peter. 'Condensation?', *everything,* vol. 2:2, Spring 1998, pp. 36–38.

Sutcliffe, Thomas. 'Those who Take Offence: A Portrait in Tyranny', *The Independent,* 29 October 1997.

Sensation: Young British Artists from the Saatchi Collection, Hamburger Bahnhof, Berlin 1998

Engberg, Bente. 'Artusindskiftet Truer', *Nekrolog,* 22–28 January 1999.

Herbstreuth, Peter. 'Die Hooligans des Kunstbetriebes', *Der Tagesspiegel,* 2 October 1998.

Kuhn, Nicola. 'Der Britische Humor Blieb Zu Hause', *Der Tagesspiegel,* 30 September 1998.

Lamoree, Jihm. 'De Nieuwe Sensatie van Saatchi', *Het Parool,* 16 January 1999.

Lösel, Anja. 'Hai Mit Kindermorderin', *Stern,* 30 September 1998.

Walde, Gabriela. 'Perverses Paradies Eines Privatsammlers', *Die Welt,* 26 September 1998.

Wendenburg, Christina. 'Schmerz, Shock und Sensationen', *Berliner Morgenpost,* 30 September 1998.

Sensation: Young British Artists from the Saatchi Collection, Brooklyn Museum of Art, New York 1999

Cembalest, Robin. 'Battle in Brooklyn', *ARTnews*, vol. 98, no.10, November 1999, pp. 61–62.

Failing, Patricia. 'Spineless or Severe', *ARTnews*, vol. 99, no. 9, October 2000, p. 60.

Heartney, Eleanor. 'A Catholic controversy', *Art in America*, vol. 87, no.12, December 1999, pp 39, 41.

Kimball, Roger. 'The elephant in the gallery, or the lessons of Sensation', *New Criterion* (USA). vol.18, no. 3, November 1999, pp. 4–8.

Macdonald, Robert R. 'Tolerence, trust and the meaning of 'Sensation'', *Museum News* (USA), vol. 79, no. 3, May/June 2000, pp. 46–53.

Nochlin, Linda. 'Saluting 'Sensation'', *Art in America*, vol. 87, no.12, December 1999, pp. 37, 39.

Rosenbaum, Lee. 'The battle of Brooklyn ends, the controversy continues', *Art in America*, vol. 88, no. 6, June 2000, pp. 39, 41, 43.

Ross, Andrew. 'The right stuff', (interview with Amy Adler), *Artforum*, vol. 38, no. 3, November 1999, pp. 45–48.

Serious Games (including Jim Campbell, Char Davies, Graham Harwood, Toshio Iwai, Bill Seaman), Barbican Art Gallery, London 1997

Laniado, Joe. 'Serious Games', *frieze*, issue 36, September/October 1997, pp. 98–99.

Settings & Players: Theatrical ambiguity in American photography (including Gregory Crewdson, Richard Prince, Collier Schorr, Cindy Sherman, Stephen Shore), White Cube², London 2001

Ammirati, Domenick. 'Real Life and Elsewhere' (with I am a camera), *Modern Painters*, vol.14, no. 2, Summer 2001, pp. 88–90.

Green, Alison. 'Photography', *Art Monthly*, no. 246, May 2001, pp.1–4.

Johnnie Shand Kydd, True Brits, Independent Art Space, London 1997

Garnett, Robert. 'Spit Fire: Photographs from the Art World, London, 1996/7' (book review), *Art*

Monthly, no. 222, December/January 1998/9, p. 39.

George Shaw, Anthony Wilkinson Gallery, London 2001

Burn, Gordon. 'England my England', *The Observer Magazine*, 21 October 2001.

O'Reilly, Sally. 'George Shaw', *Time Out*, 28 November – 5 December 2001.

Sumpter, Helen. 'Would Your Mother Like It', *The Big Issue*, October 2001.

Jim Shaw's Thrift Store Paintings, Institute of Contemporary Arts, London 2000

Farquharson, Alex. 'Inside Out' (with BA5, Cindy Sherman), *Art Monthly*, no. 242, December/January 2000/1, pp.1–6.

Searle, Adrian. 'A hundred bucks and all this could be yours', *The Guardian*, 26 September 2000, p.12.

Stallabrass, Julian. 'Collector's Pieces', *New Statesman*, 16 October 2000, pp. 42–43.

Cindy Sherman, Untitled (Bus Riders) and Untitled (Mystery), greengrassi, London 2000

–. 'Cindy Sherman', *Make*, issue 90, December–February 2000/1, p.16.

Clark, Paul. 'Cindy Sherman', *Evening Standard*, 11 January 2001, p. 63.

Farquharson, Alex. 'Inside Out' (with BA5, Jim Shaw/ICA), *Art Monthly*, no. 242, December/January 2000/1, pp.1–6.

Schwabsky, Barry. 'Cindy Sherman', *Artforum*, vol. 39, no. 5, January 2001, p.132.

Wilson, Andrew. 'Cindy Sherman', *Art Monthly*, no. 242, December/January 2000/1, pp. 33–34.

Yinka Shonibare, Camden Arts Centre, London 2000

Campbell-Johnston, Rachel. 'That bold colonial boy', *The Times*, 21 June 2000.

Grant, Simon. 'Alternative history out of Africa', *Evening Standard*, 18 August 2000.

Hubbard, Sue. 'A post-colonial look at Victorian parlour games', *Independent on Sunday*, 2 July 2000.

Yinka Shonibare, Dressing Down, Ikon Gallery, Birmingham/ Mappin Art Gallery, Sheffield/ Oriel Mostyn, Llandudno 1999

Ratnam, Niru. 'Yinka Shonibare', *Art Monthly*, no. 225, April 1999, pp. 40–41.

Yinka Shonibare, Stephen Friedman Gallery & 12 Dolland Street, London 2001

Kent, Sarah. 'Yinka Shonibare', *Time Out*, 9–16 May 2001.

Downey, Anthony. 'Yinka Shonibare', *Wasafiri*, issue 35, Spring 2002, pp. 47–50.

The Shop (Tracey Emin & Sarah Lucas), 103 Bethnal Green Road, London 1993

Daly, Pauline. Quick, Brendan. 'Crazy Tracey, Sensible Lucas', *Purple Prose*, Summer 1993.

Gregor, Muir. 'Lucas & Emin' (interview with SL & TE), *frieze*, issue 10, May 1993, p. 56.

A Short History of Perfomance: Part One (including Stuart Brisley, Bruce McLean, Hermann Nitsch, Carolee Schneemann), Whitechapel Art Gallery, London 2002

Dezeuze, Anna. 'Meat Joy', *Art Monthly*, no. 257, June 2002, pp. 1–6.

Ericksen, Dustin. 'A Short History of Perfomance: Part One', *Art & Text*, no. 78, Autumn 2002, pp. 86–87.

Withers, Rachel. 'A Short History of Performance: Part One', *Artforum*, vol. XLI, no. 1, September 2002, p. 215.

A Shot in the Head (including Francis Alÿs, Ceal Floyer, Roger Hiorns, Emma Kay, Jonathan Monk, Jemima Stehli), Lisson Gallery, London 2000

Archer, Michael. 'A Shot in the Head', *Art Monthly*, no. 239, September 2000, pp. 46–48.

Boucher, Caroline. 'And the beak shall inherit the earth', *The Observer*, 6 August 2000, p. 9.

Cork, Richard. 'A dose of eclectic shock treatment', *The Times*, 26 July 2000, p. 26.

Kent, Sarah. 'Strip Search', *Time Out*, 23–30 August 2000.

Moffat, Laura. 'A Shot in the Head', *Art Monthly*, no. 239, September 2000, pp. 47–49.

Searle, Adrian. 'Why do I feel naked?', *The Guardian*, 15 July 2000, p. 5.

(Jones, Alison. 'Jemima Stehli's Ingratiating Objects', *Make*, December 2000. no. 90, p. 23.)

Show and Tell (including Jyll Bradly, Michael Landy, Caroline Russell, Dean Whatmuff), Riverside Studios, London 1988

Bush, Kate. 'Show and Tell', *Flash Art*, March/April 1989.

Craddock, Sacha. 'Show and Tell', *The Guardian*, 19 December 1988.

Currah, Mark. 'Show and Tell', *City Limits*, 5–12 January 1989.

Gillick, Liam. 'Show and Tell', *Art Monthly*, no. 123, February 1989, pp. 22–23.

Show! Hide! Show! (Jake Chapman, Alex Hartley, Abigail Lane, Sam Taylor-Wood, curated by Andrew Renton), Anderson O'Day, London 1991

Bracewell, Michael. 'Show! Hide! Show!' (interview with A.R.), *frieze*, issue 1, November 1991, pp. 42–43.

Edwards, Natasha. 'Show Hide Show', *Artscribe*, no. 89, October 1991, p. 99.

David Shrigley, The Photographers' Gallery, London 1997

Beech, Dave. 'David Shrigley', *Art Monthly*, no. 204, March 1997, pp. 29–30.

David Shrigley, Stephen Friedman Gallery, London 2001

Brown, Neal. 'David Shrigley', *Art Review*, March 2001, p. 48.

Searle, Adrian. 'Objects' (with J&D Chapman/ White Cube), *The Guardian*, 23 March 1999, p. 9.

Sumpter, Helen. 'Deadly Doodles', *The Big Issue*, February 2001.

Wilsher, Mark. 'David Shrigley', *Art Monthly*, no. 245, April 2001, pp. 32–33.

A Silent Poetry (Alighiero Boetti, Jean-Marc Bustamante, Jenny Holzer, Roni Horn, Joel Shapiro), Timothy Taylor Gallery, London 2002

Gillick, Liam. 'A Silent Poetry', *100 Reviews (3)*, 2002, pp. 73–74.

DJ Simpson, Entwistle, London 2000

Godfrey, Mark. 'DJ Simpson', *Contemporary Visual Arts*, issue 28, 2000, p. 69.

Ross Sinclair, CCA, Glasgow 1996

Feldman, Melissa. 'Ross Sinclair'. *Art Monthly*, no.197, June 1996, pp. 37–38.

McKee, Francis. 'Ross Sinclair', *frieze*, issue 29, July/August 1996, pp. 64–65.

Ross Sinclair, Fortress/Real Life (Peckham), South London Gallery, London 2001

Fox, Dan. 'Ross Sinclair', *frieze*, issue 62, October 2001, p. 93.

Bob & Roberta Smith, Don't Hate Sculpt, Chisenhale Gallery, London 1997

Burrows, David. 'Bob & Robert Smith', *Art Monthly*, no. 210, October 1997, pp. 31–32.

Feaver, William. 'Don't Hate Sculpt', *The Observer Magazine*, 28 September 1997.

Ireson, Ally. 'Playing it Differently', *D>Tour*, issue 17, 1997, pp. 38–39.

Sumpter, Helen. 'In The Studio', *The Big Issue*, no. 248, 1–7 September 1997.

Bob & Roberta Smith, Flawed, Anthony Wilkinson Fine Art, London 1996

Burrows, David. 'Bob & Robert Smith', *Art Monthly*, no.195, April 1996, pp. 32–33.

Smith/Stewart, The Showroom, London 1996

Feldman, Melissa. 'Love Hurts', *Art Monthly*, no.196, May 1996, pp. 24–25.

Sociable Realism (including Jason Fox, Martin O'Hare, Paul Noble, David Rayson, David Thorpe, Mark Titchner, curated by Paul Noble) Stephen Friedman Gallery, London 1998

Beech, Dave. 'Sociable Realism', *Art Monthly*, no. 214, March 1998, pp. 29–30.

Some of My Best Friends are Geniuses (including Gavin Brown, Dinos Chapman, David Falconer, Russell Haswell, Bruce Louden, Sam Taylor-Wood, curated by Jake Chapman), Independent Art Space, London 1996

Muir, Gregor. 'Some of My Best Friends are Geniuses', *frieze*, issue 29, July/August 1996, pp. 73–74.

Some Went Mad, Some Ran Away... (including Ashley Bickerton, Sophie Calle, Marcus Harvey, Damien Hirst, Abigail Lane, Alexis Rockman, curated by Damien Hirst), Serpentine Gallery, London 1994

–. 'Sheep Exhibit Attack "An Artistic Statement"' (Mark Bridger), *The Daily Telegraph*, 17 August 1994.

Feaver, William. 'Murder Most Foul in all its Forms', *The Observer*, 8 May 1994, p. 14.

Pilkington, Edward. 'Life, Death and the Meaning of a Two-Tone Sheep Dip', *The Guardian*, 19 August 1994, p. 1, 19.

Wilson, Andrew. 'Out of Control', *Art Monthly*, no.177, June 1994, pp. 3–9.

Something's Wrong (including Matthew Collings, John Isaacs, Brighid Lowe, Hilary Lloyd, Bob & Roberta Smith), The Tannery, London 1994

Rushton, Steve. 'Something's Wrong at the Tannery', *everything*, no.14, July/June 1994.

Space International (including Simon Bedwell, Luis Contreras, Esther McLaughlin, Derek Ogbourne, John Russell, Clifton Steinberg, curated by BANK), 2–6 Battlebridge Road, London 1992

Searle, Adrian. 'Space International', *Time Out*, 30 September–7 October 1992.

Spellbound: Art and Film (Fiona Banner, Douglas Gordon, Peter Greenaway, Damien Hirst, Steve McQueen, Eduardo Paolozzi, Paula Rego, Ridley Scott, Boyd Webb), Hayward Gallery, London 1996

–. 'One hundred years of cinema', *The Art Newspaper* (London), no. 56, Spring 1996, p. 20.

Glover, Michael. 'Spellbound: Art & Film', *ARTnews*, June 1996.

Mars-Jones, Adam. 'Affairs of the art', *The Independent*, 27 February 1996.

Lowry, Joanna. 'Spellbound', *Creative Camera*, April/May 1996, p. 40.

Peto, James. 'Year of the moving image', *RA Magazine*, no. 50, Spring 1996, p. 20.

Quinn, Paul. 'The art of the reel', *Tate magazine*, issue 8, Spring 1996, p. 40.

Sladen, Mark. 'Spellbound: Art and Film', *Art Monthly*, no. 195, April 1996, pp. 25–27.

Stallabrass, Julian. 'Spellbound', *Burlington Magazine*, vol. CXXXVIII, no. 1118, May 1996, pp. 342–343.

Fergal Stapleton, The Agency, London 1993

Morgan, Stuart. 'Fergal Stapleton', *frieze*, issue 10, May 1993, p. 54.

Fergal Stapleton and Rebecca Warren, The Showroom, London 1997

Archer, Michael. 'Rebecca Warren & Fergal Stapleton', *Artforum*, October 1997.

Frances Stark, greengrassi, London 2002

Ammirati, Domenick. 'Frances Stark', *Modern Painters*, Spring 2002, pp. 114–115.

Wilsher, Mark. 'Frances Stark: Self-Portraiture', *What's On*, 3–10 April 2002, p. 25.

Hannah Starkey, Maureen Paley Interim Art, London 2002

FS. 'Photography in the gap', *Sleazenation*, vol. 4, issue 17, July 2002.

Güner, Fisun. 'Hannah Starkey', *Modern Painters*, Autumn 2002, p. 141.

Herbert, Martin. 'Hannah Starkey', *Tema Celeste*, no. 93, September/October 2002, p. 98.

Simon Starling, Camden Arts Centre, London 2001

DF. 'Simon Starling', *Contemporary Visual Arts*, November 2000.

Harris, Mark. 'Simon Starling', *Art in America*, May 2001.

(McKee, Francis. 'Chicken or Egg?', *frieze*, issue 56, January/February 2001.)

Georgina Starr, The Bunny Lakes, Emily Tsingou Gallery/ Bunny Lake Drive-In, 86 Brick Lane, London 2002

Schwabsky, Barry. 'Georgina Starr', *Artforum*, vol. XLI, no. 1, September 2002, p. 215.

Georgina Starr, The Bunny Lakes are Coming, Anthony Reynolds Gallery, London 2000

Beech, Dave. 'Georgina Starr', *Art Monthly*, no. 240. October 2000, pp. 32–33.

Schrock, Petra. 'Georgina Starr: The bunny lakes are coming. Variation on imagination', *Eikon* (Austria), no. 34, 2001, pp. 31–38.

Sarah Staton, Anti-paintings, Artlab, Imperial College, London 2001

O'Reilly, Sally. 'Sarah Staton', *Time Out*, no. 1595, 14–21 March 2001.

Jemima Stehli, Chisenhale Gallery, London 2000

Dorment, Richard. 'Pick of the Week: Jemima Stehli', *The Daily Telegraph*, 2 December 2000.

Harris, Mark. 'Jemima Stehli', *Art in America*, vol. 89, no. 4, April 2001, p. 150.

Kent, Sarah. 'Jemima Stehli', *Time Out*, 6–13 December 2000.

McLaren, Duncan. 'A naked woman but who's lookin', *Independent on Sunday*, 26 November 2000

Schwabsky, Barry. 'Jemmia Stehli', *Artforum*, vol. 39, no. 6, February 2001, p. 164.

John Stezaker, Care and Control, Salama-Caro Gallery, London 1991

Stallabrass, Julian. 'John Stezaker', *Art Monthly*, no. 144, March 1991.

Stop short-changing us. Popular culture is for idiots. We believe in ART., BANK, Gallerie Poo Poo, London 1998

Jones, Jonathan. 'BANK', *Untitled*, Summer 1998.

Searle, Adrian. 'Nice, but can you keep your trousers on next time?', *The Guardian*, 4 August 1998.

Williams, Gilda. 'BANK', *Art Monthly*, no. 219, September 1998, pp. 41–42.

Beat Streuli, Tate Gallery 1997

Bussel, David. 'Beat Streuli', *frieze*, issue 37, November/December 1997, pp. 84–85.

Supastore Boutique (including Matthew Higgs, Hadrian Pigott, Jessica Voorsanger, curated by Sarah Staton), Laure Genillard Gallery, London 1994

—. 'Art: must see', *The Guardian*, 18 October 1994, p. 7.

—. 'London Supastore Boutique', *Flash Art*, vol. 28, no. 179, November/December 1994.

Grant, Simon. 'Supastore, Miniatures', *Art Monthly*, no. 181, November 1994, pp. 33–35.

Tomoko Takahashi, Beaconsfield, London 1997

Stallabrass, Julian. 'Tomoko Takahashi', *AN magazine*, February 1998, p. 17.

Withers, Rachel. 'Tomoko Takahashi', *frieze*, issue 39, March/April 1998, p. 84.

Take me (I'm yours), (including Christian Boltanski, Maria Eichhorn, Gilbert & George, Douglas Gordon, Carsten Höller, Wolfgang Tillmans, Franz West, curated by Hans Ulrich Obrist), Serpentine Gallery, London 1995

Freedman, Carl. 'Take me (I'm yours)', *frieze*, issue 23, July/August 1995, pp. 73–74.

Garnett, Robert. 'Take me (I'm yours)', *Art Monthly*, no. 186, May 1995, pp. 29–30.

Joanne Tatham and Tom O'Sullivan, Cubitt, London 2002

O'Reilly, Sally. 'Joanne Tatham & Tom O'Sullivan', *Art Monthly*, no. 260, October 2002, pp. 31–32.

Joanne Tatham and Tom O'Sullivan, Transmission, Glasgow 2000

Tufnell, Rob. 'Joanne Tatham and Tom O'Sullivan', *frieze*, issue 55, November/December 2000, p. 118.

Marcus Taylor, Jay Jopling at 1–10 Summer Street, London 1992

Hunt, Ian. 'Marcus Taylor', *Art Monthly*, no. 158, September 1992, pp. 21–23.

Searle, Adrian. 'Marcus Taylor', *frieze*, issue 6, September/October 1992, pp. 51–52.

Wilson, Andrew. 'Marcus Taylor', *Forum International*, September/October 1992, p. 98.

Sam Taylor-Wood, Hayward Gallery, London 2002

Holmes, Pernilla. 'A Party Girl Grows Up', *ARTnews*, Summer 2002, vol. 101, no. 7, pp. 154–157.

Kent, Sarah. 'Partied Out', *Time Out*, 8–15 May 2002.

Smith, Emma. 'Sam Taylor-Wood', *Art Monthly*, no. 257, June 2002, pp. 31–32.

Sam Taylor-Wood, Killing Time, The Showroom, London 1994

Bracewell, Michael. 'Sam Taylor-Wood', *frieze*, issue 8, September/October 1994, pp. 58–59.

Sam Taylor-Wood, Pent-up, Chisenhale, London 1996/ Sunderland City Art Gallery 1997

Bonami, Francesco. 'Sam Taylor-Wood: brainspotting', *Flash Art*, vol. 30, no. 139, March/April 1997, pp. 96–100.

Morrissey, Simon. 'Sam Taylor-Wood', *Creative Camera*, no. 342, October/November 1996, pp. 26–30.

Williams, Gilda. 'Sam Taylor-Wood', *Art & Text*, no. 56, February-April 1997, pp. 80–81.

Sam Taylor-Wood, Travesty of a Mockery, White Cube, London 1995

Kent, Sarah. 'Sam Taylor-Wood', *Time Out*, no. 1324, 3–10 January 1996

Muir, Gregor. 'Sam Taylor-Wood', *frieze*, issue 27, April 1996, pp. 79–80.

Sam Taylor-Wood, Mute, White Cube², London 2001

Bracewell, Michael. 'Portrait of the artist as a celebrity', *Independent on Sunday*, 25 November 2001, p. 9.

Cork, Richard. 'Message from remission', *The Times*, 28 November 2001, p. 16.

Dorment, Richard. 'Spirit of the age', *The Daily Telegraph*, 22 December 2001, p. A1.

Gayford, Martin. 'Ordinary and Sublime', *The Daily Telegraph*, 28 November 2001, p. 25.

Januszczak, Waldemar. 'Cancer, mortality, art…', *Sunday Times*, 2 December 2001, p. 17.

Miller, Alicia. 'Sam Taylor-Wood', *Flash Art*, vol. 34, no. 223, March/April 2002, p. 106.

Searle, Adrian. 'The lady vanishes', *The Guardian*, 1 December 2001, p. 4.

Cerith Wyn Evans, Asprey Jacques, London 1999

Gisbourne, Mark. 'Cerith Wyn Evans', *Contemporary VisualArts*, issue 23, 1999, p. 63.

Higgie, Jennifer. 'Cerith Wyn Evans', *frieze*, issue 47, June/July/August 1999, p. 95.

Cerith Wyn Evans: Inverse, Reverse, Perverse, White Cube, London 1996

Sladen, Mark. 'Cerith Wyn Evans', *frieze*, issue 30, September/October 1996, p. 75.

(Gillick, Liam. 'Style and Council: Cerith Wyn Evans and the Devastation of Meaning', *Afterall*, 2001.)

(Hilty, Greg. 'We go round and round in the night and are consumed by fire', *Parkett*, no. 56, 1999, pp. 6–9.)

Yukinori Yanagi, Wandering Position, Chisenhale, London 1997

Kyriacou, Sotiris. 'Yukinori Yanagi', *Art Monthly*, no. 205, April 1997, pp. 22–23.

Catherine Yass, Descent, Asprey Jacques, London 2002

Godfrey, Mark. 'Catherine Yass', *frieze*, issue 68, June/July/August 2002, p. 114.

Yerself is Steam (including BANK, Matthew Higgs, Jessica Voorsanger, curated by Iain Forsyth & Jane Pollard), 85 Charlotte St, London 1996

Burrows, David. 'Yerself is Steam', *Art Monthly*, no. 199, September 1996, pp. 45–48.

Guha, Tania. 'Yerself Is Steam', *Time Out*, no. 1353, 24–31 July 1996.

Carey Young, Business as Usual, John Hansard Gallery, Southampton 2001

Suchin, Peter. 'Carey Young', *frieze*, issue 64, January/February 2002, p. 103.

Young British Artists I (John Greenwood, Damien Hirst, Alex Landrum, Langlands & Bell, Rachel Whiteread), Saatchi Gallery, London 1992

Cork, Richard. 'Tanks for the memories', *The Times*, 3 April 1992.

Craddock, Sacha. 'Schools of small fish in the Saatchi pond', *The Guardian*, 13 March 1992.

Dorment, Richard. 'Disturbing symbols of death', *The Daily Telegraph*, 11 March 1992, p. 22.

Verity, Edward. 'Is something rotten in the world of art?', *Daily Mail*, 6 March 1992.

(Garfield, Simon. 'I like it, I'll take the lot', *The Independent*, 20 March 1993, p. 29.)

Young British Artists II (Rose Finn-Kelcey, Sarah Lucas, Marc Quinn, Mark Wallinger), Saatchi Gallery, London 1993

Cork, Richard. 'Blood and guts in a new vein', *The Times*, 12 February 1993, p. 37.

Feaver, William. 'Phew! What a freezer', *The Observer*, 14 February 1993.

Januszczak, Waldemar. 'Blood and Thunder', *The Guardian*, 8 February 1993.

Richardson, Paul. 'Young Blood', *Evening Standard*, 25 February 1993.

Stallabrass, Julian. 'Young British Artists II', *Art Monthly*, no. 164, March 1993, pp. 19–20.

Young British Artists III (Simon Callery, Simon English, Jenny Saville), Saatchi Gallery, London 1994

Cork, Richard. 'Feminsim in the flesh', *The Times*, 25 February 1994.

Dorment, Richard. 'Mountains of Quivering Flesh', *The Daily Telegraph*, 9 February 1994.

Hall, James. 'Repetitive Art. Come Again?', *The Guardian*, 31 January 1994.

Kent, Sarah. 'Young Ones', *Time Out*, 2–9 February 1994.

Sewell, Brian. 'A misogynous regiment of women ...', *Evening Standard*, 28 April 1994.

Sylvester, David. 'Areas of Flesh', *Independent on Sunday*, February 1994.

Young British Artists IV (Marcus Harvey, Brad Lochore, Marcus Taylor, Gavin Turk), Saatchi Gallery, London 1995

Cork, Richard. 'Sinister twist to the everyday', *The Times*, 11 April 1995.

Garnett, Robert. 'Young British Artists IV', *Art Monthly*, no. 187, June 1995, pp. 31–33.

Packer, William. 'Artists with irritating attitudes', *Financial Times*, 11 April 1995.

Sewell, Brian. 'Young guns fire blanks', *Evening Standard*, 20 April 1995.

Young British Artists V (Glenn Brown, Keith Coventry, Hadrain Pigott, Kerry Stewart), Saatchi Gallery, London 1995

Dorment, Richard. 'Funny, but too peculiar', *The Daily Telegraph*, 20 September 1995.

Hall, James. 'Old habits die hard', *The Guardian*, 26 September 1995.

(Slotover, Matthew. 'Young British Art: The Saatchi Decade', *frieze*, issue 47, June/July/August 1999, p. 112.)

Young British Artists VI (including Jordan Baseman, Daniel Coombs, Claude Heath, John Isaacs, Nina Saunders), Saatchi Gallery, London 1996

Tozer, John. 'Young British Artists VI', *Art Monthly*, no. 200, October 1996, pp. 61–62.

Young German Artists II (including Thomas Grünfeld, Martin Honert, Thomas Ruff, Thomas Schütte), Saatchi Gallery, London 1997

Musgrave, David. 'Young German Artists 2', *Art Monthly*, no. 210, October 1997, pp. 36–38.

Zero to Infinity: Arte Povera 1962–72 (including Giovanni Anselmo, Alighiero Boetti, Jannis Kounellis, Giuseppe Penone), Tate Modern, London 2001

Coles, Alex. 'Arte Ricca', *Art Monthly*, no. 248, July/August 2001, pp. 1–5.

Farquharson, Alex. 'Zero to Infinity: Arte Povera 1962–72', *frieze*, issue 61, August 2001.

Andrea Zittel, A-Z Cellular Compartment Units, Mailbox, Ikon Gallery, Birmingham 2001

Gleeson, David. 'Andrea Zittel', *frieze*, issue 65, March 2002, pp. 85–86.

Prince, Nigel. 'Designing for Living' (with AZ/Sadie Coles HQ), *Untitled*, no. 27, Spring 2002, pp. 24–25.

Safe, Emma. 'Andrea Zittel', *Art Monthly*, no. 252, December/January 2001/02.

Zombie Golf (BANK, Dave Beech, Adam Chodzko, Maria Cook, Martin Creed, Peter Doig, Matthew Higgs, Sivan Lewin, John Stezaker), BANKspace, London 1995

Barrett, David. 'Zombie Golf', *frieze*, issue 24, September/October 1995, pp. 74–75.

Currah, Mark. 'Zombie Golf', *Time Out*, 14–21 June 1995.

Roberts, John. 'Mad for it! Bank and New British Art', *everything*, issue 18, 1996.

© 2002 by the authors and Alberta Press
Design: Silke Fahnert, Uwe Koch, Cologne
Printing: Zimmermann GmbH, Cologne (cover);
Digital Druck AG, Birkach

ISBN 3-88375-649-0
Printed in Germany